MODERN NOSTALGIA

MODERN NOSTALGIA

SIEGFRIED SASSOON, TRAUMA AND THE SECOND WORLD WAR

Robert Hemmings

EDINBURGH UNIVERSITY PRESS

Edinburgh University Press Ltd
22 George Square, Edinburgh

Typeset in Sabon and Gill Sans
by Servis Filmsetting Ltd, Stockport, Cheshire, and
printed and bound in Great Britain by
Biddles Ltd, King's Lynn, Norfolk

A CIP record for this book is available from the British Library

ISBN 978 0 7486 3306 7 (hardback)

CONTENTS

ACKNOWLEDGEMENTS

This book has benefited from the help of many. In particular I would like to thank Paul Stevens for his stubborn encouragement, my mother, Carol Ashby, and the Stevens-DeFalco family for inspiration, Sunday dinners and lakeside refuge. I feel very fortunate to work with my editors at Edinburgh University Press. I also appreciate the keen suggestions of their proposal readers, who helped nudge the project along fruitful paths.

For permission to quote from Siegfried Sassoon's published and unpublished writing I thank the Barbara Levy Literary Agency, which represents his estate, as well as Edinburgh University Press and Nipissing University's Research Services for their support in securing this permission. I am also grateful to Nipissing-Muskoka for funding my two research assistants, Jessica McDonald, and Thomas DeFalco, who parachuted in to help with the final flurry of wrapping up the typescript.

Last, and most of all, I am grateful to Amelia DeFalco for her tireless support and deft readings, her conviction and love.

INTRODUCTION

Towards the end of 1944, an English publisher asked Siegfried Sassoon to select a collection of poems by soldiers serving in the Eighth Army during the fiercely fought invasion of Italy. Sassoon reluctantly accepted. The brief and typically diffident introduction he wrote in response provides unexpected insights into his own later writing. In his prose autobiography, *Siegfried's Journey: 1916–1920*, with which he was struggling at the time of this request, he acknowledges that his own traumatic memories of combat from the First World War still held 'an awful attraction' over his mind 'in spite of [his] hatred of war'.[1] Yet readers of *Poems of Italy* find that he forges a connection with this group of soldier-poets not through a sense of shared combat experience on foreign soil, but by recalling a personal encounter. 'In the now distant-seeming days of 1942' Sassoon had the chance to meet the current commander of the Eighth Army, Sir Oliver Leese, when he was stationed at an impromptu camp struck in the park of Sassoon's Wiltshire country house.[2] The movement from the realm of combat trauma to the sequestered realm of the home is telling. The home front, not the frontline, becomes the dominant locus of Sassoon's 'Second Great War'.[3] Having established his connection to the writers he must introduce in *Poems of Italy*, Sassoon observes that the 'wholly authentic soldier poet[s] . . . are both ancient and modern in their technique'.[4] This categorical binary is typical of Sassoon's idiosyncratic simplifying; ancient refers to traditional metrical poems coming 'straight from the heart', which he favours (despite the woefully hackneyed phrase), and modern refers to 'unrhymed, irregular' poems of stark photographic realism, which he admits contribute to the collection's 'valuable report of experience from the Eighth Army'.[5] The lines he cites from a modern poem describe a German tank wreck and a crumpled letter to a lover found in the debris.[6] These lines function to indicate the 'battle and its after-effects' at the heart of the soldiers' experiences in Italy.[7] But of the seventy-two entries in the collection, he specifically names only a single poem in his introduction, one which 'particularly charmed' him.[8] This poem is called 'Nostalgia'. Technically unremarkable, 'Nostalgia' celebrates with sincerity 'the well-remembered thing' of the poet's distant home,[9] eschewing entirely direct mention of the war.

Sassoon's introduction to this anthology is a strikingly apt entrée into his own later writing. In its insularity, or at least its insulation from modernist debates about anthologies and poetics, this introduction reflects the critical stance Sassoon adopted between the wars, in which he distanced himself from modernist literary tastes. But more than his critical perspective, this introduction reflects an essential pressure in Sassoon's writing, captured in words central to Sassoon's aesthetic preoccupations: 'after-effects' and 'nostalgia'. Whenever possible, Sassoon sought in his post-First World War poetry and prose the well-remembered nuances of home, and to hold at bay the lingering after-effects of battle experience, still so hateful and awfully enthralling. That is, Sassoon's later writing manages to embody a tension between trauma and nostalgia, responding so far as possible to the traumatic impulse with a nostalgic vision. It is a necessarily selective vision.

His selective approach to the past has been unpopular with critics. Much of Sassoon's post-First World War writing, with the exception of the *Memoirs of George Sherston*, has been dismissed as belated, nostalgic, self-indulgent, historically irrelevant to a world on the verge or in the midst of international crisis. However, approaching the charges of self-indulgence and nostalgia with a more nuanced reading of the terms compels a less dismissive response to this body of work. His intense preoccupation with himself empowered a remarkable autobiographical focus, an energy that produced scores of poems (published and unpublished) and six separate books of prose that plumb the (albeit circumscribed) depths of one individual's ongoing representation of the fragmentary nature of modern subjectivity. This autobiographical focus is steeped in nostalgia; moreover, I maintain that the nostalgia of Sassoon's writing after the First World War is indelibly marked by the legacy of his traumatic experiences. It is through this very commingling of nostalgia and trauma that Sassoon's writing makes its most trenchant contributions to the expanding field of modernisms.

By focusing on Sassoon's poetry and prose of the 1920s, 1930s and 1940s, I establish a mode of continuity and exchange between nostalgia and trauma, and between literary responses to each world war. The period of my enquiry, roughly between the end of the First World War and the end of the Second, occupies a liminal space in Sassoon scholarship in which his literary identity is critically unfixed; he is no longer a war poet, and not yet truly the devout spiritual pilgrim poet he becomes in the 1950s. Yet during this period he was intensely engaged in a pursuit shared by many of the high modernist figures he preferred to distance himself from including Lawrence, Joyce, Proust and Woolf; all were involved in an ongoing interrogation of the fragmented modern subject. Rather than setting him apart from a modernist tradition, his intractable inward-looking gaze joined him to it, though in a different register.

I argue that not only do nostalgia and trauma operate from the same liminal space between memory and forgetting, but also that they are often similarly rooted in the experience of war, and more particularly, the experience of surviving war. Nostalgia, which Sassoon sought at times to deploy consciously as a curative strategy, reaches back into a past that predates the traumatic losses of war. Sassoon's self-scrutinizing autobiographical impulses, stirred by a combination of his (surprisingly modernist) literary aspirations and his unique exposure to psychoanalysis through W. H. R. Rivers, persistently seek out the distant, pre-traumatic past, the past before his war experience. But because the consolations and comforts of this era are largely illusory, not false but neither wholly true or complete, based as much on forgetting grimness as remembering gladness, Sassoon's pre-war past is ever enticing, yet resistant to a psychoanalytic process of 'working through'. The temporal and spatial distance of pre-war life did not offer the possibility of mastery, but rather held the deceptive appeal of escape from the traumatized post-war present and the lingering after-effects of war experience. The version of nostalgia embodied in Sassoon's writing contributes to an understanding of the diverse complexities of the modern subject.

As Svetlana Boym asserts in *The Future of Nostalgia*, nostalgia forges connections between the individual and the nation, 'between personal and collective memory'.[10] Surviving war is an experience Sassoon shared with modern British culture generally, as no aspect of British life was untouched by the industrial, societal, political and psychological upheavals brought about by world war. The role of nostalgia in Sassoon's representation of his survival of war, and the accommodation of traumatic experience in poetry and prose, offer insights into the adaptive possibilities of an individual and his culture staggered by two world wars. In this way, Sassoon is a case study of modern nostalgia.

Literary Nostalgias

The cultural incarnation of nostalgia as, basically, a mode of looking to the past for a stability lacking in the present is dominant in western industrialized societies. David Lowenthal identifies nostalgia's appeal as the celebration of 'an ordered clarity contrasting with the chaos or imprecision of our own times'.[11]

Other recent critics demonstrate that for nostalgia to take root, certain socio-historical conditions must prevail. Societies must be governed by a linear, not a cyclical conception of time, without the redemptive imperative of the future salvation of afterlife. That is, they must be secular. There must prevail a sense of the deficiency of the present, whether on the national level, with economic, military or imperial setbacks; the class level, with a relative diminution of power; or the personal level, with prior stages of one's life containing pinnacles of accomplishment. Finally, objects from the past must be readily accessible, be they books, buildings, town squares or country houses.[12] Each of these points is relevant to Sassoon in particular ways during the years between the wars, as I will later explore. But generally speaking, the industrializing, secular world provides fertile ground for nostalgia. Indeed the forced migration of workers from the country to the sprawling cities during the early days of the Industrial Revolution contributed to the widespread proliferation of the pathos of nostalgia on a socio-cultural plane. The recent past in one's own life, ultimately one's childhood, could offer up the impression of rural simplicity relative to the trying conditions of newfound urban adult living.[13]

From the early eighteenth century till the early twenty-first, nostalgia of this general kind has prevailed and informed the constructed relation of the past to the present in literary-cultural circles, though under different guises. Alexander Pope's move to the relative simplicity of life in Twickenham's country setting could be construed as a nostalgic response to the hectic clamour of city life, and so could the reinvigoration of the English literary tradition with a return to the classical aesthetic values of Augustan Rome. English Romantic poets reacted against neo-classical strictures by resisting the elite appeals of civic, industrial, cultural life they found inauthentic. Wordsworth's withdrawal to the Lake District was more than a geographical move away from the seat of cultural power in the South of England. It was also a retreat from industrialization and the city into the natural world, and the authentic organic communities of the rural North, as well as a homecoming.[14] Wordsworth not only retreated to the contemporary pastness of an area of England less marked by industrialization than the South; he also moved away to the space of his childhood, allowing specific physical returns to geographic sites to revivify his connection to his childhood. His poetry reflects this romantic nostalgic impulse.

Victorian nostalgia takes up Wordsworth's disdain for ruinous industrialization and embrace of rustic simplicity and directs its look backwards to a fantasy medieval England. In conjunction with this there is yearning for childhood: not one's own past, but rather an idealized state of innocence, a yearning which exists in sharp contrast to the actual exploitative experience of a typical English working-class child. The grimness of the present is measured by the despoliation of the English countryside, and the impoverishment of peasants displaced and reincarnated as workers, both adult and child. Monastic England is held up by writers like Carlyle, Ruskin and Morris as a cohering and organic past, technologically and culturally simpler and clearer than their present. But this past, favoured by writers Stephen Spender calls 'sentimentally and aesthetically . . . medievalists', is not longed for emptily, without purpose, but rather functions as an instructive model for improving the woeful present.[15] Victorian nostalgia, while disdaining industrial progress, seeks to incorporate the strength and beauty of the past into a socially progressive and aesthetically improved future.

Aesthetes of the later nineteenth century rejected the ameliorative tendencies of their earlier Victorian predecessors' nostalgic vision. Rather than constructing a past from a revival of the handicrafts of Merrie England, writers like Pater and Wilde developed a more spiritually sophisticated nostalgia out of their longing for the art and inspired genius of the Renaissance past and the classical traditions that inspired it.[16] The gap between the cultural standing of the figures of the past so celebrated by the aesthetes, and their own relatively marginal status in the industrialized and hateful present, imbues their version of nostalgia with an astringent melancholy.[17] Nostalgia of this kind obviously takes many forms in the modern period. The nostalgia of high modernists continued the aesthetes' derision for the stifling ignorance of a present culture which could not understand them in favour of the glorious order of the Renaissance. Georgian nostalgia tended toward a Victorian glorification of a distant English past as a means of improving present cultural malaise, though Georgians looked back to the perceived order of English rural society, not to the Merrie England of the medieval period. Modern nostalgia, in any of its forms, is like nostalgia from any period in so far as it registers the longing for past values to stabilize an erratic present, but with one profound difference: the widespread trauma of the world wars. Modern war enforced a destructive breach that made the past ever more inaccessible, apparently even more distant, which served to intensify the longing for it.

Like any nostalgic, Sassoon looked to the past to make sense of the present. Sassoon's nostalgia reflects the Victorianist aesthetic values he championed, the Georgian embrace of a distant English rural way of life and the modernist tradition he hated but could not escape. On the one hand, he dismissed what he saw as the arid intellectualism of modernists like Eliot, Pound and Wyndham Lewis, and others who ignored or criticized his poetry and prose of the 1930s as backward-looking. On the other hand, he sought their approbation and remained chagrined when he was thought of as yesterday's man. And yet he did look backwards; he was yesterday's man. But in some ways, so too were Eliot, Pound and Lewis, who each looked to the past, albeit beyond the nineteenth century, for order to counter the chaos of contemporaneous history, which troubled each in differing ways. Characterizing his aesthetics as happily, indeed confrontationally Victorian, Sassoon took a kind of perverse pride in distinguishing himself from the high modernists, but he shared with them a powerful nostalgic impulse. Stephen Spender once referred to nostalgia as 'the peculiar modern disease',[18] and disease, both figuratively and literally, turns out to be a fruitful way to investigate this prominent modern phenomenon.

NOSTALGIA: PATHOS AND PATHOLOGY

Once dismissed as merely a glorification of the past, nostalgia has come to be read by a range of scholars in the humanities in a more complex way as a filter through which memories of the past are ordered and shaped by forces of the present. Historian Svetlana Boym, for example, sees it as 'not merely an artistic device but a strategy of survival, a way of making sense of the impossibility of homecoming'.[19] Though Boym writes about the thwarted homecomings for those diasporic communities dispersed by the collapse of the Soviet empire, her perspective is relevant to this book. The erosion of the British empire in the 1930s and 1940s underscores the importance of nostalgia as a strategy of survival for writers like Sassoon invested in a social geography of Englishness to which homecoming was no longer possible. In this period nostalgia had already acquired its pejorative sense, indicating a futile yearning for a past way of life from which one has been permanently cut off.[20] The sense of emotion, passion and suffering in the Greek root of *pathos* is present in diluted form in the pejorative connotations of nostalgia. The *Oxford English Dictionary* (*OED*) cites David Garnett's description from 1933 of 'that violent sentimental nostalgia . . . felt by the very young [girls] about the very recent past' as evidence of 'sentimental longing *for* or regretful memory of a period of the past'.[21] Nostalgia in Garnett's usage is a useless, childish longing, more particularly the longing of a girl, a concept steeped in pathos, but its pathos is undermined by the implied immaturity of the speaker and the matching implied inutility of the period for which the speaker is pining. In this depreciatory sense, nostalgia is a feeling certainly far from the notion of masculine heroism associated with the daring exploits of an empire-builder or a soldier-poet. Yet in the period between the wars, nostalgia was sufficiently malleable to accommodate English nationalist, conservative and masculine aspirational subjectivity in search of an elusive, illusive and allusive sense of home, as Sassoon's case attests.

Nostalgia is rooted in pathology and the experience of war. In 1688, the young Swiss physician Johannes Hofer published his medical dissertation on a new disease he named by combining the Greek word *nostos*, return home, and *algos*, pain.[22] His research was based on observing symptoms in, among others, Swiss soldiers fighting on foreign soil. As later commentators like Jean Starobinski and George Rosen have noted, Hofer's disease has striking affinities with afflictions common to those in the early twentieth century suffering from a range of neuroses, including the traumatic neuroses of war, an ailment which was thought to have a psychic rather than a somatic aetiology. Hofer likened the all-consuming longing for home to 'things that impress us deeply and reappear in our dreams', and ascribed its cause 'to a disordered imagination'.[23] Hofer had noted that 'the actual occurrence of nostalgia is revealed by a continuing melancholy, incessant thinking of home, disturbed sleep or insomnia, weakness, loss of appetite, anxiety, cardiac palpitation, stupor, and fever.'[24] It is curious that Hofer's symptomatology bears an uncanny resemblance to those symptoms found at Craiglockhart, where Sassoon was hospitalized in 1917, and other war hospitals throughout Europe during the First World War; they certainly characterize some of the complaints Sassoon described in his post-war diaries and letters. That the symptoms in the war hospitals of the twentieth century were associated with various incarnations of traumatic neuroses offers further evidence of the proximity of nostalgia and trauma, a proximity that underlies much of this book.

During the eighteenth century, the classification of nostalgia was contested, with many physicians categorizing the disease as a form of insanity, pointedly distinct from melancholy. In mid-century de Sauvages published his methodical nosology, classifying it in the second order of diseases, within the deranged desires, not with traditional forms of madness.[25] De Sauvages noted three types: 'simple nostalgia' affected soldiers and students who were forced to be away from home; 'complicated nostalgia' operated in conjunction with other diseases; 'simulated nostalgia', like malingering in the modern period, was to be watched for in soldiers demonstrating symptoms that might prevent them from active duty.[26] In various forms this newly minted disease was widespread in military camps throughout Europe in the eighteenth century. The physician to the king of France studied cases of simple and simulated nostalgia among soldiers in the French army, and came up with treatments involving easily digestible foods and stimulating but not overtiring exercises, in effect reinforcing the connection between this disorder of the desires and the body.[27] A Scots surgeon in the British army, Robert Hamilton confirmed in 1781 that the condition was not merely a Swiss or continental phenomenon when he observed a recruit prone to deep and frequent sighing who complained of 'universal weakness . . . a noise in his ears, and a giddiness of his head'.[28] Languishing in an army hospital in the North of England, the soldier was unable to focus his attention beyond the topic of his past home life in Wales.[29] When the surgeon promised to secure him home leave, the symptoms dissipated remarkably, thereby confirming the positive aspects of Hofer's warning that this ailment is curable if the yearning can be satisfied, and 'incurable and fatal or at least most especially dangerous'[30] if not.

By the nineteenth century, however, there emerged a growing consensus within European medical discourse that nostalgia was absolutely associated with, as Hofer had surmised, forms of melancholy.[31] The difference between severe afflictions, insane nostalgia and minor cases, not insane, revolved around the degree to which the nostalgic vision took hold of all mental faculties.[32] In the 1890s Daniel Tuke attested in *A Dictionary of Psychological Medicine* that 'nostalgia always represents a combination of psychical and bodily disturbances,'[33] thereby affirming Hofer's position set out more than 200 years earlier. Rosen argues that the advent of cellular pathology and bacteriology, which accounted for many of nostalgia's physiological symptoms, contributed to nostalgia's fading from medical discourse by the end of the nineteenth century,[34] with the emotional phenomena that prompted Hofer's original theorizing fitting into other theoretical models: psychoanalysis, for example. However, Hofer's disease did not entirely disappear. *The Lancet* declared in 1914, several months after war began, that nostalgia had never featured as a disease in British medical discourse, as it had in French, Italian, Swiss and American treatises.[35]

In America, during the 1930s, Beardsley Ruml, a University of Chicago psychologist, argued that nostalgia was more than simply a disease and more like a fundamental condition of 'human nature',[36] linking nostalgia to primitive peoples through the dubious connection of observing symptoms in dogs.[37] But nostalgia withstood such implausible claims, and in the 1940s Willis McGann revived its pathogenic associations by connecting the frustrated desire to return home to a physiological symptom triggered in the autonomic nervous system.[38] Mention of nostalgia was absent in *The Lancet* until midway through the Second World War, when an editorial discusses the wartime proliferation of homesickness. Despite its semi-ironical, humorous tone, the editorial offers a canny overview: 'In essence nostalgia, this return-pain, consists in a longing for home expressed in mental tastes, touches, smells, sounds and pictures.'[39] The editorial's ironic treatment of nostalgia underscores its rich potential as a cultural and literary trope, while tracing its connection to corporeal sensation and disease.

Debates about the originary causes, triggers and appropriate treatments of nostalgia in the psychological and psychoanalytic journals have persisted into the twenty-first century, some making forays into its cognitive roots, others predicated upon the thwarted desire to return home, defined on personal or national grounds.[40] It is on this question of home and how to return there that the pathology of nostalgia fuses with its manifestation in cultural discourse; nostalgia can be a way of coping with the impossibility of homecoming configured temporally, spatially, individually or nationally. This preoccupation with homecoming was especially prevalent in British cultural discourse during the years between the world wars. Nostalgia, steeped with pathos, imbued with pathology, flourished in the modern period in a range of English literary production, including Sassoon's largely autobiographical work, which was shaped by the high modernists and Georgians, and which sought out the elusive sense of home shattered by the trauma of war and its lingering aftereffects.

Modernist Nostalgia

In December 1944, while Sassoon was leafing through the manuscript of poems by soldiers of the Eighth Army who had fought in the Italian campaign, Ezra Pound was in flight from those very forces, an 'evacuee' from his apartment in Rapallo, displaced by Allied bombings, working out a suite of cantos in Italian that would form the ideological framework for the *Pisan Cantos*, begun in July 1945.[41] He disdained the hateful present, fuming with the resumption of modern war which was literally destroying cultural artefacts belonging to what Pound (and others, including Mussolini) constructed as Italy's glorious Renaissance past. The 'old bitch', civilization, 'gone in the teeth'[42] that Pound lamented after the First World War, was enduring further decay. He countered this contemptuous present with a powerfully rendered yearning for a temporally distant home, which sought to revive the Italian classical past and its philosophical and ideological underpinnings.

There is a certain irony in Pound's version of modernist nostalgia. At first blush, a movement guided by Pound's cry for a new poetic idiom, shaped by a willingness among artists to embrace new forms and technologies, does not seem particularly backward-looking. But like the aesthetes and the neoclassicists before them, modernist writers like Pound yearned for the order and clarity they found in Renaissance classicism and classical antiquity. Just before the First World War, T. E. Hulme proclaimed the necessity of 'a classical revival' to 'discipline' humankind with 'order' and 'organization' to replace the soppy and moribund romanticism lingering over English poetry.[43] As Spender has it in *The Struggle of the Modern*, modernists sought to combine this understanding of the virtues of classical order with the as yet untapped potential of modern technology to transform the modern world through art.[44] And yet, this tacit acceptance of technology is combined paradoxically with 'an intense hatred and contempt for modern life'.[45] As mentioned earlier, one of the preconditions for nostalgia is a dissatisfaction with the present, but for Spender it is this degree of utter hatred for the present that distinguishes modernist nostalgics from any of their predecessors. The subjects of modernist poetry are rootless, alienated, ironically detached in the decay of the industrializing present. While previous nostalgics looked to the past for models to inspire their rejuvenated artistic actions in the present, the modernist nostalgics like Pound and Wyndham Lewis felt that their geniuses, so entrenched in the values of a past period, received no sustenance in the abhorred climate of the present.[46] This abhorrence is the source of Spender's 'peculiar modern disease' called nostalgia.[47] Sassoon too suffered from this disease. A hatred for the present produces a kind of spiritual homesickness, since the modernist's sense of belonging is to a distant past, which he or she can occupy only as a ghostly presence. This spiritual homesickness confirms the impossibility of homecoming and further galvanizes the nostalgic's yearning. My own position is that the modernist disdain for the present does not in itself distinguish modern nostalgia from its incarnations in previous periods; nostalgia is always already predicated upon an aggrieved relation to the present. What in my view distinguishes modern nostalgia is the shock of the gulf between the retrospectively constructed innocence or benevolence of the pre-traumatic past and the present staggered by the lingering after-effects of modern war.

Dangerous consequences result when nostalgia's contempt for the present is applied to the political realm, as occurred in the modern period. The use of modern technology to impose the pattern of pre-industrial society on modern society produces fascism: 'The sirens of nostalgia sang the speeches of Mussolini,' as Spender put it.[48] Pound was composing songs of this kind in the dark days of December 1944, hating the forces of the Allied present and their wanton destruction of Italian cultural landmarks. While all forms of nostalgia may not be politically conservative, it is certainly true that modernist nostalgia in these terms is rightly descried by critics as reactionary, regressive and dangerously ignoring or distorting the complexities of contemporary life in favour of the imposition of an idealized construction of past order.[49] It is noteworthy that even the Georgians, much maligned by their modernist counterparts, embody a version of modern nostalgia that, while not so openly contemptuous of the present and not so extreme politically, projects a distinctly reactionary stance.

Georgian Nostalgia

Long the whipping boy of early twentieth-century poetry, exemplars of a belated and waning stylistics incapable of negotiating the onslaught of modernity, Georgian poetry is easy fodder to the charge of pejorative nostalgia levelled against Sassoon's later writing. It is hardly surprising that such charges were levied most insistently by advocates of high modernism in the 1920s and 1930s.[50] As a young, aspiring writer, Sassoon was a good deal enthralled by the first *Georgian Poetry (1911–1912)* anthology, admiring its editor, Edward Marsh, an early personal and poetic mentor, and holding in awe one of its star attractions, Rupert Brooke. The third edition of *Georgian Poetry (1916–1917)*, prominently featured eight of Sassoon's poems, including some of his early war poems, and this volume's success did much to establish his name. Publishing war poems during this stage of the war demonstrates at least some recognition of the modern situation. But by the last anthology, published in 1922, the high watermark year of modernism, the 'new strength' of Georgian poetry had withered, and it became susceptible to charges that it was no longer aesthetically engaged with modernity. Sassoon himself felt in 1920 that it was time to get away from 'the Georgians and their conventional poetic vocabularies' and declined permission for his poems to be published in the final volume.[51]

Spender perpetuates the rigid boundary between modernists and Georgians even in the early 1960s, designating Georgians as 'non-recognizers', unable to apprehend modernity, choosing to focus on the dream of rustic peace while wilfully ignoring the wakeful nightmare of modern life.[52] While later that decade there were moves to reclaim Georgian poetry from the critical bin, even at the turn of this century 'Georgian' continues to signify an outworn, tired poetics.[53] But in fact Georgian and modernist had similarly revolutionary roots, both consciously striking out for new poetic ground, both bearing the approbation of the poetic establishment.[54] To 'break with tradition', wrote Pound in 1916, meant to 'desert the more obvious imbecilities of one's immediate elders',[55] and such breaks were cyclical, befalling each generation of intelligent artists. In deserting the immediate predecessors, less 'imbecilic' models of a more distant past were sought, thereby activating the nostalgic impulse. As early modernists deserted what they saw as Edwardian imbecilities by embracing Elizabethan classicists, Georgians deserted these same immediate elders by embracing a kind of Romanticism. Edward Marsh, the editor of the *Georgian Poetry* anthologies, inaugurates the series with these brave words from the preface: 'This volume is issued in the belief that English poetry is now once again putting on a new strength and beauty.'[56] Sloughing off broad generalities, imprecise diction and the retrograde Victorianism of Edwardian poetry,[57] Marsh proclaimed that 'we are at the beginning of another "Georgian period" which may take rank in due time with the several great poetic ages of the past.'[58] While such statements are generally invoked ironically, it is worth remembering that Georgians were actually a diverse bunch and, like their early modernist contemporaries, experimented with form (D. H. Lawrence), invoked irony (Brooke) and problematized the relation of the subject to the modern world.[59]

This is not to obscure important and undeniable differences. Georgian poetry tends to represent events as natural, not historical, and offers a reconciliatory vision of societal conflicts by looking back to the isolated individual's relation to the natural world.[60] Modernists tend to locate alienating modernity in the crowded urban world, and look back to classical forms and order to reconcile conflicts of the present. Modernism in English is typically transnational, with major practitioners including Pound, Eliot and Joyce who are not from England, and modernist nostalgia looks back to traditions of Medieval and Renaissance Italy and France, and Greek and Roman antiquity. Georgians look back and celebrate a quiet and idyllic Englishness, to the Romantic topoi of Wordsworth, which featured organic communities and individuals connected authentically to their patch of English countryside.

There are important parallels in the political implications of each of these nostalgias. I have earlier called modernist nostalgia reactionary and regressive, and it is equally possible to call the modern nostalgia of the Georgians politically reactionary, anchored in traditional class values, but also celebratory of an English cultural nationalism. Georgian poetry is steeped in a tradition that enshrines the worth and ameliorating force of the English landscape to foster a cherished organic community constituted by a sense of interconnected Englishness. While many of the poems feature an individual's interaction with this landscape, underlying this dynamic is the Wordsworthian sense of simplicity, authenticity, and liberating removal from the toil and bother of the industrializing urban culture. W. H. Davies's 'In May', for example, depicts the memory of a past encounter with the English countryside in verdant spring, which sustains him during his tribulations in city pent. Davies's speaker imagines a coastal, book-filled cottage, with a view of passing ships on one side, 'A flowery, green, bird-singing land' on the other.[61] The books, the cottage, the abundant landscape are objects of the past which act as a 'powerful talisman' of the way things were.[62] The image removes him from the alienating crowds of the city, while the order of natural world and its contiguity with the past restore him. Cows and sheep are not livestock for city abattoirs, but cosseted agents nurtured by the soft deep grasses of the countryside. At the same time, this nostalgic pastoral image is freighted with codes of English nationalism. The ships the cottage windows overlook invoke the far-reaching empire, reinforced by the reference to the Arab dreamer, while behind the green and pleasant, very English land and inside the cottage the books bespeak a tradition that connects the speaker to his literary past. I do not mean to judge an entire collection by a single poem, but rather to suggest that the appeal to a particular vision of society as a feature of a natural order apparent in this Davies poem is more or less apparent in many Georgian poems.

What the cosy nostalgic vision of 'In May' glazes over is the hardship and poverty of the rural community, which included, besides the leisured cottage-goers who might have enjoyed the views, the cowherds, shepherds and tenant labourers who worked the land, indentured and exploited to ensure the continuity of a particular way of life in the English countryside. Attendant on this nostalgic vision are the inequities of the past community upon which it is based, and which, as Marshall Berman reminds us, modernity has eradicated.[63] But then the nostalgic is not focused on the past as it was, but the past that suits the anxieties and tensions of the present.

Edward Marsh included eight Sassoon poems in *Georgian Poetry 1916–1917*, and most of these poems are preoccupied with the experience of war. But even these bellicose poems, though they may be set in France, appeal to the natural order of a particular English landscape. For example, 'The Death-Bed' features a dying soldier who escapes the pain of his wound through an opiate-induced dream of drifting gently in a rowboat upon a secluded weir 'bordered with reflected flowers / And shaken hues of summer'.[64] When the rain comes, it is not the harsh windswept rain of the French battlefield, but a 'Warm rain on drooping roses', a peaceful English rain that gently washes his life away.[65]

The trauma of the soldier's experience of modern war, his imminent encounter with death, is temporarily forced aside, or below, repressed by an insistent yearning for the landscape of home. Though this poem lacks the explicit patriotic register, it is steeped in the same Englishness as Brooke's famous, if maligned, 'The Soldier', with its appeal to English flowers, rivers and gentleness. As with almost all of Sassoon's writing between the end of the First and the Second World Wars, the nostalgia is a blend of modernist hatred for modernity's destructive capacity, most explicitly embodied through a more or less repressed traumatic memory of war experience, and a Georgian legacy of the instructive virtues that figured the English countryside as illustrative of a certain mode of English social order under threat from inescapable modernity.

Tensions between modernist and Georgian influences, between past and present, between the anxieties of peace and the struggles of war, between nostalgia and trauma dominate both Sassoon's writing between the wars and my own approach to this fertile period. In Chapter 1, I situate aspects of Sassoon's nostalgia within the rural revival movement that gathered strength in the space between the two world wars and found indirect expression in the pastoral ideals represented in Georgian poetry. In some respects this revival responds to the traumatic legacy of war, for Sassoon and the broader segment of British society that endorsed the anachronistic values of English country life.

I provide in the next chapter a historical overview of trauma as understood during the First World War, the interwar years and the Second World War. I establish the cultural context of war neuroses in Britain by tracing their roots in nineteenth-century models of traumatic neuroses and transformation into 'shell shock'. This enduring term was coined in 1915 by Charles Myers, a colleague of Rivers, who initially attributed those disturbing somatic after-effects of battle which had apparent physical cause to the physical jolt delivered to the body by the concussive power of high explosive shell-fire. As the war continued and medical officers had further opportunity to study these strange cases, leading figures like Myers and Rivers concluded that 'shell shock' in its literal meaning was inaccurate, and the damage occurred psychologically, not physically. While 'shell shock' has stuck in popular parlance, a group of British psychiatrists at Maghull and later Craiglockhart hospitals adapted continental psychoanalytic approaches in their treatment of soldiers suffering from a range of nervous disorders of war. The key Freudian concept of repression is central to Rivers's understanding of trauma, and key too for Sassoon. In this second chapter, I demonstrate the connection between Sassoon's apparently idiosyncratic and socially detached response, and the broader cultural and social response, to the threat and the renewal of modern war.

Rivers developed a therapeutic treatment for patients suffering from traumatic war neuroses that he called 'autognosis', a twofold process by which an individual 'learns to understand the real state of his mind' by accounting for both conscious and unconscious motivations, and also the environmental conditions that have produced that state of mind.[66] While Sassoon was wary of Freudian psychoanalytic ideas emphasizing unconscious depths, Rivers's articulation of 'autognosis' became the foundational framework for the ongoing autobiographical project that dominated Sassoon's writing life of the 1920s, 1930s and 1940s. In Chapter 3, I focus on the role of nostalgia in the prose autognosis of the Sherston memoirs, as well as the unsought return of war in key poems of the 1920s and 1930s. The emphasis on understanding one's environment, and one's place within it, accounts in part for the nostalgic strain of Sassoon's autobiographical project, whether in prose or poetry.

Like millions of others, Sassoon despaired at the uncanny onset of what he called the 'Second Great War', but his inclination to withdraw further into an isolated world of privileged privacy chafed against a rekindled sense of patriotism, as I detail in Chapter 4. Here I address how his thwarted sense of honour and duty found expression in the revival of his 'war poet' persona from the early days of the First World War, before his disillusionment with the government's war aims. The attendant poems, although awkward, are culturally interesting and expressive of a nostalgic longing for values effectively destroyed by the relentless damage of the 1914–18 war.

In spite of his halting efforts to produce poems for the war effort, the bulk of Sassoon's writing during the Second World War was autognostic and introspective. My analysis of key personal poems, published and unpublished, from the war years is the focus of Chapter 5. For Sassoon, to look inward was to look back into the past, and to conflate temporal and spatial metaphorical gestures. Even the Wiltshire estate to which he had essentially withdrawn in the mid-1930s becomes in his poetry a setting that draws him back in time and down archeologically into prior layers of self, towards previous imagined relations to the landscape, insulated from the fury of world war. In these poems, the war is mainly held at bay, but is always threatening to encroach and disturb traumatic sediment.

In Chapter 6 I explore the conspicuous presence of nostalgia and narcissism, concepts with psychological and literary roots, which provide tropes that illuminate Sassoon's autobiographical project. Between the mid-1930s and mid-1940s, Sassoon published three autobiographical prose volumes on the heels of completing the semi-fictionalized Sherston trilogy. In prose and in poetry, he was drawn back to his own past, attracted by the illusory prospect of 'giv[ing] the modern world the slip'.[67] But again, his purportedly idiosyncratic withdrawal shares important discursive practices with both his disdained contemporaries and literary tradition. His autobiography of this period responds to key figures in the tradition of autobiography as a genre, like Wordsworth and Pater, to psychological theorists, like Rivers, and to literary modernists, like Proust.

In the final chapter, I look closely at crucial points in his autobiographical project when Sassoon physically returns to specific sites of his past, visits which produce tropes of longing and provoke fascinating, uncanny collisions between present and prior selves. At the cusp of each of these collisions is a spatial and temporal gap, a liminal moment of heightened autognostic perception. This chapter explores these key moments in Sassoon, concluding that they are more representative and revelatory of modern (and modernist) anxieties about subjectivity, trauma and nostalgia than has been previously addressed in the scholarship of modernism.

Overall, this book offers an alternative to the perception tacitly accepted in critical circles that Sassoon's historical and cultural relevance touches the First World War only. As a case study of modern nostalgia, this analysis of Sassoon's writing of the 1920s, 1930s and 1940s demonstrates the connections between trauma and nostalgia in a culture saturated with the anxieties of war.

Notes

1. Siegfried Sassoon, *Siegfried's Journey: 1916–1920* (London: Faber & Faber, 1945), p. 69.
2. Siegfried Sassoon, 'Introduction', in Siegfried Sassoon (ed.), *Poems from Italy: Verses Written by Members of the Eighth Army in Sicily and Italy July 1943–March 1944* (London: Harrap, 1945), p. 10.
3. Sassoon's phrase from the early days of the Second World War, quoted in John Stuart Roberts, *Siegfried Sassoon: 1886–1967* (London: Cohen, 1999), pp. 277–8.
4. Sassoon, 'Introduction', *Poems from Italy*, p. 10.
5. Ibid. p. 12.
6. It is telling that Sassoon makes no connection between this poem and Keith Douglas's '*Vergissmeinnicht*', a modern poem of strikingly similar content published earlier in 1944. In spite of his friend Edmund Blunden's mentorship of Douglas, Sassoon seems not to have been familiar with Douglas's poetry, a further indication of his literary isolation during the Second World War.
7. Sassoon, 'Introduction', *Poems from Italy*, p. 11.
8. Ibid. p. 11.
9. E. G. Porter, 'Nostalgia', in Sassoon (ed.), *Poems From Italy*, p. 76.
10. Svetlana Boym, *The Future of Nostalgia* (New York: Basic, 2001), p. xvi.
11. David Lowenthal, 'Nostalgia tells it like it wasn't', in Malcolm Chase and Christopher Shaw (eds), *The Imagined Past: History and Nostalgia* (Manchester: Manchester University Press, 1989), pp. 18–32, p. 30.
12. Malcolm Chase and Christopher Shaw, 'The dimensions of nostalgia', in Chase and Shaw, *The Imagined Past*, pp. 1–17, pp. 2–3.
13. Lowenthal, 'Nostalgia', p. 20.
14. Stephen Spender, *The Struggle of the Modern* (Berkeley, CA: University of California Press, 1963), p. 31.
15. Ibid. p. 211.
16. Ibid. p. 212.
17. Ibid. p. 212.
18. Ibid. p. 214.
19. Boym, *The Future of Nostalgia*, p. xvii.
20. Jean Starobinski, 'The idea of nostalgia', *Diogenes*, 54, 1966, pp. 81–103, p. 101.

21. 'Nostalgia', *Shorter Oxford English Dictionary*, 2 vols (Oxford: Oxford University Press, 1944).
22. George Rosen, 'Nostalgia: a "forgotten" psychological disorder', *Psychological Medicine*, 5, 1975, pp. 340–54, p. 341.
23. Johannes Hofer, quoted in Rosen, 'Nostalgia', p. 342.
24. Ibid. p. 342.
25. Stanley Jackson, 'Nostalgia', in Stanley Jackson, *Melancholia and Depression: From Hippocratic Times to Modern Times* (New Haven, CT: Yale University Press, 1986), p. 376.
26. Ibid. p. 376. I discuss this point further in Chapter 1.
27. Rosen, 'Nostalgia', p. 344.
28. Robert Hamilton, 'Nostalgia', in Richard Hunter and I. Macalpine (eds), *Three Hundred Years of Psychiatry: A History Presented in Selected English Texts* (London: Oxford University Press, 1963), pp. 499–500, p. 499.
29. Ibid. p. 500.
30. Johannes Hofer, 'Medical dissertation on Nostalgia', trans. Carolyn Kiser Anspach, *Bulletin of the History of Medicine*, 2, 1934, pp. 376–91, p. 388.
31. Jackson, 'Nostalgia', p. 378; Rosen, 'Nostalgia', p. 350.
32. Jackson, 'Nostalgia', p. 379.
33. Ibid. p. 380.
34. Rosen, 'Nostalgia', p. 351.
35. ' "Nostalgie militaire" ', *The Lancet*, 28 November 1914, p. 1261.
36. This paraphrase of Ruml appears in Willis H. McCann, 'Nostalgia: A review of the literature', *Psychological Bulletin*, 38, 1941, pp. 165–82, p. 176.
37. Beardsley Ruml, 'Theory of nostalgic and egoic sentiments', *American Psychological Association*, 30, 1933, pp. 656–7, p. 656.
38. McCann, 'Nostalgia', p. 179.
39. 'In England now: A running commentary by peripatetic correspondents', *The Lancet,* 26 December 1942, p. 764.
40. See, for example, D. S. Werman, 'Normal and pathological nostalgia', *Journal of the American Psychoanalytic Association*, 25:2, 1977, pp. 387–98. Werman described nostalgia as an affective-cognitive experience involving memories of specific places from one's past that can assume pathological forms when, for example, it becomes a substitute for mourning. In 1987, H. A. Kaplan described nostalgia as 'a pleasurable affect involving warm memories of the past' that becomes pathological when one fails to accept the irrevocability of the past. See H. A. Kaplan, 'The psychopathology of nostalgia', *Psychoanalytic Review*, 74:4, 1987, pp. 465–86. In the 1990s, K. I. Batcho attempted to develop a 'nostalgia inventory' to assess the kinds of nostalgia experienced by subjects of different ages, genders and ranges of experience, observing distinctions in emotional intensity between the categories of personal nostalgia and social-historical nostalgia. See K. I. Batcho, 'Nostalgia: a psychological perspective', *Perceptual and Motor Skills*, 80:1, February 1995, pp. 131–43; and K. I. Batcho, 'Personal nostalgia, world view, memory, and emotionality', *Perceptual and Motor Skills*, 87:2, October 1998, pp. 411–32. In the twenty-first century, psychologists have situated nostalgia as a kind of hitherto understudied emotion. See Tim Wildschut, C. Sedikides, J. Arndt and C. Routledge, 'Nostalgia: content, triggers, functions', *Journal of Personality and Social Psychology*, 91:5, November 2006, pp. 975–93. Others locate nostalgia in the positive experience of successfully remembering, which is misattributed to a pleasant past. See Jason Leboe, T. Ansons, 'On misattributing good remembering to a happy past: an investigation into the cognitive roots of nostalgia', *Emotion*, 6:4, November 2006, pp. 596–610.

41. Ronald Bush, 'Art versus the descent of the iconoclasts: cultural memory in Ezra Pound's *Pisan Cantos*', *Modernism/Modernity*, 14:1, January 2007, pp. 71–95, p. 79.
42. Ezra Pound, 'Hugh Selwyn Mauberley (Contacts and life)', in Lea Baechler and A. Walton Litz (eds), *Personae* (New York: New Directions, 1990), pp. 183–202, p. 188.
43. T. E. Hulme, 'Romanticism and Classicism', in David Lodge (ed.), *20th Century Literary Criticism* (London: Longman, 1992), pp. 93–104, pp. 93, 94.
44. Spender, *The Struggle of the Modern*, p. 207.
45. Ibid. p. 208.
46. Ibid. p. 214.
47. Ibid. p. 214.
48. Ibid. p. 219.
49. Lowenthal, 'Nostalgia', p. 20.
50. Marianne Thomählen, 'Modernism and the Georgians', in Marianne Thomählen (ed.), *Rethinking Modernism* (New York: Palgrave Macmillan, 2003), pp. 77–94, p. 77.
51. Quoted in Jean Moorcroft Wilson, *Siegfried Sassoon: The Journey from the Trenches: A Biography 1918–1967*, vol. 2 (New York: Routledge, 2003), p. 98.
52. Spender, *The Struggle of the Modern*, pp. 159–60.
53. Thomählen, 'Modernism', p. 77.
54. Ibid. p. 80.
55. Ezra Pound, 'Notes on Elizabethan classicists', in T. S. Eliot (ed.), *Literary Essays of Ezra Pound* (London: Faber & Faber, 1954), pp. 227–48, p. 277.
56. E. M. Marsh, 'Prefatory note', in E. M. Marsh (ed.), *Georgian Poetry, 1911–1912* (London: Poetry Bookshop, 1912), p. v.
57. Gary Day, 'The poets: Georgians, imagists and others', in Clive Bloom (ed.), *Literature and Culture in Modern Britain, Volume One: 1900–1929* (London: Longman, 1993), pp. 30–54, p. 33.
58. Marsh, 'Prefatory note', p. v.
59. Thomählen, 'Modernism', pp. 87–9.
60. Day, 'The poets', p. 35.
61. W. H. Davies, 'In May', in Marsh (ed.), *Georgian Poetry*, p. 61.
62. Chase and Shaw, 'The dimensions of nostalgia', p. 8.
63. Marshall Berman, *All That is Solid Melts into Air* (New York: Penguin, 1988), p. 60.
64. Sassoon, 'The Death-bed', in *Collected Poems*, p. 34.
65. Ibid. p. 34.
66. W. H. R. Rivers, 'Psycho-Therapeutics', in James Hastings (ed.), *Encyclopedia of Religion and Ethics*, vol. 10 (New York: Scribner's, n.d.), p. 437.
67. Siegfried Sassoon, *The Old Century* (London: Faber & Faber, 1938), p. 125.

1

THE SPACE BETWEEN THE WARS

Rural Revival and the Georgian Legacy

Sassoon's great friend and fellow veteran, Edmund Blunden, also gained early exposure through *Georgian Poetry*, but not until after the First World War. Much of Blunden's writing, poetry and prose, exhibits the Georgian nostalgia for a simpler past when the landscape helped forge a stronger and authentic sense of Englishness among individuals and their organic communities. Paul Fussell notes that for Blunden 'the countryside is . . . as precious as English literature,'[1] invoking indirectly the comforting blend of verdant fields and books of Davies' 'In May'. Blunden's aesthetic is rooted in the English pastoral tradition, inspirited by his Georgian contemporaries, Wordsworth, Edward Young and Izaac Walton, characterizing exact observation, conventional form and metre, and precise if archaic diction, balanced in uneasy tension with subject matter often shaped by his own traumatic experiences of modernity. Two of his widely anthologized poems from the 1920s demonstrate precisely this nostalgia and this tension. In six-line fixed rhyme stanzas, the speaker of 'Forefathers', from *The Shepherd* (1922), recounts a pre-industrialized rural community of shepherds and harvesters and huntsmen. These 'men of pith and thew, / Whom the city never called',[2] are not exploited or impoverished. In this idyllic pastoral setting they watch their children play on greens, as their fathers watched them, 'As my father once watched me.'[3] Having placed himself within the rural tradition he longs for, he excises himself from it. Speaking of these men, he says: 'Here I know you by your ground / But I know you not from within.'[4] The physical space, 'the ground', marks the connection to the past, but the inner life of these forefathers has been wiped away: wiped away by the modern present, the poem implies.

'Midnight Skaters', from Blunden's next collection, *English Poems* (1925), which shares similar formal characteristics, provides a more specific and explicit reason for the breach with the past. In a similar rural landscape, though set in a different season, Blunden invokes once again a rural English community. The gathered hop-poles indicate the end of harvest that allows the rollicking leisured play upon the frozen pond by the 'Earth's heedless sons and daughters',[5] making plain by this phrase the organic connection between human subjects and the natural world. But the happy bond between men, women and nature is threatened by the figure of death, which lurks ominously below. Blunden's diction is marvellously telling: 'With but a crystal parapet / Between, he has his engines set.'[6] 'Parapet' has caught the eye of critics for its invocation of the lip of a trench,[7] which is undoubtedly a key point, but the multivalenced richness of 'engines' is remarkably apt, anchored in both the modern present and the literary past. 'Engines' referred till the early seventeenth century to skills in cunning or trickery, and until the late eighteenth century, to a 'contrivance' or 'snare'; the more familiar 'machine or instrument used in warfare' is a usage which dates from the medieval period.[8] What makes 'engines' modern is its coupling with 'parapet', which together invoke the machinery of modern war: the engines of tanks, armoured cars, aeroplanes and other machines that kept the great wheel of modern war turning. The poem ends with an apostrophe to the joyful but endangered skaters to press on and keep the threat at bay: 'Court him, elude him, reel and pass, / And let him hate you through the glass.'[9] The fragility of 'glass', which returns the reader to the associations of the 'crystal parapet', is all that separates the inspired community of skaters from the dark 'hate' of modern experience. Blunden looks back, yearns for the homely comforts of a community interwoven with the natural world, but realizes only too well that modernity – and for him and other veterans, this is most powerfully manifested through modern war – ever waits to prevent his return. Like the nostalgic tensions that persist in Sassoon's poems between the wars, Blunden's nostalgia is empowered by a yearning that is at once sharpened and embittered by the radical break struck by modern war.

Sassoon and Blunden, like many other poets who established reputations during the First World War, developed careers as prose writers in the years between the wars. Besides his highly acclaimed *Undertones of War*, Blunden wrote critical studies and biographies of (mainly) Romantic English poets, particularly poets who explored *Nature in English Literature*, the title of his 1929 study. The status of the natural world in England beyond the scope of literature was also a deeply preoccupying subject of enquiry for Blunden. In the late 1920s and 1930s, he wrote essays like 'The Preservation of England' and 'On Preservation' that sought to marshal a renewed energy to protect the English countryside from the ongoing intrusions of modernity, which contributed to a nostalgic movement that gained momentum during the interwar years. Raymond Williams identifies the 1880s as the beginning of a heightened development of the idealization of rural England as a familiar sanctuary from the anxieties of imperial ventures into unfamiliar lands.[10] Paul Fussell has noted the enduring appeal of the English countryside for soldiers of king and empire serving abroad during the First World War, whether in the poems of Sassoon, Blunden, Edward Thomas, Robert Graves, Ivor Gurney, Charles Sorley or Wilfred Owen, to name but a few, or in the popularity among non-poet soldiers of a periodicals like *Country Life*, which celebrate just this sort of idealized, happy ruralism.[11] Around the same time, but from a different perspective, A. J. Penty promulgated the view that the only possibility of a truly contented and harmonious society lay in abandoning the exploitative, individualistic values of modernity and a society of the masses and returning to the organic, collectivist values of medieval England.[12] In 1920 he wrote: 'During the Middle Ages, England had been the most prosperous and happiest country in Europe, perhaps the happiest country at any time in history.'[13] Granted, Penty was a member of the Guild Socialist movement, with an obvious affinity for historical periods in which guilds thrived, but the link between a vision of England's collectivist past with its implied connection with the natural world and its particular virtues as a nation – here England was assessed as the happiest (greatest) country in all of history – was carried forward by less socialist preservationists.

Rural revivalists had more than pragmatism behind their approaches to land husbandry or the effective recreational uses of public parkland. Imbuing the idealization of a particular understanding of the countryside with moral purpose served a distinctly right-wing conservative agenda. In *Culture and Environment*, published in 1933, F.R. Leavis and Denys Thompson glorify 'The Old England [as] the England of the organic community', laying the cause for the 'vast and terrifying disintegration' of community besetting modern life at the feet of industrial 'Progress' and mass society.[14] Their re-imagined community is organic in its pre-industrial reliance upon and interaction with the natural world, but is far from egalitarian. Thirteen years later William Beach Thomas looked back to the same imagined pre-Progressive period, identifying the social merits of the organic community: 'the English village has been as good a social unit as is found anywhere in the world. One of its social virtues is that comparative wealth is admired, not envied.'[15] The tensions and anxieties of the present that shape Thomas's construction of this past include not only the aftermath of the war, its physical, psychological and moral destruction, but also the sweeping victory in 1945 of the Labour government, and its ideological threats to the rural English social tradition, in which the countryside is figured as merely a giant dairy and granary for the city.

The roots of the rural revival reach back to the end of the previous world war. The economy of the English countryside underwent a profound change between 1918 and 1928; one-quarter of English agricultural land changed ownership.[16] Between the end of the war and 1920 alone, nearly 8 million acres were sold, signifying the largest-scale transfer of lands since the dissolution of the monasteries.[17] While some attributed this loss of rural stability to the 'lost generation' of officers from the land-owning classes wiped out in the war, the less mythical but more likely cause involved the imposition of new and severe death duties combined with a depression in the agricultural economy.[18] Within this economic climate, which fostered political debate about the merits of land nationalization, rural revivalists mobilized their deeply nostalgic response. The English countryside could only be saved by the restoration of the village community. The socio-economic stability of this treasured social unit could be ensured by the revival of the great landlord estates or even the return of the peasantry, a virtuous group of imagined tenant-labourers who admired, without envying, their lords' wealth.[19] While the pace of land exchange slowed in the 1930s and 1940s, the rural revival movement gathered strength with the threat and realization of the renewal of modern war in 1939.

Blunden's *Cricket Country*, published in 1944, is a paean not only to that most English of sports, but to its reflection of the lovely greens of English villages, to its role in the village communities, and to the subtle and unhurried – un-modern – interactions its rituals unfold. H. W. Massingham, editor of *The Nation* at the end of First World War, who published Sassoon's immediate post-war poetry, became an increasing advocate of the rural revival. During the Second World War he wrote articles and books and edited collections of essays about the importance of the countryside to the nation, articulating the political implications of a rural nostalgia. At once bemoaning the loss of pre-Enclosure innocence and embracing the private landowner class who established the enclosures, Massingham describes the 'indispensability of the squire as a warden both of the English tradition and of English husbandry'.[20] The title of the 1942 book from which this quotation is taken, *The English Countryman: A Study of the English Tradition*, indicates the potent intermingling of the ruralism, tradition and nationalism that energizes this particular articulation of modern nostalgia.

In 1933, the same year that Leavis wrote longingly about the organic community of the English village, Sassoon purchased Heytesbury House and established himself as a kind of squire figure of Heytesbury village. While Sassoon seems to have enjoyed the social privileges of this new position, his property was parkland rather than agricultural, and his responsibilities extended to leisure rather than economics. He embraced his role as host of the village cricket matches and member of the village team, and he oversaw with increasing disinterest the annual village fete. Sassoon's way of life and his approach to the natural world, if not the social world of community, embodied implicitly the rural values that Blunden explicitly articulated in his essays published in the 1930s on the preservation of rural England. In other words, Sassoon's embodiment of rural revivalism was essentially symbolic. His increasingly reclusive inclinations limited his active participation in the idealized community of the English village, organic or otherwise.

Nevertheless, his poetry and prose of the 1930s and 1940s are deeply concerned with the interaction between human subjectivity and the splendours of the natural world. While his prose typically addresses his own past and represents the topography of regions of rural England he had encountered in his pre-1914 life, his poetry invokes the consolatory capacity of the Wiltshire countryside, a topos sufficiently removed from the pressures of urban industrial modernization to connect the contemplative human subject to the rural landscape redolent of days gone by. Indeed, Sassoon's writing of his Heytesbury period invokes the manner in which the countryside reflects the values, preoccupations, concerns and anxieties of the subject.

During the Second World War, when technology brought the shadow of war to Heytesbury, with bombers flying overhead and the army requisitioning portions of his park, and even his house, for temporary camp and tank manœuvre grounds, Sassoon increasingly turned away and inwards. Though fond of his military rank – he was known as the Captain amongst the villagers[21] – he remained largely aloof from military staff (with some exceptions, including Sir Oliver Leese, commander of the Eighth Army). His past days of being an infantry officer were well buried. Instead he explored his interactions with his own personal rural revival secured by his extensive private property. As if to counter the enervating anxiety of the return to war, Sassoon's engagement with the rural revival embraced a kind of neo-Georgian sensibility similar to the sentiments invoked by Collie Knox in 1943. In an anthology called *For Ever England*, Knox celebrated his unabashed love for England, which fuses rural, nationalist and poetic interests:

> The sight of sheep filing through a hedge one by one; the symphony of the bees murmuring; the call of church bells across pasture-land – all these I love. These are England . . . 'In English hearts under an English heaven.' . . . And all this we shall come back to if we hold our heads high and follow our star, in due and blessed season. And is there honey still for tea?[22]

The evocation of this nostalgic ruralism is connected to national pride through a Georgian context by the reference to Brooke's 'The Soldier' as well as his 'Grantchester', which appeared in the first volume of *Georgian Poetry*.

Nationalism fused with the innate beauties of the English countryside was a nostalgic nationalism Sassoon could tacitly endorse in his poetry.

The Autobiographical Turn

After a brief post-First World War foray into satirical social commentary, Sassoon turned, or returned, his gaze inward and published poetry that drew on his affiliation with Edward Marsh and *Georgian Poetry*, in spite of his declared fatigue with its overused conventions. 'Keep your eye pretty steadily on some firm object,' guided Marsh, and the object that most captured Sassoon's eye was himself: more particularly, his past self. Most of his poetry of the interwar years is shaped by this nostalgic interest, nostalgic in both pathological and cultural terms. In 1928 Sassoon established himself as a prose writer with the critically and commercially successful *Memoirs of a Fox-Hunting Man*. While not an autobiography per se, this semi-fictional memoir introduces the protagonist George Sherston, a convenient persona based on Sassoon's compartmentalized understanding of selfhood – 'Sherston is only 1/5 my self,' Sassoon wrote to Robert Graves[23] – who became the centre of his first three autobiographical books. That Sherston is a fox-hunting man first and foremost is crucial. He is also an avid cricketer. He is also, eventually, an infantry officer. But it is his passionate participation in these leisured rituals of rural English life that constitutes the essence of his character. After completing this trilogy in 1936, Sassoon returned to his younger self and began another autobiographical project that would also amount to three books, drawing material from the four-fifths of his experience not covered by Sherston: *The Old Century* (1938), *The Weald of Youth* (1942) and *Siegfried's Journey: 1916–1920* (1945).

Many critics have remarked upon the persistence of Sassoon's interest in representing aspects of his own life,[24] but it is important to note that Sassoon's initial autobiographical turn coincides with a whole movement in English literary culture. *Memoirs of a Fox-Hunting Man* is part of the great war-book revival that began in the late 1920s. Autobiographical texts written by soldier-poets loosely connected to either the modernist or the Georgian movement provided an opportunity to impose a narrative meaning upon the experience of modern war. Blunden's 'pastoral prose elegy',[25] *Undertones of War*, appeared in the same year as Sassoon's first Sherston book and declared the consolatory powers of the natural world, declarations sometimes ironically undercut. R. H. Mottram's *Spanish Farm Trilogy* appeared in 1927. Ford Madox Ford and Richard Aldington, former imagists, published autobiographical novels, the *Parade's End* tetralogy (1924–8) and *Death of a Hero* (1929). David Jones's remarkable modernist poetic war narrative, *In Parenthesis*, appeared later, in 1936, saturated in a nostalgic appeal to Celtic mythology that offers order and meaning to Private Jones's alienating modern experience. Whether sympathetic to modernist or Georgian aesthetics, all of these veterans returned with varying degrees of directness to the trauma of wartime and refracted this experience through nostalgia. Sometimes the nostalgia involves looking back to a pre-traumatic past and staking claims of authenticity in an earlier period of harmony between the self and the natural world. Blunden seeks this authenticity through the solidity of natural landscapes, while Sassoon seeks it through interactions between the frail but unbroken human subject and the verdant and supporting natural world that so willingly affords carefree, leisured pastimes.

Sometimes the nostalgia involves the autobiographical genre itself, which appeals to a tradition of making meaning out of the human subject's confounding interactions with others and with the natural world. Even writers with modernist aesthetic values seem to deploy a Romantic model of autobiography as an appealing counterbalance to the fragmentation of modernity. Such models embrace the illusion of the unified and authentic individual subject, made whole through the very act of looking back and imposing linguistic order upon the splintering forces of lived experience. Robert Graves's superficially anti-nostalgic *Goodbye to all That* (1929) is nevertheless generically nostalgic in so far as it attempts to reconstitute an integrated, if iconoclastic, Romantic selfhood capable of withstanding the isolating forces of modernity, including the experience of war.[26]

But by choosing the generic form of autobiography, these veterans partake of a literary tradition that not only looks back on their prior selves, but also cannot help but recall the exemplary constructions of Romantic selfhood found in the antecedent texts of Rousseau and Wordsworth. The autobiographical subjects of *Confessions* and *Prelude* are natural men, men shaped in different ways by their intimate affiliations with the natural world. In the swell of war autobiographies of the late 1920s and 1930s, a Romantic conception of self is what Linda Anderson calls a 'nostalgic revenant',[27] called back to establish the formative prominence of the harmonic and unifying relation between human subject and the natural world.

Such privileging of the natural world's role in human subjectivity can also represent a strategic avoidance of real human intimacy. For Sassoon, the absence of sexuality in his self-representations is conspicuous. In the early 1920s, before embarking upon his Sherston memoirs, Sassoon toyed with the idea of writing an autobiographical novel about homosexuality, a '*Madame Bovary* of sexual inversion'.[28] During the 1920s and early 1930s Sassoon was embroiled in a series of passionate affairs with men that culminated with his intense, if disastrous, liaison with Stephen Tennant. Beyond his diaries and personal letters, he did not write about the swirl of sexual and emotional tensions that so enlivened and disrupted the course of his postwar life. Sexuality was off limits. Neither Sherston nor the autobiographical 'Sassoon' persona is endowed with any overt sexual feelings or conflicts. In their place readers find thoughtful and sometimes intense devotion to fellow soldiers, especially those junior in rank, and a sense of reverence and profound admiration for older men, who serve as mentor figures: Edmund Gosse, Edward Marsh, Thomas Hardy and, perhaps most influential of all, W. H. R. Rivers.

Sassoon's encounter with the eminent psychologist and ethnographer at Craiglockhart War Hospital in 1917 began one of the most important relationships of his life. He describes Rivers in the Sherston memoirs (incidentally the only character from Sassoon's life whose name he did not alter for transfer to Sherston's semi-fictional world) as the solution to the memoirs and the 'solution' to his life. Sassoon made this assessment in 1936, fourteen years after Rivers's death, indicating his enduring legacy, in both his lived experience and its (semi-fictional) representation. The enduring legacy of Sassoon's war experience, which prompted his introduction to Rivers in the first place, is one of the underlying tensions of Sassoon's life not fully represented in his autobiographical writings. In the Sherston memoirs, Sassoon describes some of his hateful and inescapable encounters with death as a soldier, but he is at pains to downplay their after-effects on the development of Sherston's self, as if the impact of these encounters were contained in the moments of their unfolding. In the case of his post-Sherston autobiographies, both the war experience and its legacy are entirely forsaken, as the recollecting Sassoon looks back beyond his war experience to an idyllic and idealized childhood and youth. Trauma, like sexuality, is a significant absence in Sassoon's autobiographical writing.

Traumatic knowledge unsettles the autobiographical project. Recent criticism of autobiography articulates a shift, initiated by feminist writing and scholarship, from the confessional to the testimonial mode, in which witnessing and its ethical imperatives shape the autobiographical discourse. Within such a shift, the relation between the speaker and the listener is paramount, as both work to uncover the meaning of the testimony that cannot be fully known by the speaker alone.[29] Such an act of testimony can then work collaboratively towards attaining traumatic knowledge, which occurs belatedly, in so far as it cannot be fully understood or known during the time of its immediate experience, but only afterwards, during its persistent and lingering after-effects. However, Sassoon's autobiographical writing resists the testimonial mode. He remains immersed in the confessional manner of the autobiographical tradition, with not only little consideration of a specific and collaborating listener, but also a kind of active resistance to and denial of the workings of trauma in his own constructed selfhood. Nevertheless, I maintain that trauma plays a fundamental role in Sassoon's autobiographical poetry and prose. In the years during and preceding the Second World War, the trauma of his experience as a soldier during the First seems to empower the distinctly nostalgic inclination of almost all that he wrote. To understand more fully Sassoon's articulation of nostalgia, a better understanding of his experience of trauma is necessary.

Notes

1. Paul Fussell, *The Great War and Modern Memory* (Oxford: Oxford University Press, 1975), p. 258.
2. Edmund Blunden, 'Forefathers', *The Shepherd* (London: Richard Cobden-Sanderson, 1922), p. 14.
3. Ibid. p. 14.
4. Ibid. p. 14.
5. Edmund Blunden, 'Midnight Skaters', *English Poems* (London: Richard Cobden-Sanderson, 1925), p. 28.
6. Ibid. p. 28.
7. See, for example, Paul Fussell, *Great War*, p. 258.
8. 'Engines', *Shorter Oxford English Dictionary*, 2 vols (Oxford: Oxford University Press, 1944).
9. Blunden, 'Midnight Skaters', p. 28.
10. Raymond Williams, *The Country and the City* (New York: Oxford University Press, 1975), p. 281.
11. See Paul Fussell, 'Arcadian recourses', in Paul Fussell, *Great War*, pp. 231–69.
12. William Stafford, '"This Once Happy Country": Nostalgia for pre-modern society', in Malcolm Chase and Christopher Shaw (eds), *The Imagined Past: History and Nostalgia* (Manchester: Manchester University Press, 1989), pp. 33–46, pp. 34–5.
13. A. J. Penty, quoted in Stafford, 'Happy Country', p. 34.
14. F. R. Leavis, quoted in Malcolm Chase, 'this is no claptrap, this is our heritage', in Chase and Shaw, *The Imagined Past*, pp. 128–46, p. 133.
15. William Beach Thomas, quoted in Chase, 'this is no claptrap, this is our heritage', p. 132.
16. Chase, 'this is no claptrap, this is our heritage', p. 134.
17. Ibid. p. 135.
18. Ibid. p. 135.
19. Ibid. p. 134.
20. H. W. Massingham, quoted in Chase, 'this is no claptrap, this is our heritage', p. 138.
21. Jean Moorcroft Wilson, *Siegfried Sassoon: The Journey from the Trenches: A Biography 1918–1967*, vol. 2 (New York: Routledge, 2003), p. 284.
22. Collie Knox, *For Ever England: An Anthology* (London: Cassell, 1943), pp. 180–1.
23. Siegfried Sassoon, in Paul O'Prey (ed.), *In Broken Images: Selected Letters of Robert Graves, 1914–1946* (London: Hutchinson, 1982), p. 208.
24. See, for example, Paul Fussell, *Great War*; Bernard Bergonzi, *Heroes' Twilight*, 2nd edn (London: Macmillan, 1980); Paul Moeyes, *Siegfried Sassoon: Scorched Glory: A Critical Study* (New York: St Martin's, 1997).
25. Fussell, *Great War*, p. 252.
26. The autobiographical subjects of these books by soldier-poets tend not to experiment with form or ponder alternate and unpredictable meanings that arise from their written representations of lived experience in order to undermine the construction of authenticity, as postmodern autobiographical subjects might (Linda Anderson, *Autobiography* (London: Routledge, 2001), p. 53). Yet even postmodern autobiographical theory invokes nostalgia by insisting on the inevitability of return; the 'I' constitutes itself only through return, Derrida posits (quoted in Anderson, *Autobiography*, p. 82).
27. Anderson, *Autobiography*, p. 59.

28. Siegfried Sassoon, *Diaries 1920–1922*, ed. Rupert Hart-Davis (London: Faber, 1981), p. 53.
29. Shoshana Felman, *What does a Woman Want? Reading Sexual Difference* (Baltimor, MD: Johns Hopkins University Press, 1993), pp. 14–16. See also Felman and D. Laub, *Testimony* (London: Routledge, 1992).

2

RIVERS, MYERS AND THE CULTURE OF WAR NEUROSES

Trauma

Early conceptions of traumatic neurosis have a great deal in common with the aetiology of nostalgia. In 1688 Johannes Hofer attributed the disease to an 'afflicted imagination', noting in patients the persistence of melancholy, relentless preoccupation with home, disturbances of sleep, images of home recurring in dreams, loss of strength and appetite, fever, heart palpitations and stupor.[1] He also speculated that a physiological alteration of channels transferring 'spirits' between brain and body underlaid these symptoms. In nineteenth-century Europe, similarly strange symptoms, partial paralyses and other bodily malfunctions arose in those who experienced industrial or railway accidents. In Britain, this was called 'railway spine'. In America, during the Civil War, a soldier's nervous exhaustion on the battlefield was attributed to 'windage', the incalculable result of exposure to the shock waves of cannon fire. The transforming power of these shocking interactions between the human subject and the machinery of modernity compelled early physicians of the modern industrial age to assume that the trauma of the accident must have produced some underlying organic change. This assumption was slow to leave medical epistemology. In the last decades of the nineteenth century, physicians began to explore more closely the connection between the memory of the shocking experience and the ensuing alteration of the self. Hofer's idea that the impressions which lead to nostalgia can reappear in our dreams is an almost exact prefiguring of the relation between traumatic experience and dream in psychoanalytic terms. In discussing the history of 'traumatic neuroses' in 1910, Thomas Glynn noted that many physicians have held it to be 'a disease of the imagination',[2] and by recalling Hofer's phrase, implies a parallel between trauma and nostalgia.

During the First World War, English military physician Charles Myers transformed the diagnosis of windage into 'shell shock', attributing the severe somatic impairments of combat veterans to an imperceptible alteration to the nervous system caused by the concussive force of high explosive shellfire. But, given the difficulties of proving a somatic cause, many physicians abandoned an organic approach to aetiology in favour of exploring the effects of traumatic experience upon memory and its legacy upon self-understanding. This psychological or psychoanalytic turn in understanding the impact of war experience upon the human subject retained influence until well after the Second World War. Physicians in the service of the military, like Charles Myers and W. H. R. Rivers, gave shape to these psychological models in Britain, building on the work of relatively obscure British physicians and adapting controversial psychoanalytic ideas from the Continent.[3]

From traumatic neuroses to shell shock, war neuroses, war stress, battle fatigue and post-traumatic stress disorder, notions of trauma have dominated the twentieth-century understanding of the psychological impact of war. Of course, trauma transcends military experience and informs discourses of family violence, child abuse, slavery and AIDS, to name but a few, and in recent years has become a privileged psychic phenomenon and mode of enquiry in the humanities and social sciences. In these terms, trauma refers to an overwhelming experience of catastrophe to which the response occurs not immediately, but in a series of delayed and repetitive after-effects.[4] Andreas Huyssen considers trauma, along with the abject and the uncanny, the 'master-signifiers' of the 1990s, 'all of which have to do with repression, specters, and a present repetitively haunted by the past'.[5] Like nostalgia, but in a different register, trauma is 'located on the threshold between remembering and forgetting, seeing and not seeing, transparency and occlusion'.[6] This liminality, together with the prominence of repression, spectres and a present haunted by the past are all very much features of Sassoon's post-First World War writing, features aligned more closely with the dominant concerns of modernism than he or his critics would concede.

In 1917, Sassoon was sent to Craiglockhart War Hospital and came under the care of Rivers, who taught him the dangers of repression and the importance of articulating, without fixating upon, one's conscious and unconscious anxieties. Sassoon never fully mastered the lesson. Decades later, Sassoon describes the understanding of wartime trauma he gleaned from Rivers and Craiglockhart:

> Shell shock. How many a brief bombardment had its long-delayed after-effect in the minds of these survivors, many of whom had looked at their companions and laughed while inferno did its best to destroy them. Not then was their evil hour, but now; now, in the sweating suffocation of nightmare, in paralysis, in the stammering of dislocated speech.[7]

He had himself experienced the 'sweating suffocation of nightmare', and well understood the persistence of the 'evil hour' of now, the present haunted by the past. For Sassoon and other veterans, the war did not end with their withdrawal from the frontline or with the Armistice. Six years later, in 1924, T. E. Lawrence wrote to Robert Graves:

> What's the cause that you, and Sassoon . . . and I can't get away from the War? Here you are riddled with thought like an old table-leg with worms: [Sassoon] yawing about like a ship aback: me in the ranks, finding squalor and mistreatment the only permitted existence; what's the matter with us all? It's like the malarial bugs in the blood, coming out months and years after in recurrent attacks.[8]

What was the matter with them all? Lawrence's pathological metaphor of 'recurrent attacks' contains the answer. In a word, trauma.

Traumatic Neuroses and Modern War

Wartime investigations into the nature of soldiers' functional disorders followed the pattern of debate about the nature of psychological ailments in peacetime. Since the middle of the nineteenth century, physicians had observed nervous disturbances in victims of industrial and railway accidents who had sustained no discernible physical injury.[9] The physical essence of the disturbance suggested by the anatomical components of its early names, 'railway spine' or 'railway brain', was carried into the more general term which supplanted them later in the nineteenth century: 'traumatic neuroses',[10] where 'trauma' derives from the Greek word meaning 'wound'.[11] Symptoms of traumatic neuroses were typically separated into neurasthenia, including insomnia, nightmares, restlessness, excessive irritability, melancholia (all of which Sassoon complained about in his diaries), tingling sensations, vertigo, and memory loss; and hysteria, including stooping gait, paralysis, seizures, temporary blindness, deafness and mutism.[12] Before the turn of the century, the prevailing belief was that neurasthenic or hysterical symptoms were caused by some hitherto undiscovered organic injury, or trauma, sustained during an accident.[13] This belief that psychological trauma had physiological roots guided the theorizing of psychological ailments in Britain early in the First World War.[14]

Military medical authorities throughout Europe were overwhelmed by the sheer volume of soldiers incapacitated by nervous disorders of war, which were identified with a proliferation of terms, including 'shell shock', 'war strain', 'war neuroses', 'neurasthenia', 'hysteria' and 'anxiety neuroses'. Traditional medico-military treatments included 'sympathy, firmness, isolation, suggestion in various forms, hypnosis', though these were often ineffective.[15] Generally, regardless of the term, authorities regarded such disorders with suspicion. Even before the war, Thomas Glynn indicated the degree of mistrust associated with trauma: 'That which in medico-legal work is called a traumatic neurosis would be regarded in ordinary life as a fraud.'[16]

Similarly wary of 'insidious malingering', healthy soldiers masquerading as casualties, military physicians such as Babinski, Leri, Dejerine and Yealland treated patients by means of moral punishment, 'persuasion' often involving enforced hunger, isolation and painful electrical faradization (application of electrical current to the body).[17] In Germany and Austria such treatments were common, favoured by physicians like Koslowski and future Nobel Prize laureate Wagner-Jauregg.[18] Ironically, this harsh materialist approach to nervous disorders contained within itself an implicit acknowledgement of the Freudian theory it opposed so desperately. As the German psychiatrist Ernst Simmel commented: 'They make a torture of the treatment in order to force the neurotic "to flee into health".'[19]

Charles Myers and 'Shell Shock'

Within months of the outbreak of the war, the editors of *The Lancet* speculated upon the widespread incidents of nerve-related casualties among the soldiers at the front. Could such physical factors as the repeated concussions of air from high explosive shellfire affect the nervous system in some imperceptible but substantial way and in such a fashion that otherwise normal individuals would become susceptible to mental breakdown? With 'insufficient data' at present to resolve the speculation, the editors invited further discussion of this perplexing situation. Early the following year, *The Lancet* published 'A Contribution to the Study of Shell Shock' by Charles Myers, who first applied the enduring term to nerve-related casualties of war.

Once a student of W. H. R. Rivers, Myers was at work in a psychological laboratory at Cambridge in the early days of the war, studying phonographic recordings of the music of 'primitive Australian tribes'. By the end of August 1914 he found this work becoming increasingly irrelevant and unimportant in the face of the developing war.[20] In the patriotic fervour that swept England and Europe in the late summer of that year, there was no difficulty finding physicians for medical corps; the War Office was not accepting any physician older than forty for service abroad. Myers had to travel to France of his own accord and curry favour among his influential friends until he found a position in the Duchess of Westminster's Hospital Unit. Finally he could visit a tailor in Paris and order his khaki uniform.[21]

Over the next weeks and months Myers observed the casualties that led to his publication in *The Lancet*. In three case studies he found that the physical shock from nearby exploding shells had caused the hysterical symptoms of 'loss of vision, smell, and taste', and the neurasthenic symptom of loss of memory.[22] At this early stage in the investigation, the organic aetiology of the condition was yet to be doubted seriously. By the middle of 1916, Myers had seen more than 2,000 cases of 'shell shock'.[23] His experience allowed him to formulate the following comprehensive definition:

> After a man has been buried, lifted or otherwise subject to the physical effects of a bursting shell or other similar explosive, he may suffer solely from concussion (which should be termed 'shell concussion'), or solely from mental 'shock' (so-called 'shell shock'), or from both of these conditions in succession.
>
> If 'shell shock' occurs, it will give rise to one or more of the following groups of mental symptoms, namely, (i) hysteria, (ii) neurasthenia, (iii) graver temporary 'mental' disorder.
>
> But 'shell shock' and these three groups of accompanying symptoms . . . do not depend for their causation on the physical force (or the chemical effects) of the bursting shell. They may also occur when the soldier is remote from the exploding missile, provided that he be subject to an emotional disturbance or mental strain sufficiently severe.[24]

The most important aspect of this definition is the emphasis on severe 'emotional disturbance' or 'mental strain' as a root of the condition. Sudden fear or horror – any 'psychical trauma' or 'inadjustable experience' – is sufficient to activate the condition.[25] Myers admitted that the term 'shell shock' was 'singularly ill-chosen' since the condition may not be caused by a shell, and may not even be attributable to a single 'shock'. Dissatisfied with the term's abuse, he made motions to have the War Office officially ban 'shell shock' as a diagnostic condition.[26] His suggestions for new terms were ignored until the War Office eventually accepted NYDN ('Not Yet Diagnosed, Nervous') in June 1917 as the initial diagnostic term for frontline medical officers to indicate a soldier suffering from some aspect of war neuroses.[27] Nevertheless, Myers's evocative initial designation endured.

Rivers, Maghull and the English Psychoanalytic Approach

Rivers had returned to England in the spring of 1915 from ethnographic field work in the South Pacific, and in the summer joined Myers and Elliot Smith at the Maghull Military Hospital in Manchester.[28] Maghull, like Craiglockhart, was one of nineteen hospitals[29] for war neuroses established during the war to accommodate the flood of psychological cases from the front. Since his training in Germany in the early 1890s, Rivers had been interested in Continental approaches to neuroses[30] and once back in England had become an early advocate of Freudian ideas.[31] Writing of this time together at Maghull, Smith recalled a stimulating 'society in which the interpretation of dreams and the discussion of mental conflicts formed the staple subjects of conversation'.[32]

In their book, *Shell Shock and its Lessons* (1917), Smith and T. H. Pear acknowledged the popular (if misleading) currency of 'shell shock', which they redefined broadly to include 'all those mental effects of war experience which are sufficient to incapacitate a man from the performance of his military duties'.[33] The authors did not seek out the physiological alterations caused by the concussions of shellfire, but emphasized the psychological impact of exposure to battle. At Maghull Smith, Pears, Rivers and Myers looked beyond the traditional and ineffective treatments,[34] prescribing instead 'psychological analysis and Re-education'.[35] By 'Re-education' they referred to the development of practical strategies for coping with life, working through problems, an approach which became a key feature of Rivers's 'autognosis', which I discuss further in Chapter 3. The chief lesson of shell shock for Smith and Pear was that mental disease is a far-reaching societal problem, in times of peace as well as war. They upbraid the British medical establishment for being unable to help patients suffering from ailments which may have no apparent physiological cause but are 'real' enough to them. As Rivers later affirmed, 'the essential causes of the psycho-neuroses of warfare are mental, and not physical.'[36] The work of Freud and Breuer in the early 1890s was largely responsible for introducing the idea that the root of traumatic neuroses might have a mental or psychological source, and not necessarily a physical one: 'Hysterics suffer mainly from reminiscences,' the authors famously claimed.[37] In *Studies on Hysteria* (1895), Freud and Breuer insisted that the 'operative cause' of traumatic neuroses 'is not the trifling physical injury, but the affect of fright – the psychical trauma'.[38] Myers's subsequent experience with more than 2,000 cases of shell shock, combined with his participation in an intellectual environment open to the ideas of Freud and Breuer, led him to realize that shell shock could be brought about by a severe 'emotional disturbance' without any physical or chemical injury.[39] At Maghull, Rivers, Myers and their colleagues were concerned less with the aetiology of traumatic neuroses than with an effective treatment of it that would enable their soldier-patients to return to duty,[40] though not necessarily back to the trenches.[41]

In 'Freud's Psychology of the Unconscious', a paper presented in March 1917 at the Edinburgh Pathological Club, six months after he moved to Craiglockhart,[42] Rivers set out to clear up the misunderstanding that surrounded the British medical establishment's suspicion of Freudian ideas,[43] and to reveal their potential utility.[44] He demonstrated how Freud's ideas could be validated by general observations of human behaviour as exemplified by himself or his friends, and he downplayed the contentious issue of sexuality, insisting that it was not as central to Freudian thought as either his avid supporters or his vehement detractors made out. Rivers emphasized the 'naturalness' of unconscious experience in human existence and the role of instinctual impulses in the unconscious, foregrounding what he found to be the most striking aspect of Freudian thought: the active nature of forgetting, especially forgetting unpleasant experience and suppressing it in the unconscious. But unlike the typical case studies of Freud, who traced his patient's illness back to childhood traumas or sexual development, Rivers focused on the emotional conflicts of frontline experience that produced the 'flight to illness'.

Rivers held that, like the neuroses of peacetime, war neuroses were the result of not fully successful 'attempts to solve the conflict between [the] warring elements' of instincts and their controlling forces.[45] Accordingly, he saw war neuroses as a product of the conflict between the soldier's instinct of self-preservation and the sense of duty that endangered his survival; the instinct to avoid danger in active service produces fear, which is held by 'the ordinary standard of our social life' to be unmanly, 'disgraceful'.[46] The 'healthy' solution to this conflict, Rivers thought, involved the suppression of instinctive fear and its absorption into the unconscious mind, leaving the soldier able to perform his dangerous duty. When the 'unwitting' or unconscious act of suppression had to be attempted by a conscious effort of repression, neuroses resulted.

In December 1917, at the Royal Society of Medicine, Rivers presented a paper called 'Repression of War Experience', the essence of which Sassoon expressed in his famous poem with the same title. In his paper Rivers cautioned against the harmful effects of the standard medical advice for psychologically disturbed soldiers: avoid all thoughts of the war and you will be right as rain. The attempt to banish or repress the effects of painful experience from the mind not only did not work, but actually exacerbated the neurosis. The mental discomfort and depression which resulted from the conflict that produced the neurosis tended to 'crystallise' round some incident of trauma the patient had experienced.[47] The haunting memory of this experience often displaced the original affect of fear by producing its own affect of horror, guilt or shame of survival. During waking hours the conscious mind worked fervently to banish these powerful affective memories. During sleep, however, the repressed images returned with a vengeance in 'dreams or nightmares', when 'the painful affect, together with the experience round which it has crystallised, dominate the mind'.[48] Such distress often drove the sufferer to increased efforts of conscious repression until finally a 'comparatively trivial shock, illness or wound' caused a breakdown and the loss of ability to deal with the original conflict. The victim would be plunged into a fully developed state formerly called neurasthenia, but now, following Freud, more generally known as anxiety-neurosis,[49] due to exaggerated levels of anxiety, the *Angst* of the German language, which forms one of the state's most striking and characteristic symptoms.[50] Because of the vital aetiological role of repression in this condition, Rivers suggested that an apt name for it would be repression-neurosis, but 'war neurosis' was the term that caught on.

In early July 1917, during the frantic days of working out his public protest against the war, Sassoon wrote the poem that he later, once under Rivers's influence, retitled 'Repression of War Experience'.[51] The speaker of the poem is a wounded soldier who attempts to figure a moth as a talisman to keep his mind from wandering to darker subjects, but the scorching of its wings by a candle returns him to precisely where he does not want to be: 'No, no, not that, – it's bad to think of war, / When thoughts you've gagged all day come back to scare you.'[52] As the moth 'bumps and flutters' against the reflection of candlelight upon the ceiling, and is trapped there to beat against the illumination and not pass through it, it symbolizes the surviving soldier's plight. It is not his experience exactly that traps him; rather, the reflection of that experience through unbidden memories entraps him in a cycle of repression and repetition. Though he had not yet been sent to Craiglockhart nor met Rivers, Sassoon had observed first-hand in others the terrifying, lingering consequences of war experience that were now the focus of Rivers's work.

Uncanny Doublings

The internal dialogue of Sassoon's poem embodies the conflict Rivers described between natural instincts and cultural forces that control them. Rivers's model of an individual constituted by warring parties posits a subjectivity of duality (or multiplicity), which echoes the notion of the double, a common trope in war poems and memoirs, as well as a key figure in Freud's version of the uncanny. Freud opens his 1919 essay with a series of definitions of 'uncanny' from various languages, including English: 'Uncomfortable, uneasy, gloomy, dismal, uncanny, ghastly; (of a house) haunted; (of a man) a repulsive fellow'.[53] Each of these words readily applies to the experience of trench warfare. Freud describes 'Dismembered limbs, a severed head, and hand cut off at the wrist . . . all these have something peculiarly uncanny about them,'[54] and 'all these' are constituent of the haunting experiences faced by veterans of the Western Front. Certainly, such imagery figures prominently in the war writings of soldier-poets like Sassoon's 'Counter-attack', Rosenberg's 'Dead Man's Dump', Graves's 'A Dead Boche' and the grimmer pages of Blunden's *Undertones of War*.

Freud further describes the uncanny effect generated by an effacing of the distinction between imagination and reality, when something one once regarded as imaginary seems to become reality.[55] Recollections of ordinary conditions on the front were at times saturated with images previously limited to the imaginary texts of classical antiquity, Dante's *Inferno* or other journeys to the underworld. Sassoon drew images from these imaginary textual antecedents when attempting to describe the battlefield from the Western Front: '[The landscape] loomed limitless and strange and sullenly imbued with the Stygian significance of the War. And the soldiers who slept around us in their hundreds – were they not like the dead[?]'[56] Freud pointed out that 'the over-accentuation of psychical reality in comparison with material reality' was an aspect of the uncanny that commonly featured as a symptom of neuroses,[57] and of war neuroses especially. When the distinction between imagination and lived experience is breached, the uncanny floods in.

The dissolution of boundaries between imaginary and actual worlds contributes to perhaps the most prominent feature of Freud's uncanny: the double. The double can arise from an inability to determine one's 'real' self reliably; it can occur when the subject identifies himself or herself with someone else so that doubt arises about which self is the subject's own, or when there is a splitting or dividing or replicating of the self.[58] In Freud's view, owing to 'the primary narcissism which dominates the mind of childhood and primitive man', the double was in these early stages a positive force, a protection against the extinction of death, 'an assurance of immortality'.[59] But when this early stage has passed, for the individual adult or for civilization as a whole, then the double becomes a thing of potential terror, 'the uncanny harbinger of death'.[60] Invoking the inner conflict that Rivers seized upon, Freud related the double to war experience more explicitly in his 'Introduction' to *Psycho-Analysis and the War Neuroses*. He described the internal conflict between the pre-war ego and the ego of the soldier that arises when the soldier's duty puts the subject in life-threatening situations. In this conflict the soldier ego becomes the 'newly formed parasitic double', endangering the subject's survival.[61] The 'parasitic double' hearkens back to an image from *Studies on Hysteria* of trauma infiltrating the psyche like a 'foreign body' and wreaking havoc from within. This internalized conflict of the double is also present in Elliot Smith's discussion of a soldier suffering from shell shock: 'There are warring elements inside as well as outside him: he is trying to fight the enemy with an army which has mutinied.'[62] The army-in-mutiny metaphor conveys the self's sense of a loss of agency by its own unruly hand. To conceptualize the conflict as one between a 'self' and its 'parasitic double', as Freud did, can enrich one's reading of war writers who grapple with the lingering effects of their uncanny experience.

Certainly the double's associations with death are inescapable in Sassoon and other war writers: Blunden and Graves, for example. 'One might even say', Freud stated in his 'Introduction' cited above, 'that in the case of the war neuroses the thing feared is after all *an inner foe*.'[63] It is 'the inner foe' who conjures up 'the crowds of ghosts among the trees' in Sassoon's 'Repression of War Experience'.[64] It is the 'inner foe' who haunts Blunden in 'Another Journey from Béthune to Cuinchy':

I see you walking
To a pale petalled sky,
And the green silent water
Is resting thereby;
It seems like bold madness
But that 'you' is I.[65]

In Graves's 'Recalling War' it is the 'inner foe' who unleashes 'the inward scream, the duty to run mad'.[66] The 'duty' to madness works well to yoke together the soldier's duty to the army and the all-too-common result of this obedience. There are many other examples in the poetry and prose of these three, and of countless other war writers. But in Sassoon's memoirs, as I will discuss in Chapter 3, he also invokes the double from childhood, which is a kind of nostalgic resurrection of the double's positive role as protector against the fear of immortality.

Trauma: The Historical Return

During the First World War, and into the early 1920s, there were many articles in British medical journals about the aetiology, prognosis and treatment of casualties related to trauma. As one writer says, 'the neuroses incidental to the great war made the world neurosis-minded.'[67] The 'Report of the War Office Committee of Enquiry on Shell Shock', published in 1922, the year that Rivers died suddenly, coincided with a reduction in publishing activity on this topic in the important journals.[68] The report offered some important conclusions about neurotic illness related to war. The Committee aimed to lay to rest, permanently, the application of the misleading term 'shell shock' (though including it in their title seems a strange way to assure its removal from medical discourse). They also insisted that incidents of neuroses or mental breakdown must be recorded by the Army Medical Corps as cases of general disease, like, say, tuberculosis, and not as cases of battle casualty. The insistence on this 'disease' classification was likely related to issues of liability compensation.[69] In 1918 there were 32,000 veterans in Britain receiving pensions for 'functional nervous or mental disease'; by 1921 this figure had more than doubled to 65,000.[70] In 1938 there were still 29,000 drawing pensions, making this disorder the most expensive for the Ministry of Pensions, apart from 'Wounds and Amputations'.[71] After the flurry of articles published during wartime and in the early post-war years, study of this ailment subsided. Subsequent to 1922 there was relatively sparse coverage of the traumatic neuroses of war in British medical journals, until the Second World War revived interest in the subject.

The War Office Committee on Shell Shock made some noteworthy recommendations about the treatment of war neuroses. They approved a variety of therapeutic approaches: 'the simplest forms of psycho-therapy', including suggestion and persuasion, combined with such 'physical methods' as baths, massage and electricity.[72] However, the Committee explicitly did 'not recommend psychoanalysis in the Freudian sense'.[73] That the military could not commit the time and resources required for in-depth psychoanalytic treatment was not surprising, but one wonders if the same prejudices that made Freud unpopular during the war – his being Austrian, his 'pan-sexual' perversion and so on – did not also contributed to the Committee's blanket dismissal.

By the time traumatic neuroses reappear in medical discourse in the later 1930s, with war once again a possibility, Freud had fled Vienna for Britain after the Nazi invasion of Austria in 1938 and his ideas were no longer deemed 'enemy ideas'. Charles Berg, a Harley Street Freudian psychologist, published a collection of his articles and case histories in *War in the Mind* (1941), including a section on 'War Neuroses' in which he discussed several case studies of veterans whose symptoms, stemming from their First World War experience, became reactivated during the late 1930s' threat of war. In one former serviceman, the repressed anxiety of his war trauma was more dynamic and active than its forgotten memory. Conscious anxiety-provoking thoughts in the present about the possibility of a new war with Germany forged a connection with the unconscious memories of the war past. On a more passive level, the sounds of traffic invoked echoes of bursting shellfire. The memories and extreme anxiety of the past experience were thus drawn up into the conscious mind with confounding consequences. During treatment, this patient, overwhelmed by anxiety, struggled to flee Dr Berg's consulting rooms 'just as though it were Cambrai in 1917 and not London in 1938'.[74] Such temporal juxtaposition becomes a dominant trope in Sassoon's writing of the 1930s and 1940s.

When the Second World War was under way, the medical establishment in Britain was far better prepared for the inevitability of psychological strain in soldiers. With the advent of airborne warfare and the alarming prospect of widespread bombardment of civilian targets, there was also the expectation of extensive afflictions of war neuroses in civilians. That civilians forced to sit passively through an aerial bombardment fared better than soldiers undergoing similar conditions was attributed to the lack of gain a civilian would receive from illness. Psychological illness in a soldier could remove him from the battle zone, but for a civilian there was no escape when the battle zone was where he lived and worked.[75] Nevertheless, the medical community prepared itself for the worst. At Cambridge, a series of lectures on war neuroses was given by T. A. Ross to general practitioners during 1940 to demystify the phenomenon of war neuroses by stressing the causal significance of gain through illness. Also at Cambridge early in the Second World War, Charles Myers published *Shell Shock in France 1914–1918*, conceding that the new war elicited from the unconscious legion anxieties and clouded memories of his own traumatic experiences of the First World War.

Abram Kardiner's *War Stress and Neurotic Illness* (1947) established the dominance of Freud's ideas in understanding trauma during the recurrence of world war. Kardiner underwent analysis with Freud shortly after the publication of *Beyond the Pleasure Principle*[76] and was a keen student. He eventually adapted his psychoanalytic learning from the master into a version of ego psychology, which became the American incarnation of Freudian ideas. But Kardiner's approach to the impact of war experience upon an individual psyche offers insightful contributions into the understanding of trauma. Anticipating Cathy Caruth's articulation, Kardiner described how the originary traumatic event cannot be apprehended at its moment of being; at that moment meaning is disrupted. What the trauma rehearses again and again is the attempt to adapt to the residual stimuli of the originary event, which are displaced through various symptomatic routes, such as nightmare and 'an altered conception of the outer world and of the self'.[77] Kardiner argued that the self, disturbed by excessive stimuli from the external world, 'contracts' and its ability to adapt to the residue of these stimuli is reduced.[78] Sassoon's life after the war, as well as his post-war writings, can be seen to illustrate Kardiner's explanation of the post-traumatic workings of his war experience. His reclusiveness, especially in the later 1930s and 1940s, and the obsessive introspection and nostalgic direction of his poetry and prose after 1926 both mark a contraction of Sassoon's construction of self. The notion of 'repetition compulsion' is certainly pertinent to a writer who, in Paul Fussell's words, embarked upon an 'obsessive enterprise' in which he spent half his life 'plowing and re-plowing the earlier half'.[79]

Ernst Simmel, who contributed to the Symposium on War Neuroses at the 1918 Psycho-Analytic Congress in Budapest while serving as a medical officer in the German army, had emigrated to America after the war. In a 1943 article, Simmel looked back on how trauma was understood during the First World War. The intervening twenty-five years had provided a growth in knowledge about the dynamics of ego psychology which allowed him to gain perspective on some of the early discoveries of psychoanalysis. He stressed two fundamental points. Most basically, anxiety was of 'cardinal significance' in the origin of all mental disturbance,[80] a point with which Rivers, Myers, Ross and Berg would have agreed. And more specifically, 'the "repetition compulsion" is a fundamental factor in all traumatic neuroses,'[81] which accorded very much with Kardiner. Simmel concluded his article by quoting Freud's introduction to *Psycho-Analysis and the War Neuroses* and invoking an image that is also relevant to this project: 'One can dare say that in war neuroses, what is feared is an inner enemy.'[82] For Sassoon, this foe lurking within – a consequence of his traumatic experience of battle – lurked still during the post-war years and the years leading up to the Second World War. Rivers, and the memories of Rivers, helped to shore up Sassoon's defences against this inner enemy.

Sassoon's Rivers

The first signs of the appearance in Sassoon's writing of the inner foe that Freud conceptualized came in his diary in the early spring of 1916, more than a year before he met Rivers. The peacetime lover of nature was transformed by the death of a friend into a daring and reckless killer: 'I used to say I couldn't kill anyone in this war; but since they shot Tommy I would gladly stick a bayonet into a German by daylight.'[83] He came to know 'the lust to kill'[84] and the desire 'to smash someone's skull'.[85] To recognize and acknowledge such unexpected and powerful feelings had serious repercussions, some of which Sassoon sounded out in an unpublished poem called 'Peace' written in his diary:

> In my heart there's cruel war that must be waged
> In darkness vile with moans and bleeding bodies maimed;
> A gnawing hunger drives me, wild to be assuaged,
> And bitter lust chuckles within me unashamed.[86]

This chuckling 'bitter lust' was a troubling sensation, a kind of inner foe that conflicted with his peaceable survival instincts. Indeed the poem, as well as entries elsewhere in his wartime diary, articulate the internalized 'cruel war' between instinctual aggression and the forces inhibiting its expression, which were weakened by combat. This inner conflict had lasting repercussions, introducing him to the temporal instability characteristic of trauma. A diary entry almost a year later confirms the persistence of the feelings described in 'Peace': 'while I lie awake staring at the darkness of the tent my own terrors get hold of me and I long only for life and comfort.'[87] He felt 'scarred and tortured' by the 'nerve-strain' of his frontline experience; yet he supposed that 'all this "emotional experience" (futile phrase)' might be valuable in the future,[88] but 'leads nowhere now (but to madness)'.[89] Recovering from a head wound in 4th London Hospital at Denmark Hill, Sassoon recorded his mental distress:

> And when the lights are out . . . and the white beds are quiet with drowsy figures, huddled out-stretched, then the horrors come creeping across the floor: the floor is littered with parcels of dead flesh and bones, faces glaring at the ceiling, faces turned to the floor, hands clutching neck or belly; a livid grinning face with bristly moustache peers at me over the edge of my bed, the hands clutching my sheets. Yet I found no bloodstains there this morning . . . I don't think they mean any harm to me. They are not here to scare me; they look at me reproachfully, because I am so lucky, with my safe wound, and the warm kindly immunity of the hospital is what they longed for when they shivered and waited for the attack to begin, or the brutal bombardment to cease . . . I wish I could sleep.[90]

Such a hallucinatory experience, a common symptom of war neuroses, affected Sassoon only intermittently, however, and several weeks after recording these nocturnal visitations, he wrote in his diary: 'For a while I am shaking off the furies that pursued me.'[91] But it was also clear that he was unsure about how long he could engage in this inner 'cruel war'.

In July 1917, already decorated with an MC, Sassoon was sent by the military authorities to Craiglockhart War Hospital outside Edinburgh. Their motives were political. Eventually published in twelve newspapers, including *The Times*, and read out in the House of Commons, Sassoon's statement against the war was a potentially damaging document. The War Office sought to limit the damage by declaring that the author of 'A Soldier's Declaration' was suffering from shell shock and therefore not of sound mind.[92] Sassoon dismissively referred to Craiglockhart as 'Dottyville' and insisted that there was no psychological basis for his confinement in 'the truly awful atmosphere of this place of washouts and shattered heroes'.[93] Entrusted to the care of the eminent ethnographer and psychologist, W. H. R. Rivers, Sassoon would recall in the mid-1930s how both of them had joked about the 'anti-war complex' from which he was reputedly suffering.[94] He asked Rivers outright if he was a shell shock case and reports that Rivers replied, 'Certainly not.'[95] Compared to some of his dramatically incapacitated fellow 'inmates' in that 'live museum of war neuroses',[96] he insisted his mental health was relatively untroubled, which was also Rivers's initial assessment after their first meeting on 23 July 1917.[97] However, Sassoon himself was very anxious about the state of his nerves, as shown by his wartime diaries and the later memoirs, as well as his continuing reliance after Craiglockhart on Rivers as a 'guiding spirit'.

In the third volume of the Sherston memoirs, Sassoon downplays the psychological damage he suffered in the war, in a way subrogating his encounters with internal foes with his encounter with Rivers. For example, he addresses trauma in *Sherston's Progress* (1935) in a lightly ironic and intriguingly equivocal way when, as Sherston,[98] he recalls an aspect of Rivers's treatment:

> About my own dreams he hadn't bothered much, but as there may be someone who needs to be convinced that I wasn't suffering from shell-shock, I am offering a scrap of dream evidence, which for all I know may prove that I was![99]

The exclamation mark almost invites the pre-emptive assertion of the final clause to be read at face value. While Sassoon preferred to emphasize the political motivations behind the War Office's decision to send him to Craiglockhart and to dismiss his experience of mental anguish as merely part of his 'anti-war complex' – the light-hearted diagnosis offered by Rivers with a smile during one of their interviews[100] – after his release from the hospital, he made a note in his diary which casts doubt on that jocularity. He wrote that 'after the strain and unhappiness of the last seven months [at Craiglockhart]' he would stop brooding about the war's futility and instead indulge in 'light-hearted stupidity' and 'peacefulness'.[101] It was, he said, 'the only way by which I can hope to face the horrors of the front without breaking down completely'.[102] And yet, despite his resolve, the obstinate concern about complete breakdown persisted; contemplating his return to the Western Front, he determines: '*I will not go mad*'.[103] Like many veterans, including his friends Edmund Blunden, Robert Graves and T. E. Lawrence, Sassoon feared the onset of madness, which itself can be a sign of war neurosis.[104] Five months later, in May 1918, he seems actually to acknowledge that what he had experienced was indeed a breakdown: 'I must never forget Rivers. He is the only man who can save me if I break down again.'[105]

Rivers provided Sassoon with a strategy to keep madness and that inner enemy at bay, which he in effect adapted to suit his latent mysticism just as he converted Rivers from a psychological to a spiritual mentor. In his paper 'Repression of War Experience', Rivers warned of the pitfalls of obsessive self-absorption and expressed the limitations of the talking cure: 'in my opinion it is just as harmful to dwell persistently upon painful memories or anticipations, and brood upon feelings of regret and shame, as to attempt to banish them wholly [through repression] from the mind.'[106] Rivers approached the treatment of neuroses, including war neuroses, through what he called autognosis and re-education. By autognosis he meant 'the process by which the patient learns to understand the real state of his mind and the conditions by which this state has been produced'.[107] This search for self-understanding had to be combined with re-education, 'a process in which the patient is led to understand how his newly acquired knowledge of himself can be utilized'.[108] The therapeutic techniques of autognosis certainly resonate in Sassoon's post-war writing, but there is more than gratitude for a psychologist's insights behind his veneration of 'the great and good man who gave me his friendship and guidance'.[109] It is not only because Rivers had died suddenly that he was the only person in the Sherston memoirs whose name was not altered to suit its semi-fictionalized construct: 'If he were alive I could not be writing so freely about him. I might even be obliged to call him by some made-up name, which would seem absurd.'[110] Sassoon's indebtedness to Rivers is clear in the way he adopts the concepts of autognosis and re-education, adapting them to suit his impressionistic, subjective, poetic and ultimately spiritual temperament.

Some critics have deemed *Sherston's Progress* aesthetically disappointing compared to the first two volumes of the trilogy, or have found the religious overtones of its title and the concluding scene disingenuous.[111] However, it is not religion as such, I believe, that underlies the allusion to Bunyan in the book's title and epigraph – 'I told him that I was a Pilgrim going to the Celestial City'[112] – but the almost spiritual nature of Sassoon's devotion to Rivers and his psychological insights. Rivers saw a relationship between medicine and religious beliefs, between the psychiatrist and the priest, between the cathartic benefits of the talking cure and confession:[113] 'catharsis is the most important psycho-therapeutic agent in the process of confession, whether this form part of a religious rite or of a manifestly medical procedure.'[114] For Rivers, both approaches to human distress were underwritten by the crucial element of 'faith' focused on 'the personality of the physician or priest'.[115] Early in *Sherston's Progress*, Sherston is told that 'Rivers was evidently some sort of great man,'[116] and soon after meeting him, he says: 'All I knew was that he was my father-confessor, as I called him.'[117] At the end, recovering from a head wound in hospital, he is troubled by self-destructive thoughts, but when Rivers enters the ward 'My futile demons fled him – for his presence was a refutation of wrong-headedness.'[118] He 'exorcis[ed]' Sassoon's 'demons' without saying anything – 'his smile was benediction enough.'[119] The goal of Sherston's 'progress' in this volume – and in everything Sassoon wrote before his conversion to Roman Catholicism – is his version of the state of enlightenment promised by the therapeutics of autognosis and re-education: to 'know the world for what it is, and ourselves for what the world has made us'.[120] When he did convert in 1957, he redirected his faith from physician to priest, an adjustment entirely in keeping with Rivers's conception of the healing capacity of faith, regardless of its guise.[121]

Visions of War's Return

By ending the Sherston trilogy with the dispersal of his menacing 'demons', Sassoon attempts to endow his alter ego with a sense of hope that in 1918 he himself did not quite possess. He admitted in a letter that the ' "Slateford" [i.e. Craiglockhart] part needed a bit of fudging in places',[122] and outside testimony suggests that the 'fudging' might well have involved the severity of his condition. In a 1936 letter, Rivers's sister described her brother's account of his visit to Sassoon in July 1918 at Lancaster Gate Hospital in London: 'W[illy] told us he sat up all night with him in London. Must have been much worse than he says [in *Sherston's Progress*].'[123]

For Sassoon and other veterans the war did not end with their withdrawal from the frontline or with the Armistice. In his celebrated autobiography, Robert Graves recalls how he and Edmund Blunden suffered from 'war shock' in autumn 1919 at Oxford when they 'talk[ed] each other into an almost hysterical state about the trenches . . . The war was not yet over for us.'[124] Two years later Blunden was on the point of breakdown and his employers at the *Nation and Athenaeum* booked him on a journey to Argentina, ostensibly to write a travel book, but actually to provide him with the relief a change of scene might bring.[125] But in language similar to Sassoon's, Blunden reported being troubled by his own 'futile demons', even at sea: 'Still the dreams came; the war continued.'[126] Even during the day, the memory of traumatic war experiences

> is as sombre and as frightening as they were themselves in their aspect and their annals. They come unbidden, and when they will come, the mind is led by them as birds are said to be lured by the serpent's eye. A tune, a breath of sighing air, an odour – and there goes the foolish ghost back to Flanders.[127]

In his diaries Sassoon frequently – and tellingly – resolved not to think about the war. On 30 June 1921, for example, he wrote: 'I've given up thinking about the War. I am clear of it all, steadily settling down into a new state of mind,' but in the very next sentence he admitted that 'the War comes back on me occasionally.'[128] Before long he complained of living in an 'Atmosphere of nerve-twitching exhaustion'.[129]

Even while claiming that he did not suffer from shell shock and citing Rivers's affirmation of this denial as supporting evidence,[130] he describes two recurring dreams in *Sherston's Progress* that demonstrate the lingering unconscious effects of his war experience. In the first instance he recounts a 'battle dream', as Rivers would have called it,[131] in which he and his battalion are adrift in the mud of the Ypres Salient, surrounded by the 'unmitigated horror' of the battlefield, and he feels sure of imminent death.[132] Yet even in the depth of 'dream-despair', he notices a 'queer thing': the distressing dream allowed him to 'add[] a very complete piece of war experience to my collection'.[133] Here he seems to be drawing on Rivers's view of the unconscious as 'a storehouse of experience associated with instinctive reactions',[134] with memories drawn from unconscious as well as conscious sources, avidly collected, almost cherished, perhaps even fetishized, each new 'addition' increasing the overall worth of the 'collection'. 'Dream-despair' offers him a glimpse of the ongoing vitality of his memory collection, which animated even as it disturbed his post-war life, especially as the portents of a new war began to gather.

The second dream in *Sherston's Progress* recurred, with subtle variations, every two or three months: 'The War is still going on and I have got to return to the front.'[135] He is upset because he is ill-equipped for this return; he is anxious because he cannot find his service kit, and he worries that he has forgotten how to perform his duties. Sometimes in this dream the anxiety is so intense that he bursts into tears as he frantically searches for his equipment. In spite of his fears and doubts, in the dream he often returns to the front, though it is a strangely altered front, 'always in England – the Germans have usually invaded half [of] Kent', and he is 'tak[ing] out a patrol', feeling 'quite keen about it'.[136]

Sassoon's treatment of dreams in *Sherston's Progress*, a volume whose 'solution' he attributed to Rivers,[137] is noteworthy for its lack of psychoanalytic analysis. In *Conflict and Dream*, Rivers argued that a dream is an attempt by the unconscious to solve an underlying conflict that has been occupying the dreamer.[138] He observed that the affective symptoms of a recurring dream or nightmare prevail until the conflict underlying the dream is satisfactorily resolved.[139] Through his work with hundreds of soldiers during the war, Rivers learned that encouraging a patient to 'talk through' his trauma, to revisit it consciously, produced in accordance with Freudian theory abreactive benefits that lessened the affective intensity of the nightmare. As a patient slackened his repression, his battle dreams would often evolve into recurring nightmares whose manifest content was transformed by the dreamwork into a setting less directly representational of the scene of trauma. The greater the transformation, the weaker was the affective intensity.[140] For Rivers, a nightmare that jolts the sleeper awake bathed in sweat represented an unsuccessful solution to the conflict, for 'When a conflict is solved in a dream, there is no affect.'[141] The process of transformation sets the patient on the road to recovery. Although it is hard to believe that Rivers and Sassoon did not talk about dreams at Craiglockhart and after, there is no record in the correspondence or the diaries of such conversations or any direct references to the ideas in *Conflict and Dream*. Sassoon's own dream interpretations are intriguing as much for what he does not say as for what he does. Even in the diaries, he describes his dreams rarely and briefly, with perfunctory interpretations, if any at all.[142] In *Sherston's Progress* he gestures towards Rivers's ideas by claiming that the recurrent 'battle dream' at Ypres ended once he had written his 'account of military service',[143] thereby demonstrating implicitly the psychoanalytic principle of abreaction endorsed by Rivers. He might have suggested that in creating the narrative Sassoon drew the repressed memories from the unconscious, where their affective energies had disturbed his sleep, into the conscious mind that was then enabled to face and to some extent resolve the underlying conflict, dispelling the recurring dream or at least transforming it.

The recurring anxiety dream of the war still going on, Sassoon explains, 'obviously dates from the autumn of 1917',[144] when he decided to leave Craiglockhart and return to active service – a decision he describes as a 'potential death-sentence'.[145] Not very startlingly, the dream 'proves' to him the underlying conflict between honour and patriotic duty, on the one hand, and 'The instinct of self-preservation', on the other,[146] implying the presence of the inner foe. That the dream situates the front in Kent, the land of his childhood, is the kind of detail that Rivers would have seized on, but it escapes Sassoon's commentary. His reluctance to tap deeply into psychoanalytically informed dream interpretation in his autobiographical prose, poetry, or diaries suggests not a turning away from Rivers's influence, but a change in its tenor. Rivers is the 'solution' to *Sherston's Progress*; his psychological ideas seem to have given Sassoon some insight into the persistent after-effects of his frontline service, and they can also help Sassoon's readers to understand the 'complex egotistical personality', as Spender called it, at the heart of his post-war writing. But the source of his influence over Sassoon lies, I think, in the adaptability of his teachings that stressed the common ground between the talking cure and confession, between the healing powers of faith in psychological principles and faith in religious truths. Sassoon was thereby able to view dreams as windows into not only psychological but also spiritual truth, which he increasingly sought as he aged, and still maintain his emotional allegiance to Rivers.

Something in Rivers's character, perhaps his powers of empathy or generosity of spirit,[147] inspired devotion in Sassoon, and in his eyes transformed the ethnographer and psychologist into a kind of spiritual mentor. Thus Rivers became what Sassoon needed him to be. As he wrote in 1936, 'Rivers is the solution . . . [to] my own life up to 1922 – and since then too, for his spirit . . . has been my guide in many dark places.'[148] His use of 'spirit' and 'dark places' marks his movement toward a conception of existence that transcends the disturbing vagaries of material and psychological exigencies, and seems to embrace a mystical vision of life that probably served as a precursor to his Catholic conversion. In a poem from the early 1930s dedicated to Rivers, Sassoon describes the 'strange survival' of his 'ghost' who 'revisits' him at night, perhaps to 'once more harmonize and heal'.[149] He feels 'His influence undiminished'[150]; indeed, it seems strengthened and expanded in this poem. The warmth of this encounter with Rivers's spirit contrasts sharply with the chilling ghostly intruders who haunted him at Denmark Hill hospital in 1917. Increasingly he saw Rivers in the light of spiritual guide rather than therapist. That soon after Rivers's shocking death he read Freud and tried to untangle 'Freudian perplexities' suggests his desire to understand what had been important to his friend rather than to understand himself. When he invokes dreams in his poetry, for example, Sassoon sometimes uses the language of psychoanalysis, not for psychoanalytic purposes, but apparently as a means to articulate the spiritual stirrings he saw in dreams, as well as in homage to his friend and a reminder of the comfort that he still found in the memory of Rivers. Nevertheless, Sassoon's application of Rivers's twin notions autognosis and re-education were crucial, I believe, to his autobiographical poems, and to an important extent influenced his general understanding of poetry after the First World War.

Notes

1. Johannes Hofer, 'Medical dissertation on nostalgia', trans. Carolyn Kiser Anspach, *Bulletin of the History of Medicine*, 2, 1934, pp. 376–91, pp. 381, 386.
2. Thomas Glynn, 'The traumatic neuroses', *The Lancet*, 2, 1910, pp. 1332–6, p. 1333.
3. Ironically, at the end of the twentieth century and early in the twenty-first, the controversial diagnosis of post-traumatic stress disorder (PTSD) at once encompasses

the psychological legacy of trauma while accommodating the potential physiological aetiology. Studies by Van der Kolk and Van der Hart posit that the source of PTSD resides in some organic inhibition of particular brain functions, possibly the hippocampus. See Bessel A. Van der Kolk and O. Van der Hart, 'The intrusive past: The flexibility of memory and the engraving of trauma', in Cathy Caruth (ed.), *Trauma: Explorations in Memory* (Baltimore, MD: Johns Hopkins University Press, 1995), pp. 158–82. Some historians even suggest that the return of the physiological in the psychiatric understanding of traumatic experience announces, at long last, the end of that confounding diversion known as psychoanalysis. See Edward Shorter, *A History of Psychiatry: From the Era of the Asylum to the Age of Prozac* (New York: John Wiley, 1997).

4. Cathy Caruth, *Unclaimed Experience: Trauma, Narrative, and History* (Baltimore, MD: Johns Hopkins University Press, 1996), p. 11.
5. Andreas Huyssen, *Present Pasts* (Stanford, CA: Stanford University Press, 2003), p. 8.
6. Ibid. p. 8.
7. Siegfried Sassoon, *Sherston's Progress* (London: Faber & Faber, 1983), p. 51.
8. T. E. Lawrence, *The Letters of T.E. Lawrence*, ed. David Garnett (London: Cape, 1938), p. 463.
9. Glynn, 'Traumatic neuroses', p. 1332.
10. 'Traumatic neuroses', *The Lancet*, 1, 1891, p. 160.
11. 'Trauma', *Shorter Oxford English Dictionary*, 2 vols (Oxford: Oxford University Press, 1944).
12. Glynn, 'Traumatic Neuroses', p. 1333.
13. H. Oppenheim, 'The neuroses: Hysteria; neurasthenia or nervous weakness; the traumatic neuroses (neuroses of accident)', in H. Oppenheim, *Text-Book of Nervous Diseases*, trans. Alexander Bruce, 5th edn, vol. 2 (Edinburgh: Otto Schulze, 1911), pp. 1051–180, p. 1163.
14. From the mid-1880s till the 1910s, there were occasional contributions to *The Lancet* and the *British Medical Journal* that challenged the organic assumptions underlying the aetiology of traumatic neuroses and hysteria then widely accepted in Britain. Dennis De Berdt Hovell argued in the 1880s that traumatic neurosis was essentially a psychological condition ('Obituary: Dennis De Berdt Hovel', *British Medical Journal*, 1, 1888, p. 1303). In the 1890s Herbert Page argued that a patient's nervous system could be genuinely disrupted without evidence of physical injury, that the emotional disturbance resulting from a shock could be more important than a physical injury ('On the medical aspects of traumatic neuroses', *The Lancet*, 1, 1895, p. 876).

    But the voices more characteristic of the British medical community insisted upon the organic basis of the condition. Rivers observed that, before the war, Freud's ideas were largely reviled, due in large part to their foundation upon the theory of infantile sexuality (W. H. R. Rivers, *Instinct and the Unconscious*, 2nd edn (Cambridge: Cambridge University Press, 1924), p. 3). Myers observed that British neurologists in the years before the First World War were 'usually ignorant of normal or abnormal psychology, [and were] content to treat patient symptoms and signs by persuasion or force' which typically worsened the patient's condition (Charles Myers, *Shell Shock in France 1914–18 (Based on a War Diary)* (Cambridge: Cambridge University Press, 1940), pp. 20–1). Leonard Woolf recalled the treatment Virginia Woolf received during the years 1913–15 from the top practitioners in the field, including Henry Head, a neurological colleague of Rivers; their utter lack of success suggested to Woolf that what the medical establishment 'knew amounted to practically nothing. They had not the slightest idea of the nature or the cause of Virginia's mental state' (Leonard Woolf, *Beginning Again: An Autobiography of the Years 1911–18* (London: Hogarth, 1972), p. 160). Virginia Woolf's damning portrayal of Dr Bradshaw in *Mrs Dalloway* conveys the perception that even after the war British specialists were still intent on treating the patients suffering from war neuroses 'by persuasion or force.'

15. G. Elliot Smith and T. H. Pear, *Shell Shock and its Lessons*, 2nd edn (Manchester: Manchester University Press, 1917), p. 53.
16. Glynn, 'Traumatic neuroses', p. 1333.
17. Martin Stone, 'Shell shock and the psychologists', in W. F. Bynum, Roy Porter and Michael Shepard (eds), *The Anatomy of Madness* (London: Tavistock, 1985), pp. 252–63, p. 253.
18. K. R. Eissler, *Freud as an Expert Witness: The Discussion of War Neuroses between Freud and Wagner-Jauregg*, trans. Christine Trollope (Madison, CT: International University Press, 1986), p. 203.
19. Sandor Ferenczi, Karl Abraham, Ernst Simmel and Ernest Jones, *Psycho-Analysis and the War Neuroses* (London: International Psychoanalytical Press, 1921), p. 43.
20. Myers, *Shell Shock*, pp. 1–2.
21. Ibid. p. 4.
22. Charles Myers, 'A contribution to the study of shell shock', *The Lancet*, 1, 1915, pp. 316–20, p. 316.
23. Myers, *Shell Shock*, p. 25.
24. Ibid. p. 25.
25. Ibid. p. 26.
26. Ibid. p. 96.
27. Ibid. p. 26.
28. Richard Slobodin, *W. H. R. Rivers* (New York: Columbia University Press, 1978), p. 53.
29. By the summer of 1918, there were 'six special neurological hospitals for officers and thirteen for other ranks' (Ted Bogacz, 'War neurosis and cultural change in England, 1914–1922: The work of the War Office Committee of Enquiry into "Shell-Shock"', *Journal of Contemporary History*, 24.2, 1989, pp. 227–56, p. 235).
30. Slobodin, *W. H. R. Rivers*, pp. 13–14.
31. Like Freud, Rivers began his medical training in neurology, and this field offered both men an important mutual influence: the British neurologist, John Hughlings Jackson. Rivers revered Hughlings Jackson as a 'father-figure' (as Rivers himself was to be revered as a 'father-figure' by Sassoon), and was deeply affected by his death in 1911 (Slobodin, *W. H. R. Rivers*, p. 45). Freud's early work on aphasia is particularly indebted to the ideas of Hughlings Jackson, whom Freud 'regarded as his mentor in this sphere' (Kenneth Dewhurst, *Hughlings Jackson on Psychiatry* (Oxford: Sandford, 1982), p. 107). Indeed, Hughlings Jackson's conceptual understanding of brain functions, which Freud praised in his neurological writings, helped Freud give shape to his theories (C. W. Wallesch, 'Hughlings Jackson and European neurology', in Christopher Kennard and Michael Swash (eds), *Hierarchies in Neurology: A Reappraisal* (London: Springer-Verlag, 1989), pp. 17–23, p. 22). For instance, Freud's first reference to 'regression' can be traced to the Jacksonian idea of 'reduction' (Dewhurst, *Hughlings Jackson*, p. 108).
32. G. Elliot Smith, quoted in Slobodin, *W. H. R. Rivers*, p. 55.
33. Smith and Pear, *Shell Shock and its Lessons*, pp. 1–2.
34. Ibid. p. 53.
35. 'Psychological analysis' is their tamed version of 'psychoanalysis', a term they avoid because of their perspective that 'few terms in medicine have aroused so

much misunderstanding, so much criticism, well-informed and ill-informed – and so much enmity' (Smith and Pear, *Shell Shock and its Lessons*, p. 73).

36. W. H. R. Rivers, *Instinct and the Unconscious*, 2nd edn (Cambridge: Cambridge University Press, 1924), p. 3.
37. Joseph Breuer and Sigmund Freud, *Studies on Hysteria*, 1893–95, trans. James Strachey and Alix Strachey, ed. Angela Richards (London: Penguin, 1991), p. 58.
38. Ibid. p. 56.
39. Myers, *Shell Shock*, p. 25.
40. Like other physicians serving the army, Rivers was troubled by the ethical constraints his military uniform placed on his imperatives as a medical practitioner. His relationship with Sassoon, for instance, caused him to question the validity of his position against a negotiated peace, insisting that the war must go on till the defeat of German militarism. His doubts and his conversations with Sassoon crept into his dream life, as he recorded in a passage of *Conflict and Dream* entitled 'The "pacifist" dream' (W. H. R. Rivers, *Conflict and Dream*, ed. George Elliot Smith (London: Kegan Paul, 1923), pp. 165–75).
41. Arthur Brock, 'The re-education of the adult: The neurasthenic in war and peace', *Sociological Review*, 10, 1918, pp. 25–40, p. 36.
42. Slobodin, *W. H. R. Rivers*, p. 59.
43. After the war, prejudice against Freudian psychoanalysis was still widespread, even within ostensibly supportive circles. In editing an important book of essays about dream life that Rivers had been working on shortly before his death in 1923, Elliot Smith felt moved to defend the genealogy of Rivers's ideas. While Rivers was the first president of the British Psycho-Analytic Society and his attitude may initially appear to be essentially Freudian, Smith insisted it was drastically different; it was clear and logical and 'prunes' from psychoanalytic dream theory 'most of the repulsive excrescences that have brought upon it so much odium' (Rivers, *Conflict and Dream*, pp. vi-vii). Certainly there are some important differences between Rivers and Freud, but they do not obscure Rivers's profound indebtedness to Freud's ideas.
44. Rivers, *Instinct*, p. 159.
45. Ibid. p. 119.
46. Ibid. p. 121.
47. Ibid. p. 123.
48. Ibid. p. 123.
49. Ibid. p. 124.
50. In *Beyond the Pleasure Principle* Freud distinguishes between anxiety (*Angst*), fear (*Furcht*), and fright (*Schreck*):

    > 'Anxiety' describes a particular state of expecting the danger or preparing for it, even though it may be an unknown one. 'Fear' requires a definite object of which to be afraid. 'Fright', however, is the name we give to the state a person gets into when he has run into danger without being prepared for it; it emphasizes the factor of surprise. (Sigmund Freud, *Beyond the Pleasure Principle*, in James Strachey (trans.) and Angela Richards (ed.), *On Metapsychology* (London: Penguin, 1991), pp. 269–338, pp. 281–2)

    He then concludes that the qualities of preparedness or expectation prevent 'anxiety' alone from producing traumatic neurosis; he attributes traumatic neurosis to a 'fright' one does not expect and for which one cannot prepare. The mental shock or surprise of a railway accident is Freud's prime example. Drawing upon his exposure to victims of wartime trauma, Rivers saw the production of war neuroses as a combination of 'anxiety' and 'fright'. Frontline conditions demand of the soldier a constant state of anxiety which strains his mental resources until a 'comparatively trivial' fright may overwhelm him.

51. Jean Moorcroft Wilson, *Siegfried Sassoon: The Making of a War Poet: A Biography (1886–1918)*, vol. 1 (London: Duckworth, 1998), p. 378.
52. Siegfried Sassoon, *Collected Poems 1908–1956* (London: Faber & Faber, 1961), p. 89.
53. Sigmund Freud, 'The "uncanny" ', in James Strachey (trans.) and Albert Dickson (ed.), *Art and Literature* (London: Penguin, 1991), pp. 335–76, p. 341.
54. Ibid. p. 366.
55. Ibid. p. 367.
56. Siegfried Sassoon, *Memoirs of an Infantry Officer* (London: Faber & Faber, 1965), p. 80.
57. Freud, 'Uncanny', p. 367.
58. Ibid. p. 356.
59. Ibid. p. 357.
60. Ibid. p. 357.
61. Sigmund Freud, 'Introduction', in Ferenczi, *Psycho-Analysis and the War Neuroses*, pp. 1–4, pp. 2–3.
62. Smith and Pear, *Shell Shock and its Lessons*, p. 71.
63. Emphasis added; Sigmund Freud, 'Introduction', in Ferenczi, *Psycho-Analysis and the War Neuroses*, p. 4.
64. Sassoon, *Collected Poems*, p. 89.
65. Edmund Blunden, *Undertones of War* (London: Penguin, 1982), p. 250.
66. Robert Graves, 'Recalling war', *No More Ghosts* (London: Faber & Faber, 1941), p. 51.
67. Abram Kardiner, *The Traumatic Neuroses of War* (Washington, DC: National Research Council, 1941), p. ix.
68. These general observations are based on an examination of volumes of *Index Medicus* covering the years 1914–45.
69. In Germany, from the early days of Oppenheim, the issue of traumatic neuroses was embroiled in legal liabilities. It is therefore not surprising that German medical literature during the 1920s and 1930s features many articles on neuroses, and the condition is invariably bound up in litigious issues of compensation or pension. See Paul Lerner, 'Pension war: Nervous veterans and German memory in Weimar Republic', in Paul Lerner, *Hysterical Men: War, Psychiatry, and the Politics of Trauma in Germany, 1890–1930* (Ithaca, NY: Cornell University Press, 2003), pp. 223–48.
70. Emanuel Miller (ed.), *The Neuroses in War* (London: Macmillan, 1940), p. 8.
71. Ibid. p. 32.
72. Quoted in Miller, *The Neuroses in War*, p. 223.
73. Miller, *The Neuroses in War*, p. 223.
74. Charles Berg, *War in the Mind: The Case Book of a Medical Psychologist*, 2nd edn (London: Macaulay, 1948), p. 178.
75. Ernst Simmel, 'War neuroses', in Sandor Lorand (ed.), *Psychology Today* (New York: International University Press, 1944), pp. 227–48, p. 232.
76. Peter Gay, *Freud: A Life for Our Time* (New York: Norton, 1988), p. 388.
77. Kardiner, *Traumatic Neuroses*, p. 347.
78. Ibid. p. 253.
79. Paul Fussell, *The Great War and Modern Memory* (New York: Oxford University Press), p. 92.
80. Simmel, 'War Neuroses', p. 240.
81. Ibid. p. 242.

82. Ibid. p. 248.
83. Siegfried Sassoon, *Diaries 1915–1918*, ed. Rupert Hart-Davis (London: Faber & Faber, 1983), p. 52.
84. Ibid. p. 52.
85. Ibid. p. 53.
86. Ibid. p. 52.
87. Ibid. p. 133.
88. Ibid. p. 133.
89. Ibid. p. 133.
90. Ibid. pp. 161–2.
91. Ibid. p. 167.
92. Wilson, *Siegfried Sassoon*, vol. 1, p. 384.
93. Sassoon, *Diaries 1915–1918*, p. 189.
94. Sassoon, *Sherston's Progress*, p. 12.
95. Ibid. p. 12.
96. Ibid. p. 12.
97. Leaving the space following the heading 'Disease' blank, Rivers noted:

    > The patient is a healthy-looking man of good physique. There are no physical signs of any disorder of the Nervous System. He discusses his recent actions and their motives in a perfectly intelligent and rational way, and there is no evidence of any excitement or depression.
    >
    > . . . His views differ from that of the ordinary pacifist in that he would no longer object to the continuance of the War if he saw any reasonable prospect of a rapid decision. (W. H. R. Rivers, 'Medical Case Sheet', ts. *Document Archive: Siegfried Sassoon*. Imperial War Museum, London)

    The fact that Sassoon was free from any 'physical signs' of nervous disease set him apart from many of Rivers's other patients. Rivers knew that a rational, non-depressive demeanour and the lack of physical symptoms were not conclusive proof of an undamaged psyche, but there is no record of him ever stating that Sassoon suffered from 'any disorder of the nervous system', either during the Craiglockhart period or afterwards.
98. In *Siegfried's Journey*, the third volume of his non-fictive autobiography, Sassoon acknowledges the extent to which 'George Sherston's' experiences, memories and accounts represent his own:

    > My experience during the next three weeks [of 1917], which ended in my being sent to a shell shock hospital, have already been related in *Memoirs of an Infantry Officer* [the volume preceding *Sherston's Progress*]. I am thankful not to be obliged to drag my mind through the details again. Siegfried Sassoon, *Siegfried's Journey: 1916–1920* (London: Faber & Faber, 1945), p. 55.
99. Sassoon, *Sherston's Progress*, p. 48.
100. Ibid. p. 12.
101. Sassoon, *Diaries 1915–1918*, p. 197.
102. Ibid. p. 198.
103. Ibid. p. 238.
104. Rivers noted that the hallucinatory symptoms of neuroses often gave rise to the patient's anxiety over 'approaching insanity' (W. H. R. Rivers, 'Psycho-Therapeutics', in James Hastings (ed.), *Encyclopedia of Religion and Ethics*, vol. 10 (New York: Scribner's, n.d.), p. 437). In *Shell Shock and its Lessons*, Elliot Smith made a point that he said 'cannot be too much emphasized': while the soldier-patient may be quite sane, he may take 'the abnormal phenomena' of his

war neurosis to be signs of 'incipient . . . or established insanity' (Smith and Pear, *Shell Shock*, p. 68). Other writers who undertook case studies during the interwar years drew similar conclusions. T. A. Ross, a psychiatrist whom Sassoon met in the early 1930s and who worked in war hospitals during the war, put the point even more emphatically: 'all people with neurosis at some period of their illness think that they are about to go mad' (T. A. Ross, *Lectures on War Neuroses* (London: Edward Arnold, 1942), p. 85). Abram Kardiner, whose first study of traumatic war neuroses was based largely upon observations of cases of chronic neuroses from the First World War, also noted the preponderance of the fear of insanity among his patients (Abram Kardiner and Herbert Spiegel, *War Stress and Neurotic Illness* (New York: Hoeber, 1947), p. 100).

105. Sassoon, *Diaries 1915–1918*, p. 246.
106. Rivers, *Instinct*, p. 203.
107. Rivers, 'Psycho-Therapeutics', p. 437.
108. Ibid. p. 440.
109. Sassoon, *Sherston's Progress*, p. 15.
110. Ibid. p. 28.
111. See Bernard Bergonzi, *Heroes' Twilight*, 2nd edn (London: Macmillan, 1980), p. 154, and Paul Moeyes, *Siegfried Sassoon: Scorched Glory: A Critical Study* (New York: St Martin's, 1997), pp. 186–97.
112. Sassoon, *Sherston's Progress*, p. 9.
113. Rivers, 'Psycho-Therapeutics', p. 433.
114. Ibid. p. 437.
115. Ibid. p. 436.
116. Sassoon, *Sherston's Progress*, p. 13.
117. Ibid. p. 35.
118. Ibid. p. 149.
119. Ibid. p. 149.
120. Ibid. p. 150.
121. This conversion is duly noted in the secondary sources. See Felicitas Corrigan, 'Introduction', *Siegfried Sassoon: Poet's Pilgrimage* (London: Gollancz, 1973), pp. 15–42, and John Stuart Roberts, *Siegfried Sassoon: 1886–1967* (London: Cohen, 1999) for readings of Sassoon's life, and the bulk of his post-First World War writings, as aspects of a journey toward religious enlightenment.
122. Siegfried Sassoon to Geoffrey Keynes, letter, 8 September 1943, Papers of Siegfried Sassoon, Manuscript Department, Cambridge University Library.
123. Kathleen Rivers to Ruth Head, letter, 6 September 1936, private collection.
124. Robert Graves, *Good-bye to All That* (London: Cape, 1929), pp. 358–60.
125. Barry Webb, *Edmund Blunden: A Biography* (New Haven, CT: Yale University Press, 1990), p. 131.
126. Edmund Blunden, *The Bonadventure: A Random Journal of an Atlantic Holiday* (London: Cobden-Sanderson, 1922), p. 42.
127. Ibid. p. 65.
128. Siegfried Sassoon, *Diaries 1920–1922*, ed. Rupert Hart-Davis (London: Faber & Faber, 1981), p. 73.
129. Ibid. p. 75.
130. Sassoon, *Sherston's Progress*, p. 48.
131. Rivers, *Conflict and Dream*, p. 92.
132. Sassoon, *Sherston's Progress*, p. 49.
133. Ibid. p. 49.
134. Rivers, *Instinct*, p. 38.
135. Sassoon, *Sherston's Progress*, p. 49.

136. Ibid. p. 49.
137. Siegfried Sassoon to Ellis Roberts, letter, 9 September 1936, Sassoon Collection, Harry Ransom, Humanities Research Center (HRHRC), University of Texas, Austin.
138. Rivers, *Conflict and Dream*, p. 17.
139. Ibid. p. 39.
140. Ibid. p. 67.
141. Ibid. p. 71.
142. For example, in the summer of 1922, he recounted in his diary a 'Curious dream' in which he comforted Sacheverell Sitwell after hearing news that his brother Osbert (with whom Sassoon had been feuding) had died of some terrible disfiguring disease, news which provoked in him a mournful incantation that he repeated 'again and again' (Sassoon, *Diaries 1923–1925*, ed. Rupert Hart-Davis (London: Faber & Faber, 1985), p. 230). Sassoon supposed that the dream 'proves' that he was actually fond of Osbert Sitwell, and concluded with a comment typical of his interpretative gestures: 'But I can't think of what suggested the dream, unless it was memory of the illness-complex he suffers from' (Sassoon, *Diaries 1920–1922*, 1981), p. 230). Similarly, a dream in which he tossed a book of his poems into the sea, felt regret and dived in to rescue it, was swept away by a current but managed to struggle back to the shore, prompted: 'I suppose the dream expressed a conflict between athletic and intellectual interests!' (Sassoon, *Diaries 1923–1925*, p. 23). The exclamation mark suggests his wariness about taking the interpretive enterprise too seriously. Other examples of his dream descriptions appear in the published diaries (Sassoon, *Diaries 1920–1922*, pp. 200, 222, 227–8, 232; Sassoon, *Diaries 1923–1925*, pp. 147, 271).
143. Sassoon, *Sherston's Progress*, p. 49.
144. Ibid. p. 49.
145. Ibid. p. 50.
146. Ibid. p. 50.
147. Slobodin, *W. H. R. Rivers*, p. 63.
148. Sassoon to Ellis Roberts, letter, 9 September 1936.
149. Sassoon, *Collected Poems*, p. 221.
150. Ibid. 221.

3

WITNESSING AND SURVIVAL: THE CHALLENGE OF 'AUTOGNOSIS' IN THE INTERWAR YEARS

'To know Myself – this fragment of to-day –
To pluck the unconscious causes of unrest
From self-deceiving nature.'

Siegfried Sassoon, 'Autognosis', 1921

In his writing between the wars Sassoon was strongly influenced by Rivers's concept of autognosis, the twofold process by which an individual 'learns to understand the real state of his mind' by accounting for both conscious and unconscious motivations, and also the environmental 'conditions by which this state has been produced'.[1] The epigraph for this chapter comes from Sassoon's 1921 diary, where it is followed by comments asserting the importance of being 'a watchful critic' of his own behaviour: 'I must be both action and the audience; "produced" by environment.'[2] His words echo Rivers's sense of the combined influence of internal and external forces that shape self-understanding, but Sassoon comes to adopt a version of autognosis that incorporates his increasingly nostalgic inclinations. Although his published poetry of the early 1920s was predominantly satirical, culminating in his 1926 collection *Satirical Poems*, his diaries during these years make it clear that he was intrigued by the potential of autognosis to enrich his poetry but at the same time wary of uncovering and writing about 'the unconscious causes of unrest'.

In his youth, Sassoon was advised by his uncle, Hamo Thornycroft, about writing poetry: 'Let your thoughts ring true; and always keep your eye on the object while you write.'[3] After he met Rivers, the 'object' on which he typically fixed his eye was himself, and under Rivers's influence he strove in his own circumscribed way 'to pluck unconscious causes of unrest from self-deceiving nature' through the act of poetic self-reflection and, later, semi-fictionalized memoirs.[4] Sassoon's growing autobiographical project really began with his encounter with Rivers. In this chapter, I demonstrate that Sassoon's adaptation of autognosis informs the intensive self-scrutiny that became the hallmark of his writing during the interwar period. His diaries record his perception that his 'real state of mind' was a site contested by various aspects of self: the present recollecting self, the selves of his pre-war past and, more problematically, the selves of his wartime past. Not until he engaged in poetic form with his repressed 'Fusiliering self' and his traumatic memories was he able to pursue autognosis in his writing, inflecting it with his own nostalgic impulses.

The Heart's Journey (1928) is the first collection of poetry in which the internal motivations of autognosis are treated in a sustained way, while in *The Road to Ruin* (1933) he demonstrates a concern with the external forces that impinge upon the poet's 'real state of mind'. An appreciation of the interdependence of constitutive forces within the self and without is further illustrated in his treatment of dreams in *Vigils* (1935). While he draws on psychoanalysis by adopting some of its terminology, his poetry of this volume demonstrates his growing belief that dreams are windows not only into the unconscious self, but also into a spiritual existence that opened the way for his eventual religious conversion. The transcendent significance of dreams in this poetry provides further evidence of the evolution of Rivers from psychological to spiritual guide for Sassoon, a change that reflects the particular needs of his own version of self-understanding. In Chapter 2, I mentioned Rivers's idea that a patient's faith in his psychologist is as central to the therapeutic process as a believer's faith in his priest. Rivers, wholly the scientist, understood religion in distinctly cool, scientific terms as 'a group of processes, the efficacy of which depends on the will of some higher power . . . Religion differs from magic in that it involves the belief in some power in the universe greater than that of man himself.'[5] But he also believed that 'no treatment of the subject of mind and medicine would be complete which ignores religion,'[6] which suggests that he would have endorsed Sassoon's adaptation of autognosis to foster an acceptance of spiritual beliefs.[7] I conclude this chapter with a discussion of Sassoon's awareness of the contemporary situation, the historical and literary conditions that affected his literary apprehension of self. Although frequently criticized by reviewers (and later critics) for being removed from the contemporary scene, he was more concerned than has been previously recognized with both the international political situation and the relation of his writing to the changing literary environment.

The Return of the War: Key Poems of the 1920s

Due to his own traumatic experiences and to Rivers, Sassoon was well aware of the fragmenting nature of modern subjectivity. In a diary entry from February 1922, he stated his autognostic goal explicitly:

> I have formed an inflexible resolve to reveal my real self; my inner self; my secret self; the self that never sees the light of day . . . The question now arises – which of my selves is the more worthy of survival? Which of my selves is writing this exordium? And, having written it, how can it be responsible for what future selves may reveal?[8]

This resolve and understanding of identity based on distinct, multiple and compartmentalized selves found expression in much of his post-war poetry. 'A Fragment of Autobiography', a poem published only privately (1923), attempts to trace the relationship of three versions of self – past, present and future – as they are affected by present experience and by memories and spectres of the past. The poem opens in a moment of leisured rumination, as the present-day Sassoon reads Hardy by firelight. He recalls a time when he did not like Hardy, and is suddenly confronted by his unsophisticated 1910 self, a sportsman in cricket gear who 'stands before him'.[9] The 1920 self tries to engage the 1910 self in conversation, but the latter shows no signs of recognition or interest in anything beyond his cricket bat, the weather and scoring runs. 'WAR! . . . Can't I sting you into life with that? . . .' :[10] not even the exclamatory explosion of capitalized letters or the gaps of ellipses can shock the 1910 self into imagining an existence beyond the sporting life. The present self continues:

> Good-bye; I won't detain you now; I know
> You want to read *The Sportsman* on the lawn.
> Go out and gobble strawberries. I'm a ghost;
> A face that yawns in fireless wintry dawn.[11]

The 1920 self dismisses his 'visitor' to leisured, epicurean satiety and acknowledges that 'I'm a ghost.' But just who is 'a ghost'? Where is the 'I' to be situated? The 'I' has all along been the present 1920 self, the present narrative persona of the poem; the 1910 self is the ghost that appears before him. With the dismissal, the two selves collapse into the weary countenance that faces the bleak onset of day. The present self apprehends the constitutive legacy of 1910 and sees the inevitability of its own participation in a repetitive pattern of non-recognition. The poem concludes as the 1920 self imagines a time ten years hence when he will haunt the memory of a 1930 self, as much a 'stranger' then as his earlier self is to him now.[12] 'A Fragment . . .' provides an early example of Sassoon's technique of juxtaposing different temporal versions of self which reveals the interconnectedness of past and present. While he strove for self-revelation explicitly in his diary, with its private or semi-private audience,[13] in his published poetry his tactics were more guarded. In the summer of 1923, some months after *Recreations* was printed, Sassoon advised J. C. Squire that he felt that this poem was 'too personal to publish . . . I am quite sure I don't want "Frag. of Auto." to appear.'[14]

His determination to apply autognostic principles to his writing had obvious limitations. Against his resolution to transparency were two imposing sites of occlusion: homosexuality and war memories. When he first contemplated prose autobiography, he seriously considered articulating an inner, 'secret self' – his homosexuality – which part of him longed to express with candour and even pride. In the early twenties, E. M. Forster lent him a copy of the unpublished novel *Maurice*, which he found both moving and inspiring.[15] In his diary he contemplated again writing a Proustian novel of memories which would reveal his true feelings unmasked and unburdened. He imagined this work as a '*Madame Bovary* of sexual inversion . . . a *Tess* created from my own experience!'[16] Several years later, after reading J. R. Ackerley's *Prisoner of War* (1925), a play about a tormented homosexual officer, he told a friend at the Reform Club that he wanted to write an unabashed autobiography on the same theme.[17] The desire to express his homosexuality haunted him for years, but in his diary in 1939 he noted that 'Homosexuality has become a bore; the intelligentsia have captured it.'[18] It did not feature explicitly in any of his writing published during his lifetime, its absence an indication of the extent of his withdrawal and reclusion.

Before he began writing the first volume of the Sherston memoirs in 1926, Sassoon was adamant that 'I've given up thinking about the War. I am clear of it all, steadily settling down into a new state of mind, craving only for development in the technique of expression in verse and in prose.'[19] His new friendship with Edmund Blunden, a fellow veteran whose gentle wisdom struck him as uncannily like Hardy's, whom he revered, both helped and hindered his desire to put his war experience behind him: 'Little Blunden makes me more inclined to label myself "literary" . . . [and] encourages me to work on what (he suggests) is a "rich vein", i.e. autobiographical poems. Probably he is right.'[20] Blunden's advice gave a literary nuance to the autognostic ideas of Rivers, and inspired Sassoon to refine his autobiographical verse. During a visit with Blunden in East Anglia the war and a particular kind of Englishness preoccupied conversation: 'for three days B. and I talked about county cricket and the war and English poetry and our own poetry.'[21] Even as Sassoon proclaimed that he had finished with thinking about the war, it none the less returned.

In spite of his resolve to express the complexity of his 'real self', he also resisted explicitly incorporating the wartime soldier aspect of self into his poetic representations of subjectivity. Like the ghost of 1910 from 'A Fragment . . .', he had to be stung into it. Such a sting came in a letter he received in late

February 1926 from J. C. Dunn, his old Medical Officer, who was compiling a regimental history and sought a brief prose contribution from Sassoon. Wary of getting caught up in war memories, he initially refused Dunn's request, but the request stimulated his poetic energies in unexpected ways. He wrote 'A Footnote on the War: On Being Asked to Contribute to a Regimental History', which was not published during his lifetime. The poem enacts the disruptive disinterment of repressed memories of war. Its key trope is exhumation, uncovering spatial and temporal layers buried in the sediment of time. The poem is a 'footnote' – that is, something which appears below the main body of text – but since there is no regimental history to appear beneath, the 'footnote' becomes the text and the first act of exhumation, uncovering what is buried, or more precisely what should be buried.

'A Footnote on the War' operates in a series of contrasts between peace and war, proceeding deeper into the buried past till it reaches a point beyond articulation. It opens with a contrast between the Sunday morning in London of the present, with Sassoon inside and protected, and the 'gory' French Front of 'nine years ago', when he was outside and exposed.[22] Dr Dunn appears in the poem as a friendly oasis in the 'doubly-damned' setting of the past, but his request dredges up this past into the immediate present: 'Now here's his letter lying on my table.'[23] Sassoon wonders with trepidation, 'What can I unbury? . . . / Seven years have crowded past me since I wrote a / Word on [the] war.'[24] He is reluctant to exhume his own 'wounding memories of the dead' because

> in those seven odd years I have erected
> A barrier, that my soul might be protected
> Against the invading ghosts of what I saw
> In years when Murder wore the mask of Law.[25]

Returning none the less to his wartime diary, he tells himself that 'My Fusiliering self has died away,' and the 'scribbled entries' of the diary are 'moribund – remote / From the once-living context of his mind'.[26] Again compartmentalizing aspects of himself, he sees the 'Fusiliering self' as dead and buried beneath the protective 'barrier' he has 'erected'. Even as he seeks to ward off the 'invading ghosts', he finds himself conjuring them up: 'a fair-haired Cameronian / Propped in his pool of blood while we were throwing / Bombs at invisible Saxons'.[27] This 'plutonian / Cartoon' has a haunting intensity that he cannot 'join up' with the present comforts of his music room.[28] At the end he wills himself to turn away from the horrors of this past:

> War's a mystery
> Beyond my retrospection. And I'm going
> Onward, away from that Battalion history
> With all its expurgated dumps of dead:
> And what remains to say I leave unsaid.[29]

And yet, even as he resolves to move 'Onward, away from that Battalion history', he cannot help articulating at least some of the things that he determines to 'leave unsaid'.

While he was contemplating the disturbances to his 'real state of mind' stirred up by Dunn's request, he met with a former comrade, Ralph Greaves, and this meeting produced another poem. In 'To One Who was With Me in the War', published in *The Heart's Journey*, the second person pronoun has a dual function: it is Ralph Greaves, but it is also an uncanny double. With this accompanying figure, Sassoon embarks on a tentative journey back, 'exploring sunken ruinous roads' of traumatic memory,[30] seeking out, in uncanny terms, 'that which ought to remain secret and hidden but has come to light'. 'Remembering, we forget':[31] the pervading tension between remembering and forgetting retrieves 'visual fragments' from the past, the disconnected characteristics of which are reinforced typographically with ellipses, long dashes and wide indents.[32] It was 'too long ago', and yet the charged memories of battle fill the survivors with 'a sense of power', but remembering some fragments compels the forgetting of others, back and forth the poem oscillates until the speaker and his double are led to a culminating uncanny encounter. Along the memories of soaked trenches the two figures wander past 'men / Whose names we've long forgotten' until they encounter a commanding officer huddled against the rain. This officer 'turns his head / And shows you how you looked, – your ten-years-vanished face',[33] producing the hall-of-mirrors effect of a strange and spectral encounter between the double figure and its own double, and the persona looking on, perturbed. The poem ends in a similar fashion to 'A Footnote', with a gesture towards the 'unsaid'; an ellipsis announcing a shift in time is followed by the final words of the poem, 'What's that you said?'[34] Here the unsaid is not quite what cannot be said, but what, as befits traumatic knowledge, cannot be fully understood.

'To One Who was With Me in the War' is placed two-thirds of the way through *The Heart's Journey*, immediately preceding 'On Passing the New Menin Gate', Sassoon's scathing condemnation of the Ypres war memorial as 'a pile of peace-complacent stone' that belittles the staggering losses of life.[35] These two poems are the only ones in the collection dealing directly with the war, and both are fixed upon the problem of accommodating traumatic memories of the past. While 'To One Who was With Me in the War' articulates individuals' struggles to contain 'much that was monstrous', 'On Passing the New Menin Gate' passes judgement on a society's attempt to contain a massive and futile 'immolation' within a 'sepulchre of crime'. This dubious stone structure is implicitly contrasted with the enduring legacy of Stonehenge, addressed in poem IX of the collection, and Stonehenge's unadorned simplicity and openness are symbolic of a prior incarnation of humankind, purer, more integrated with the cosmos and the natural world. The new Menin Gate is an edifice complicit in that which it vainly seeks to oppose. The traumatic past cannot, Sassoon contends, be so readily contained; the names engraved on stone, though remembered, trivialize those whose honour their imprint seeks to restore. These two poems, which articulate without fixating upon the traumatic experience of war, are enfolded in *The Heart's Journey*, buffered by poems that emphasize the more distant past and non-bellicose memories. Sassoon does not shy away from mortality elsewhere in the collection, but with the exception of these two poems, death and its attendant wraiths, spectres and ghosts, migrate from the battlefield and are domesticated into a normalized and civilian framework.

As he wrote in 1937 of frontline experience, it is 'hateful and repellent, unforgettable and inescapable'. The experience remains, to recall Huyssen, in the 'repression, specters, and a present repetitively haunted by the past'. But onwards Sassoon resolved to move, away from mourning the losses of dead, away from the trauma of war, a movement into the liminal space 'between remembering and forgetting, seeing and not seeing, transparency and occlusion': that is, into the space of modern nostalgia.

Prose Autognosis

Through much of the 1920s Sassoon had, in his desultory way, developed his skills as a prose writer, largely through the diary he started during the First World War, receiving encouragement from literary friends as diverse as Edmund Gosse, Osbert Sitwell, T. E. Lawrence and E. M. Forster. His plans for a 'Madame Bovary of sexual inversion' evolved into hopes to write 'a powerful, realistic modern novel full of gloom and grandeur and tragic truthfulness' with a cosmopolitan, non-sporting poet as the central character.[36] Though his prose books developed differently, it is significant that both of these unrealized plans are autobiographical in nature. In the 1920s Sassoon was very much the cosmopolitan and romantic poet (who had largely given up the sporting life), and whose emotional and sexual adventures had led him through the fashionable destinations of Europe. His diaries record these interactions. But when it came to writing his 'novel', these aspirations collapsed under the weight of his nostalgic vision. The autobiographical impulse, fused with nostalgia, drove his self-reflexive and autognostic inclinations back deeper into his past, beyond the too-near 1920s, ripe with emotional and sexual confusions and tensions, past the war years and their traumatic turmoil, back to the safety of a reconstructed childhood assembled from selected memories.

In the autumn of 1926 Sassoon returned to his childhood home in Kent to visit his mother and during this visit he felt himself 'invaded by all the strangeness of the past'.[37] As meetings earlier in the year with his former comrades had disturbed lurking memories of his war experience, encounters with his mother and his former neighbours led to vivid recollections of the calmer, earlier past of peace and childhood. Sassoon harnessed the power of this 'strange invasion' for *Memoirs of a Fox-Hunting Man*. Early in the writing process he realized that these childhood recollections must be shown to lead up to his war experience.[38] The second Sherston volume, *Memoirs of an Infantry Officer* (1930), which would contain the passage of prose initially prompted by the request from Dr Dunn, explores the heart of Sassoon's traumatic war experience, but it is significant that the war is figured as an encroachment on the sporting and leisured rural world of his childhood and youth.

Sassoon created his autobiographical persona – roughly one-fifth of himself, as he suggested to Graves – in sharp contrast to his initial novelistic aspirations of sexual candour. While George Sherston is an enthusiastic (or obsessed) sportsman, he is without sexual appetite or inclination, without interest in the art of poetry. This and other biographical divergences between Sassoon and Sherston, including Sherston's status as an orphan raised by his aunt, help the recollecting Sassoon to focus his attention on reconstructing his idyllic past. The epigraph from Shakespeare's *Richard II* is aptly chosen: 'This happy breed of men, this little world'. John of Gaunt's idealizing vision of England, with its emphasis on happiness, masculinity and the autonomy of the English world, exactly suits the setting Sassoon creates. In contrast to the post-war 1920s, replete with unemployment, ripplings of unrest in the Empire and labour disputes, including the divisive General Strike, Sassoon's 1890s were a golden time for a particular English social geography of rural leisure featuring the acquisition of the right horses, the thrill of point-to-point races and long, hotly (but decently) contested cricket matches. Sassoon's gentried class was secure within the pinnacle of British imperial dominance, and this security underwrites Sherston's pursuit of leisure in an isolated world of boys and men. Female characters do exist, but they are functional and peripheral to the male-dominated world of fox-hunting and cricket, which are both in turn preparations for Sherston's, and Sassoon's, ultimate masculine realm, the army. Young Sherston reluctantly attends a local dance, and the girls in frocks are mere distractions from the guest who commands Sherston's fawning attention and leaves him tongue-tied and blushing: a boy two years older than him and already an accomplished little sportsman. The most significant female character, especially early in the narrative, is Sherston's aunt. While she may hold the purse strings, the groom-gardener Dixon holds the reins that both guide young Sherston in his horsemanship and deftly manipulate his aunt into supporting his masculine pursuits. Aunt Evelyn is a hapless female bystander and unwitting enabler of the sporting hobbies Dixon so skilfully instils in her nephew. As such Dixon serves as a father-figure, foreshadowing Rivers's role in the third volume of memoirs, and as a mentor who pursues through sport the harmony the natural world affords to the privileged social classes.

The Sherston volumes provide a vision of Englishness consistent with the Englishness Blunden sought to preserve in his essays and poetry. In language that reverberates with the words of Shakespeare's John of Gaunt, Blunden writes that 'We are the luckiest of races in our surroundings' and that 'when all is said and balanced [Nature] is happy in England.' The younger generation of modern England must be educated, Blunden implores, in 'a proper, a spiritual, patriotism'.[39] Blunden's implied corollary is that the English are happy in nature, away from the broil of modern urban industrialization. Through the woods on horseback or between the wickets on the village green, young Sherston learns the same joys of being English. Distinctly absent from Sassoon's vision are references to the social conditions that might cloud the golden age he reconstructs. Tom Richardson, the historical person on whom Dixon is based, had a son who recorded his own memoirs of a fox-hunting man's groom's son in Edwardian Kent, which describes the darker realities of the organic community of rural England. The majority of the community contributed to the farming economy that sustained rural life, and conditions for them were far from idyllic:

> Most of them lived in cottages which were not much more than hovels, with no sanitation other than a nasty little building situated at the extreme end of the garden . . . Water supply was from a shared well and had to be hauled up on a windlass and carried in buckets . . . [vegetable gardens were] a necessity of existence for [cottagers] and not just a means of beating old 'so and so' at the annual Brenchley Horticultural Show.[40]

Sherston's Aunt Evelyn is interested in precisely such horticultural events. In recollecting her lack of consideration for his boyish interests, Sherston remarks that 'the world was less democratic in those days,'[41] and this statement serves as blanket disclaimer to any sense that the recollections will pursue a fair and full disclosure of the past and its undemocratic division of privilege and leisure between the gentry and the working classes. Pursuing such socio-economic discrepancies has no place in Sassoon's nostalgic recreations. If it is ever mentioned, social hardship is connected to the industrialized metropolis. On changing trains at Waterloo station, Sherston notices the sprawling and 'dilapidated tenements and warehouses' with a certain air of disgust: 'Poverty was a thing I hated to look in the face; it was like the thought of illness and bad smells, and I resented the notion of all those squalid slums spreading out into the uninfected green country.'[42] Poverty is not so much a social ill or condemnation of societal values, than a vague, distasteful and inconvenient contagion that threatens Sassoon's treasured recreation of a particular social geography of England.

In the nostalgic confines of Sassoon's first autognostic journey in prose, home and its sensual particulars are the shimmery high points. Sassoon's portrayal of the resplendent pastoral comforts of his childhood home, refracted through the semi-fictional lens of Sherston, is an implicit response to what Svetlana Boym identifies as modern nostalgia's object of mourning: the absence of a physically and spiritually realized sense of home, 'an enchanted world with clear borders and values'.[43] The key moments where the recollecting subject attains a sense of quasi-spiritual interfusion with the natural world always occur at home. Sherston's exploits at public school, based upon Sassoon's alma mater, Marlborough, and his chequered career at Cambridge play no role in the narrative. What is more important is the renewed appreciation of home he gains upon returning there from periods away at school.

Back for the summer holidays, Sherston is attuned to the relative comforts of home and its harmonic integration into the natural world:

> My window was wide open when I went to bed, and I had left the curtains half-drawn. I woke out of my deep and dreamless sleep to a gradual recognition that I was at home and not in the cubicled dormitory at Ballboro'. Drowsily grateful for this, I lay and listened. A cock was crowing from a neighbouring farm; his shrill challenge was faintly echoed by another cock a long way off.
>
> I loved the early morning; it was luxurious to lie there, half-awake, and half-aware that there was a pleasantly eventful day in front of me . . . Presently I would get up and lean on the window ledge to see what was happening in the world outside.[44]

What he sees are starlings nestled in the jasmine, and the distant treetops reaching toward the brightening morning sky. The eventful day that awaits him involves a purloined slice of cake from the pantry and a dramatic village cricket match. There is in this passage a Proustian sensitivity to the luxuriousness of embracing the quiet pleasures of a privileged life in the country.

Having decided to leave Cambridge without a degree and secured his aunt's support of his decision not to pursue legal studies in London, Sherston finds himself back in his home county, en route to a cricket match:

> The air was Elysian with early summer and the shadows of steep white clouds were chasing over the orchards and meadows; sunlight sparkled on green hedgerows that had been drenched by early morning showers. As I was carried past it all I was lazily aware through my dreaming and unobservant eyes that this was the sort of world I wanted. For it was my own countryside, and I loved it with an intimate feeling, though all its associations were crude and incoherent. I cannot think of it now without a sense of heartache, as if it contained something which I have never quite been able to discover.[45]

Again the landscape of rural England is the object of his dreaming, intimate love. 'Now', now that the recollecting Sherston is separated from this beloved countryside, he can think of it only with pangs of heartache. This is what Boym calls 'reflective nostalgia', in which the *algos*, the pain of separation from the home, animates the nostalgic who dwells in 'the imperfect process of remembrance.'[46] This passage is also noteworthy for its explicit literary reference. While figuratively 'Elysian' refers to a place of perfect happiness, which is the primary meaning in this passage, it also invokes death, as 'Elysium' is literally the resting place of the blessed dead in Greek mythology. Like the photograph of Watts's 'Love and Death', which hangs in Aunt Evelyn's drawing room and repeatedly captures Sherston's attention, the Elysian air of this richly nostalgic passage draws together perfection and death, reifying the painful longing for a home, a time and a place that have irrevocably passed, to which one can never properly return.

In Watts's painting, the figure of the beautiful boy, Love, cannot bar the shrouded figure from entering the house, but Watts depicts them in stasis upon the threshold. All has yet to be lost. In a similar fashion, Sassoon constructs the nostalgia of the pre-war past to hold off his shrouded memories of traumatic war experience. Sassoon's version of modern nostalgia in part expresses pangs for an absent absolute, for Boym's home that is both physical and spiritual, the edenic unity of time and space before entry into history'.[47] Through much of *Memoirs of a Fox-Hunting Man* Sherston dwells, like the boy, Love, in a prelapsarian Edenic time and space, but with the declaration of war and Sherston's ready enlistment in the army, death looms inevitably, marking an entry into traumatic history.

This movement from love to death, from nostalgic reconstruction to traumatic history, is also borne out in the transformation of uncanny doubles in this narrative from representing affirmers of life to portenders of mortality. In the book's first chapter, Sherston recalls how, as a child, he combated loneliness with the invention of an 'ideal companion who became much more a reality' than the unfriendly children he met at the few parties his aunt allowed him to attend.[48] This 'other boy', this 'dream friend', is integral to young Sherston and 'made his childhood unexpectedly clear'.[49] In his childhood Sherston's imaginary friend protects and completes him, blurring the distinction between reality and imagination. This imaginary friend, an uncanny double that is at once a part of Sherston and not Sherston, offers an early example of the splitting of the subject so prevalent in Sassoon's autobiographical project. Later in his apprenticeship as a fox-hunting boy, he meets Dennis Milden, who serves as another example of the positive uncanny double of childhood. Milden is 'another boy of about my own age', whose prowess with horses fills Sherston with awe and admiration:[50] 'already I was weaving Master Milden into my day dreams, and soon he had become my inseparable companion in all my imagined adventures.'[51] Milden replaces Sherston's 'ideal companion', penetrating his dream world and completing his adventure fantasies. Both Milden and

Sherston's young imaginary friend represent uncanny doubles that dominate the childhood mind and offer protection against death.

After his Ballboro' career Sherston meets his next ideal companion, Stephen Colwood, another gifted horseman who is sufficiently like Sherston that they are mistaken for brothers. But beyond the space of childhood, this uncanny double becomes a harbinger of death. Colwood sees active service before Sherston, and chummy and encouraging letters between the two anticipate a jolly reunion, which is spoiled by news of Colwood's death in action. Love and death fuse as Colwood's demise coincides with the arrival of Sherston's 'new companion',[52] the beautiful Dick Tiltwood, whose 'cheerful companionship' sustained Sherston through the tedium of army life.[53] Tiltwood's presence wards off thoughts of death, and together the pair ride through the French woods when they can, imaginary fox-hunters of peacetime. But following Colwood's death comes the death of Dixon, who had written to Sherston hoping to transfer to his regiment, and soon too the inevitable death of Dick, and of the happy and innocent way of life Sassoon's nostalgic vision struggled to reconstruct.

With the war's rapidly accumulating destruction, death ascends over love and Sherston's uncanny double becomes internalized, what Freud would call his 'parasitic double' that seeks out deathly encounters: 'I had more or less made up my mind to die.'[54] The concluding image of *Memoirs of a Fox-Hunting Man* features Sherston in a trench, immersed in a life without comfort and thinking of his last visit to Aunt Evelyn. Her comforting home and the community of supporting country characters represent a rural England whose values exist in sharp contrast to his growing disillusionment with Christianity and the role of the church in the war. The failure of Sherston's parasitic double to prevail and become a timely harbinger of death is assured by the existence of the recollecting narrator who has survived, but the disillusionment of the final chapters promises the future prominence of death in Sherston's military exploits as they unfold. This promise is realized in Sassoon's second Sherston volume, *Memoirs of an Infantry Officer*, in which the nostalgically drawn pre-war landscapes are juxtaposed with the devastated landscapes of battle-torn France and Flanders, until the disillusionment erupts into Sherston's 'Soldier's Declaration' against the conduct of the war. Sherston's incarceration into Slateford War Hospital at the outset of the final Sherston volume facilitates the appearance of W. H. R. Rivers into his life, a new father-figure to replace Dixon and help Sherston to negotiate the after-effects of his war experience. Rivers's benedictory capacity affirms a new spiritual possibility of life to counter the feuding inner demons released by Sherston's war experience. Fittingly, Sherston's very last words summarize the lessons of Rivers in a homily: 'it is only from the inmost silences of the heart that we know the world for what it is, and ourselves for what the world has made us.'[55] It is a succinct reiteration of autognosis.

UNCANNY RETURNS: POETRY OF WAR AND DREAMS IN THE 1930S

The effort of representing his frontline experience and his public protest against the war in *Memoirs of an Infantry Officer* left Sassoon exhausted,[56] and he resolved to concentrate on writing poetry for the next year at least.[57] In poetry, where he sought to express other aspects or versions of his self, he might be able to avoid dredging up wartime memories. But the residual influence of his 'war book' could not be so easily dropped. In the early 1930s, the war also intruded obliquely during the personal crisis that ensued from the acrimonious and protracted unwinding of his relationship with Stephen Tennant.[58] In 1932, Tennant was diagnosed as neurasthenic and admitted to the Cassel Hospital for Functional and Nervous Disorders under the care of T. A. Ross, a colleague of Henry Head.[59] During his infrequent visits to Cassel, Sassoon walked the halls of a civilian version of Craiglockhart, which must have stirred memories of his own troubled time in a neurasthenic hospital. Sassoon told Head that he believed the root of Tennant's neurosis lay in a 'tragic disability' that caused 'most of his irrational restlessness',[60] a belief confirmed by Ross, who attributed his patient's plight to 'one great [unidentified] shock' that took place during his formative years.[61] Sassoon observed that Ross's psychoanalytic approach provided some temporary benefits,[62] but these did not prevent Tennant from treating Sassoon badly. After declining to receive his visits, Tennant refused to respond to Sassoon's letters and enlisted Ross to write the letter that ended the relationship. Bearing witness to the debilitating effects of his lover's trauma was difficult for Sassoon. When their mutual friend, Edith Olivier, comforted Sassoon, she observed that in his despair he was awash with rekindled memories of the war.[63]

Sassoon's next book of poetry, *The Road to Ruin* (1933), reflects these irrepressible memories obliquely and responds to the political unrest disrupting Europe in the early 1930s. While Hitler's ascent to power in January 1933 was not widely condemned in England,[64] Sassoon was among those who feared the new German government and he revived his 'war poet' persona to warn against a future war.[65] Sassoon uses a prelude and an epigraph to situate and justify the belated reappearance of his protesting voice. On the title page, two six-line stanzas provide an insight into the character of the voice that follows:

> My hopes, my messengers I sent
> Across the ten years continent
> Of Time. In dream I saw them go, –
> And thought, 'When they come back I'll know
> To what far place I lead my friends
> Where this disastrous decade ends'.[66]

But his messengers do not return. Waiting, 'like one in purgatory', he is visited by a 'ghost' of these hopes who urges him to steer others from the ruinous path they are on.[67] The ten-year journey of his hopes recalls the temporal shifts of 'A Fragment of Autobiography' through which he sought to integrate his self-understanding. The 'ghosts' of the prelude are both a spectre who has seen into the future, and one from the past, the speaker, a phantom of Sassoon's own previous self, the 'war poet'. It is noteworthy that Sassoon's bleak assessment of the 1930s anticipates Auden's oft-quoted 'low dishonest decade' from 'September 1, 1939'. The ubiquity of Auden's poem in anthologies compared to the relative obscurity of Sassoon's collection supports the obvious point, to which I will return later in this chapter, that Sassoon's aesthetic tastes differed then, and continue to differ, from the prevailing literary tastes. What Sassoon might disdain as Auden's showiness, and the open connections Auden draws between his political discontent and his inner subjectivity, are precisely what is lacking in Sassoon's poems and contributes to their lack of favour among readers. The axiomatic (and oversimplified) critical gulf that divides writers of the 1930s into left-leaning social realists like Auden and high modernists like Pound and Joyce left Sassoon somewhere in the middle, antagonistic towards both camps. Nevertheless, the historical issues that energize the better-known and younger poets of the 1930s also engaged Sassoon's imagination, albeit on a different register. For Sassoon, talk of war, even war in the future, always drew his gaze backwards to the First World War.

The epigraph of *The Road to Ruin*, taken from Albert Einstein's 1933 public discussion with Freud of the question 'Why War?',[68] identifies a 'small but determined group, active in every nation', that regards warfare as an opportunity to advance its interests and enlarge its authority.[69] Einstein's words initiate a return to the target Sassoon had attacked during the First World War with his poetry and his public protest: the political elite and the war profiteers, 'who have the power to end [war] . . . [and who are responsible for] political errors and insincerities'.[70] The epigraph foregrounds the external, socio-political causes of war that Sassoon denounces in the six short poems that follow. The imagery is abstract, emphasizing external dangers, like peoples 'pledged to live / With Violence, Greed, and Ignorance', who inaugurate 'A super-savage Mammonistic State'.[71] Given the influence of Rivers and Head, it is striking that Sassoon did not cite in this volume, or mention in his letters, Freud's response to 'Why War?', which attributes the fundamental cause of war to the individual's innate capacity for violence based on the destructive instinct, a projection of the death instinct on to an external object.[72] Having himself experienced, in Freud's words, the 'lust for aggression and destruction' in the trenches,[73] and having had his memories of war recently stirred up by the end of his relationship with Tennant and the composition of *Memoirs of an Infantry Officer*, Sassoon was all too familiar with the individual's role in the roots of war. By choosing Einstein's words over Freud's for the epigraph and emphasizing socio-political causes, Sassoon created a buffer that allowed him to avoid his complicity in the inner roots of war identified by Freud.

There is something cumbersome and belated about the revived protesting persona in *The Road to Ruin*. Sassoon may have realized this, since most of his poetry in the 1930s avoids overt political stances and pursues that 'rich vein' of autobiographical material suggested by Rivers for psychological reasons and by Blunden for literary ones. The poems of *Vigils* (1935) still reflect his understanding that the 'real state of mind' depends upon both inner unconscious forces and external forces – literary, socio-political, historical, spiritual – which shape it. In particular, his treatment of dreams exhibits the importance of both internal and external influences in his version of autognosis, while also reflecting the shift in Rivers's ongoing influence from psychological to spiritual guide. In the summer of 1922, the year Rivers died, Sassoon noted in his diary his eagerness to learn how the past three years 'impressed themselves on my below-the-surface life (subconscious).[74] Have I digested and assimilated them yet? (When I have done so they will reappear in poetry or prose?) I get vague clues from my dreams.'[75] But consistent with his underlying resistance to the full implications of autognosis as Rivers saw it, there is little follow-up in the diaries or the poetry to this interest in 'below-the-surface life'. The brief discussion of recurring dreams in *Sherston's Progress*, noted in the previous chapter, is the most extensive dream interpretation to be found in his published work. And though he was troubled by upsetting dreams and nightmares long after his war service, disturbing dreams are relatively rare in Sassoon's poetry, which makes them all the more interesting when they do occur, especially when they are connected with some of the ideas Rivers expressed in *Conflict and Dream*.

At Craiglockhart in 1917, Sassoon wrote of 'those dreams from the pit' and the 'noiseless dead' that invaded one's sleep, asking sardonically, 'Do they matter?'[76] The 'pit' is both the trenches of the Western Front and the unconscious, the force of which he had only recently become aware in his talks with Rivers. As he relaxed his 'barriers' against his war memories and tapped into the 'rich vein' of autobiography, Sassoon became open not only to his own traumatic experiences, but to his unconscious, where they had sunk and festered. In 'To One Who was With Me in the War', the horrors of battle have receded in calendar time, but the 'after-thoughts' send one's mind back 'Beyond Peace, exploring sunken ruinous roads' that lead to the unconscious and to encounters with distressing passers-by.[77] Poems steeped in trauma appear even in 1935 in the middle of *Vigils*: 'War Experience' assembles the 'ghastly glooms / Of soul-conscripting war',[78] and 'Ex-Service' evokes 'dream voices' from 'swindled ghosts . . . crying / From shell-holes in the past'.[79] In this version of a 'dream from the pit', these unsettled and plaintive voices issue from 'shell-holes', signifying a topography of the unconscious impressed by the traumatic past. Poem 17, which follows these two poems of experience, presents a dialectic of self in which the poet seeks sanctuary from the 'muttering mind-wrought voices' that have been invading the 'silence' of his sleep.[80] He desires to 'Break silence . . . Call for lights' and 'Prove these persistent haunting presences wrong / Who mock and stultify your days and nights',[81] but even the coming of dawn that 're-creates' his bedroom cannot dispel them. With the intrusion of traumatic memories, his unconscious is reduced and darkened to 'that garret of uneasy gloom / Which is your brain',[82] and the silence of night trembles with eerie utterances emanating from within it. The dreams in these poems, Rivers might well have said, convey the troubling results of an unresolved inner conflict with the traumatic past, but Sassoon tends to baulk at interpretation or analysis, perhaps wary of what it might reveal.

In *Vigils*, Sassoon demonstrates the potential of dreams to influence his autognostic course not only from within the unconscious, as Rivers would have it, but also from without. I mentioned above that there are poems in *Vigils* in which dreams are charged with the residual energies of trauma, but elsewhere in the collection he keeps the nocturnal intrusions of his war experience at bay, though his unconscious is still haunted by voices of the past. Nostalgic dreams of happy childhood reconfigure the unconscious as a 'quiet house' rather than the 'garret of uneasy gloom' that generates and contains his war dreams:

> But dreams have a secret strength; they will not die so soon:
> They haunt the quiet house through idle afternoon;
> And under childhood skies their summer thoughts await
> The rediscovering soul returning tired and late.[83]

These dreams of innocence, of 'Standing in the strangeness of that [childhood] garden air',[84] share with his war dreams a 'secret strength', enticing him to return to the past, but here a more distant and safer past.

In the last half of the collection, Sassoon moves to reclaim hope from the voices and visions that both harrow him as a man and empower him as a poet. The titles of these poems suggest their positive associations: 'The Gains of Good', 'Vibrations', 'The Merciful Knight' and 'Heaven', which is followed by 'Credo', the first line of which reads: 'The heaven for which I wait has neither guard nor gate.'[85] In the final two poems, 'Presences Perfected' and an 'Ode' to the city of God, the dead, whose voices haunt his 'mind-sight', have a heavenly purpose that strives for harmony as they remind him that his 'shriven self survives'.[86] The design on the title page of the first edition of *Vigils* may represent this modest sense of hope; a large hourglass, with equal amounts of sand top and bottom, is superimposed upon a scythe. The detail is clean, exact and precise; the symbolism suggests that contemplative life has replaced a life of action, while rumination has replaced cutting irony.

The poems in *Vigils* are thus haunted by grief and remembrance: 'Again the dead, the dead again demanding' to be accounted for, 'demanding' that the poet allow himself, in his 'strange survival', to be reconciled to his participation and complicity in their fate.[87] To achieve this reconciliation, Sassoon orchestrates through dreams the haunting voices into a chorus of spiritual redemption. '"We Shall Not All Sleep"', for example, looks back to war and forward to Christian salvation. The title recalls a line in John McRae's 'In Flanders Fields', the most popular poem of the First World War, but the quotation marks suggest an exactness of reference, which is found in St Paul's First Letter to the Corinthians: 'We shall not all sleep, but we shall all be changed, in a moment, in the twinkling of an eye, at the last trumpet.'[88] Paul's words of Christian transcendence indicate the direction Sassoon was taking in his attempts to turn trauma into hope and strength in his own life.

The dreams of visitors from the past, even the traumatic past, now offer comfort. In Poem 22, for example, he asks, 'And how, revisitants by life envisioned, / Can what we are empower your quiet returning?'[89] The answer is hinted at in the poem 'Revisitation (W.H.R.R.)', a homage to Rivers, now also among the dead who revisit his 'heart's room': 'in strange survival stands / Your ghost, whom I am powerless to repay.'[90] All Sassoon can glean from this 'revisitation' is the 'feel[ing of] his influence undiminished',[91] though not unchanged. He had once relied on Rivers to provide answers, to banish his demons, his doubts and fears, but his friend's power to 'harmonize and heal' is now offered in terms more spiritual than psychological. In 'Revisitation' Sassoon imagines that Rivers's spirit resides in a heavenly realm 'where the grace / Of human sainthood burns'.[92] From *Vigils* on, he is more open than before about the ability of poetic dreams to at once imbue the traumatic past with nostalgic inflections and elicit 'vague clues' to his spiritual yearnings.

Looking Back: Sassoon's Aesthetics

The reception of *Vigils*, first printed privately in May 1934 and then published by Heinemann in the late autumn of 1935, contributed to Sassoon's realization that he differed from the prevailing tastes of his time. T. E. Lawrence was enthusiastic and sensed that Sassoon was in control of his emotions as never before: 'I can feel the solidity of the war-anger and the peace-bitterness under the feet, as it were, of these poems: they are all the better for it, but so far from it.'[93] Lawrence knew from his own war experience how stubbornly the past clung to oneself, and how necessary it was to struggle with it and master it. Other reviewers, who did not share Sassoon's war experience, could not see the connection of *Vigils* with the present or future. The *Times Literary Supplement* noted 'a slackening of tension and reflectiveness of mood' in many of 'these backward-glancing poems'.[94] And while the writer in the *London Mercury* responded to the poems' 'melancholy elegance' and 'sad music', he concluded that 'now [Mr. Sassoon] has more definitely than ever turned his back on the contemporary situation . . . [He] has no forward vision.'[95] *The Road to Ruin* had also been criticized as backward-glancing, even by Lawrence, who nevertheless respected the poems' ability to 'frighten'.[96] The critical consensus in the mid-1930s was that Sassoon's concern with the First World War, as exemplified in the Sherston memoirs, was an 'obsession',[97] and that his 'acute sensibility . . . has not yet recovered from [it]'.[98]

The cool reception of his post-war poetry was, I think, an important 'condition' that shaped Sassoon's 'real state of mind' and influenced his writing in two important and interrelated ways: it fuelled his reclusive nature and entrenched his 'old-fashioned' aesthetic values. Feeling at odds with the modern world, which through the war had shaped his character and his writing so irrevocably, produced in Sassoon a profound ambivalence towards the contemporary situation. This uneasiness, combined with his continued commitment to self-understanding, including an acceptance of the inescapable role of external influences, led to a pattern of engagement and withdrawal that characterizes his relation to the international political and literary debates of the period.

In the same month that *Vigils* was privately printed, Sassoon, newly married, retreated to Heytesbury House in Wiltshire, on the edge of Salisbury Plain, where he would live for the rest of his long life. His friends worried that this move would only encourage his tendency to solitariness, brooding and self-pity, but this retreat was different.[99] He was not alone, and he saw his wife, at least to begin with, as a 'perfect companion', and his new house and grounds as 'a perfect place'.[100] Sassoon expended a great deal of energy and resources in transforming the sprawling early Georgian country manor house set in 170 acres of parks and downs into 'a little private Utopia'.[101] He had the house refurnished, recarpeted and rewired, and revived the grounds by planting small forests of sycamore, ash and birch trees.[102] Heytesbury functioned as a bastion against the world Sassoon had come to disdain. In contrast to the hurly-burly of London, Heytesbury provided a calming atmosphere in which he felt 'like some Trollope character', happily thriving in an old-fashioned existence.[103] Both Heytesbury House and his marriage to Hester Gatty, which surprised not only his friends but himself as well, held the promise of 'health and peace and safety'.[104] But they also brought him closer to the threat of the emotional exhaustion he strove to escape after the wrenching break-up with Tennant. In the weeks before the wedding Sassoon confessed that 'the "emotional impact" has been rather strong, [and] I know that it would take very little to reduce me to nervous exhaustion again.'[105] He was also fearful about the impression his nervous condition might make on his wife: 'I am terrified of getting nervy [and] then passing on my nerviness to Hester, (who, it must be remembered, was *almost* a nervous invalid last winter).'[106] His fears, unhappily, were realized as tensions in the marriage soon began to disrupt the idyllic existence he had hoped to cultivate.

Sassoon's move to Heytesbury House embodied an aspect of the cultural nostalgia of the 1930s that Blunden, Massingham and others endorsed: the preservation, or reclamation, of an organic English rural community order. During the middle of the Second World War, Blunden wrote *Cricket Country*, his paean to 'the ever changeful, changeless game . . . the prime English eccentricity',[107] and cites Sassoon as both an exemplary sportsman and a committed upholder of the 'native heath'.[108] For Blunden, and he implies for Sassoon too, cricket is not only England's national sport, but a bastion of social tradition capable of warding off the vicissitudes of modernity. Blunden writes:

> At a period when Estate is in some disfavour we may well understand why [Sassoon] has chosen it, much in its old form; and while the world echoes with systems, new societies, governances and proposals for them he continues his practical creed of the country house with as much as is workable of its locally useful influence. He can let his meadows, plant his woodland, employ husbandry, preside on occasions, be the friend of the village, study his literary and artistic concerns, and entertain and refresh the minds of others who share those interests. Included in his little principality, as it always used to be in such places, is the cricket ground – and the proper name of the team is the Estate.[109]

At Heytesbury House, Sassoon played the role of the country squire responsible for the welfare of the village way of life, symbolically celebrated on the cricket ground he maintained and protected from the encroaching menace of modern road-making strategies that sought to requisition the land. The pragmatics of being at the helm of this organic rural community, whose order reaches back to happier times before the Industrial Revolution, resolutely resists the modern world of new systems, societies and governances. The position also afforded Sassoon the opportunity to pursue his literary concerns, but not without obstacles.

Even in splendid country solitude, his country life posed a challenge to finding the ruminative space necessary for his 'poetic' or 'real' self. Less than two years after the marriage and the move to Heytesbury, Sassoon admitted to a friend that 'I am feeling nervy, as I have been so little alone this summer, and never seem to get a chance to relax and ruminate.'[110] Writing at this time in the guise of Sherston:

> my main difficulty [as professional ruminator] has been that I absorb so much that I am continually asking to be allowed to sit still and digest the good (and bad) things which life has offered me. A ruminator really needs two lives; one for experiencing and another for thinking it over. Knowing that I *need* two lives and am only allowed one, I do my best to *lead* two lives; with the inevitable consequence that I am told by the world's busybodies that I am 'turning my back on the contemporary situation.'[111]

Sherston returns to the difficulty of maintaining a duality of inconsonant selves that occupies Sassoon's poetic expression, though in vague terms that conflate private and public lives. Increasingly, Sassoon's responsibilities to his family and the village became a distracting burden to his 'ruminations', as much as the intellectual busybodies who spurned his poetry.

In *Rhymed Ruminations*, published privately on the eve of the Second World War, the first poem, 'Brevities', begins, significantly (if unfortunately): 'I am that man who with a luminous look / Sits up at night to write a ruminant book.'[112] When he informed Keynes that he had completed his selections for this volume, he put it in these terms: 'Yes, I suppose the ruminations are quite well ruminated.'[113] Clearly, 'ruminate' is a seminal word in Sassoon's lexicon. From the Latin root *rumen*, 'throat', 'to ruminate' means to chew again what has been lightly chewed and swallowed, or figuratively, 'to bring something up again and again for mental consideration'.[114] Apparently attesting to its physiological root, he once described his ruminative self as 'a mental muncher and cogitator'.[115] What seems essential about this term to Sassoon is the notion of retrospection, the 'need' to think 'over and over', 'again and again' the implications of his life experiences in order to digest their real meaning. Only then might he be free from the nervous disquietude that threatened his peace; only then might the possibilities of spiritual redemption, which he did not yet fully accept, provide the comfort for which he yearned.

Notwithstanding his desire for ruminative solitude, he continued to take part in public debates about international politics and aesthetic values. He visited London occasionally but kept up with current events, mostly through newspapers, personal letters and the wireless. Despite his reconstruction of a rural life out of a Trollope novel, Sassoon was seduced by modern technology, in particular the motorcar, which facilitated his many tours of the countryside and his revisitations of important sites from his childhood, and the wireless, with which he kept abreast of developments from beyond his idyllic rural enclave. In 1936 he appeared on behalf of the Peace Pledge Union at the Albert Hall and read from his war poems, asking his audience, 'Have you forgotten yet?'[116] He was also sensitive to the abuse of language inherent in propaganda, from the left or the right. Nazi rhetoric drew his ire, as expressed in an uncollected poem, 'Theme and Variation', published in the spring of 1935:

> In a world simply seething with troubles
> Our three most unburstable bubbles
> Are Hitler & Goering & Goebbels.[117]

The mock-serious title followed by lines of unabashed doggerel pointedly disparages the self-inflated, grandiloquent figures under attack. The twisting of Goebbels' name in each of the tercets to rhyme with babbles, squabbles and roubles directs its derision fittingly at the head of Nazi propaganda. Sassoon regarded 'Theme and Variation' as 'facetious lines on a serious subject'.[118] The poem is in keeping with other such interventions that make it clear that, though he had slipped away from the metropolitan centre of modernity to Heytesbury Park, he was not ignorant of the 'contemporary situation'.

Sassoon was exasperated by 'the superior intellectuals who are busily turning up their priggish little noses at *Vigils*'.[119] His personal letters are full of incredulity at the acclaim heaped upon modernists in favour of those he regarded as 'real' writers like Walter de la Mare and Max Beerbohm, not to mention himself. His sense of his own marginalization by changing literary tastes served only to entrench his opposition to those tastes. He railed against the modernists' lack of humour, which he took as a sign of emotional barrenness. Contemporary poets were 'all too anxious to be clever and smart. I wish some of the younger bards had more sense of humour.'[120] He was horrified by what he called the 'wild bosh' that appeared in *The Year's Poetry 1935*,[121] which he agreed to review in *The Spectator*. By exaggerating his indebtedness to antiquated traditions, he erected a kind of nostalgic aesthetic, transforming into virtues what the new generation regarded as his poetic flaws. He concocted a character, 'Aunt Eudora', who was unrepentantly Victorian in her upbringing and tastes, with whom he entered into a light-hearted discussion that focused on particularly trying passages from poems by William Empson, W. H. Auden and others, and concluded with a condemnation of the self-conscious and highly artificial nature of contemporary poetry. Demonstrating exactly the arid solemnity that so galled Sassoon, Michael Roberts replied to the editor, despairing of the older poet's blithe approach to so important a subject as poetry. Sassoon responded with his own letter to the editor, and by reviving Aunt Eudora in two further articles in support of his own defiantly old-fashioned position that 'true poetry always seems so natural,' since it is 'memorable, indirectly descriptive, and fused by emotion'.[122] Ridiculing the contrived, scientific ways of modernist verse and bemoaning its uncritical acceptance of Freud and 'morbid psychology', he wrote of the younger poets that 'they watch the Unconscious like a cat watching a mouse-hole.'[123] While there is certainly some tongue in cheek behind this pithy critique of the 'undelighting moderns'[124] which may mitigate the condemnation of Freudian psychology, its underlying attitude suggests how far his feelings for Rivers, still his guiding light, had evolved from a psychological influence into a spiritual one. The modernists' scientific distrust of the simple spiritual faith imputed to Aunt Eudora's world view had the effect of making Sassoon into, if not a believer, then one willing to understand himself by looking beyond the unconscious to the possibility, at least, of spiritual being.

Early in 1936 Sassoon agreed to contribute a foreword to an edition of Isaac Rosenberg, whose poetry he found to be exemplary – natural, memorable, fused with emotion – precisely the kind of poetry so noticeably absent from contemporary literary offerings. Singling out 'Break of Day in the Trenches' for its 'poignant and nostalgic qualities', he describes 'front-line existence' in a self-revealing way as 'hateful and repellent, unforgettable and inescapable'.[125] Though he chose not to address his memories of this grim experience in his autognostic writing after *Sherston's Progress*, this experience irrevocably broke the connection to the quaintly old-fashioned world of 'Aunt Eudora', the golden age before 1914, a breach which mobilized his nostalgic, recollecting gaze to this prior world in his prose autobiographies that followed.

In *On Poetry*, a lecture presented in May 1939 at the University of Bristol, Sassoon aligns himself with a tradition of 'simplicity' stretching back through Hardy to Wordsworth and Milton.[126] As self-consciously and defiantly 'old-fashioned' as his 'Aunt Eudora' creation,[127] Sassoon seeks to counter the obscurantism and artificiality of 'the cult of incomprehensibility' that he saw in modernism.[128] In 'Aliveness in Literature', published in the *Fortnightly Review* in November 1940, he reiterates his conservative aesthetic position. Stressing the mechanization of modern culture, he distances himself from the 'ultra-mechanized' air war over Britain that seemed to draw all citizens into the field of battle, deadening their sensibility as the obscure intellectualism of modern writing had started to do on a different level.[129] What becomes apparent from his contributions to the literary debate is his apparent obliviousness to the gap between the aesthetic values he wants to embrace and his own 'inescapable' modern experience. He cannot turn the clock back to the 1870s, but he can deploy his nostalgic vision to reconstruct a version of the past as a bulkhead to ward off modernity.

Sassoon's final critical contribution to the contemporary literary scene before the end of the Second World War was '*The Dynasts* in Wartime', a brief article commissioned by the *Spectator* that appeared in 1942. Disclaiming competence 'to offer even a tentative opinion on the analogies between "the First and Second German Wars" . . . and those of the Napoleonic Period',[130] he brings to bear on the subject of war his traditional literary values, which he contrasts with values of modernism. He finds it 'somehow comforting . . . that Wordsworth . . . [was] kept awake at night by comparable anxieties', and cites lines from Swinburne and Meredith which could be repeated in 1942 with no loss of effect.[131] It is Hardy's epic drama, however, that he recommends as a literary balm to the traumas of contemporary life: '*The Dynasts* can help us towards a sense of proportion and perspective when we try to acclimatise and adapt our minds to the biological struggle for survival in which we are involved.'[132] He finds particularly appealing Hardy's use of transcendent controlling spirits and patterns of historical repetition. Even before his conversion, as one perhaps sees in his poetry of the 1930s, he believed in immanent spiritual entities at work in the universe, 'powers of darkness . . . in conflict with powers of light'.[133] Unconscious repetition is at the heart of Hardy's 'panoramic masterpiece' and 'shows us all', Sassoon says, 'in relation to our tormented chapter of history'.[134] In *The Dynasts*, England is under threat of invasion by a European dictator and its leaders are shown seeking strength from past battles:

> Unprecedented and magnificent
> As were our strivings in the previous war,
> Our efforts in the present shall transcend them,
> As men will learn.[135]

While Hardy 'can have had no expectation that history would repeat itself in the twentieth century' or that Napoleon would have a 'claimant-successor',[136] Sassoon can read the 'unprecedented' efforts of 'the previous war' as evidence of Hardy's prescience. He finds solace and hope in reading of the defeat of Napoleon by England's 'tough, enisled, self-centred, kindless craft'.[137]

Sassoon concludes '*The Dynasts* in Wartime' with a poetic image resonant with repetition. He describes an eighteenth-century hourglass that once belonged to Hardy, recalling how he had seen Hardy turn the clock over and watch the growing pyramid. Now that very hourglass is in his possession, and as he turns it over and watches the sands shift, he thinks how 'they measured the hours while Napoleon came and went. They will make their casual contribution to Chronometry when aggression has again received its proper repayment.'[138] The questionable reasoning of this observation does not impair the image's power, which, like poetry itself, is governed by the multidimensional power of repetition. Sassoon implies that 're-reading' *The Dynasts* in wartime,[139] like inverting an antique hourglass, is an act of revisiting the past, measuring out the present in a pattern of comforting familiarity.

Sassoon's aesthetic traditionalism can be seen as another version of his need to return to the past to find meaning in the present, another dimension of his nostalgia. His relation to the contemporary socio-political, historical and literary conditions that 'produced' his real state of mind was certainly important to Sassoon and his autognostic autobiographical project, but what is crucial is his nostalgic attitude to these conditions. The past was important to Sassoon not in and of itself, but in so far as it could provide sustenance for the modern present he found so barren, politically, socio-economically, aesthetically and, increasingly, personally. The historical return of war offered little reprieve.

Notes

1. W. H. R. Rivers, 'Psycho-Therapeutics', in James Hastings (ed.), *Encyclopedia of Religion and Ethics*, vol. 10 (New York: Scribner's, n.d.), p. 437.
2. Siegfried Sassoon, *Diaries 1920–1922*, ed. Rupert Hart-Davis (London: Faber & Faber, 1981), p. 47.

3. Siegfried Sassoon, *The Old Century* (London: Faber & Faber, 1938), p. 288.

   It is interesting that Sassoon records how this advice was reiterated by Edward Marsh before the First World War: 'It seems a necessity now to write either with one's eye on an object and one's mind at grips with a more or less definite idea', in Siegfried Sassoon, *The Weald of Youth* (London: Faber & Faber, 1942), p. 138.

4. Sassoon, *Diaries 1920–1922*, p. 47.
5. W. H. R. Rivers, *Medicine, Magic and Religion* (London: Kegan Paul, 1924), p. 4.
6. Ibid., p. 144.
7. In light of Sassoon's conversion, it is interesting to note that Rivers was struck by the fact that a penitent Catholic was required to seek the cause of his transgression in 'apparently minor faults' of character, a practice that he accorded with 'most modern systems of psycho-therapy', which led him 'to the place of religion in psychological medicine' (Rivers, *Medicine*, p. 143). This suggests to me that, despite his scientific approach to religion, Rivers would have encouraged in Sassoon any fledgling religious notions they may have discussed.
8. Sassoon, *Diaries 1920–1922*, p. 104.
9. Ibid. p. 21.
10. Ibid. p. 22.
11. Ibid. p. 22.
12. Ibid. p. 22.
13. Sassoon showed his diary to close friends, like E. M. Forster, to seek advice on improving his prose (Siegfried Sassoon, *Diaries 1923–1925*, ed. Rupert Hart-Davis (London: Faber & Faber, 1985), p. 36).
14. Quoted in Geoffrey Keynes, *A Bibliography of Siegfried Sassoon* (London: Hart-Davis, 1962), p. 57. 'Fragment of Autobiography' did not appear publicly until Hart-Davis included it as a prelude to the first volume of the published diaries (Sassoon, *Diaries 1920–1922*, pp. 20–1).
15. Mark Bostridge, rev. of *Siegfried Sassoon: The Making of a War Poet* by Jean Moorcroft Wilson. *The Independent On-line*, 26 May 1998, n.p.
16. Sassoon, *Diaries 1920–1922*, p. 53.
17. Sassoon, *Diaries 1923–1925*, p. 234.
18. Sassoon, *Diaries 1920–1922*, p. 53n.
19. Ibid. p. 73.
20. Ibid. pp. 161, 51.
21. Ibid. p. 174.
22. Siegfried Sassoon, *The War Poems*, ed. Rupert Hart-Davis (London: Faber & Faber, 1983), p. 147.
23. Ibid. p. 148.
24. Ibid. p. 148.
25. Ibid. p. 148.
26. Ibid. pp. 148–9.
27. Ibid. pp. 149–50.
28. Ibid. p. 149.
29. Ibid. p. 150.
30. Siegfried Sassoon, *Collected Poems: 1908–1956* (London: Faber & Faber, 1961), p. 187.
31. Ibid. p. 187.
32. Ibid. p. 186.
33. Ibid. p. 187.
34. Ibid. p. 187.

35. Ibid. p. 188.
36. These are Sassoon's words from his notes towards an incomplete fourth volume of autobiography, quoted in Jean Moorcroft Wilson, *Siegfried Sassoon: The Journey from the Trenches, 1918–1967*, vol. 2 (New York: Routledge, 2003), p. 175.
37. Ibid. p. 176.
38. Ibid. p. 178.
39. Edmund Blunden, 'The preservation of England', in Edmund Blunden, *Votive Tablets: Studies Chiefly Appreciative of English Authors and Books* (London: Cobden-Sanderson, 1931), pp. 353–4, p. 358.
40. John Richardson, quoted in Jean Moorcroft Wilson, *Siegfried Sassoon: The Making of a War Poet*, vol. 1 (New York: Routledge, 1999), p. 70.
41. Siegfried Sassoon, *Memoirs of a Fox-hunting Man* (London: Faber & Faber, 1928), p. 11.
42. Ibid. p. 81.
43. Svetlana Boym, *The Future of Nostalgia* (New York: Basic, 2001), p. 8.
44. Sassoon, *Fox-hunting Man*, p. 52.
45. Ibid. p. 76.
46. Boym, *Nostalgia*, p. 41.
47. Ibid. p. 8.
48. Sassoon, *Fox-hunting Man*, p. 11.
49. Ibid. p. 11.
50. Ibid. p. 34.
51. Ibid. p. 40.
52. Ibid. p. 268.
53. Ibid. p. 270.
54. Ibid. p. 311.
55. Siegfried Sassoon, *Sherston's Progress* (London: Faber & Faber, 1983), p. 150.
56. Siegfried Sassoon, quoted in James F. Stewart, *A Descriptive Account of Unpublished Letters of Siegfried Sassoon in the University of Texas Collection*, diss., University of Texas, Austin (Ann Arbor, MI: UMI, 1972), p. 212.
57. Stewart, *Unpublished Letters*, p. 217.
58. For an account of this relationship see Philip Hoare, *Serious Pleasures: The Life of Stephen Tennant* (London: Hamish Hamilton, 1990).
59. Hoare, *Serious Pleasures*, p. 171.
60. Quoted in Hoare, *Serious Pleasures*, p. 174.
61. Ibid. p. 174.
62. Ibid. p. 172.
63. Laurence Whistler, *The Laughter and the Urn: The Life of Rex Whistler* (London: Weidenfeld & Nicolson, 1985), p. 174.
64. See, for example, A. J. P. Taylor, *The Origins of the Second World War* (London: Penguin, 1963).
65. He was serious enough about his prophetic announcements that he considered asking the League of Nations to publish the six poems of this volume in a pamphlet (Stewart, *Unpublished Letters*, p. 222).
66. Sassoon, *Collected Poems*, p. 199.
67. Ibid. p. 199.
68. This pamphlet was part of a programme sponsored by the Permanent Committee for Literature and the Arts of the League of Nations. The Committee instructed the International Institute of Intellectual Co-operation to arrange for an exchange of letters between important intellectuals 'on subjects calculated to serve the common interests of the League of Nations and of intellectual life'

(quoted in Albert Einstein and Sigmund Freud, *Why War?*, in Sigmund Freud, *Civilization, Society, Religion*, trans. James Strachey and ed. Albert Dickson (London: Penguin, 1991), pp. 341–62, pp. 343–4). Einstein was one of the first to be approached by the Committee, and it was his idea to correspond with Freud. Their letters were published together in 1933 (appearing simultaneously in French, German and English). Freud, apparently, was not pleased with his own response; he found the format contributed to 'a tedious and sterile discussion' (ibid. p. 344).

69. Albert Einstein, quoted in Sassoon, *Collected Poems*, p. 200.
70. A complete text of 'A Soldier's Declaration' appears in Siegfried Sassoon, *Memoirs of an Infantry Officer*, (London: Faber & Faber, 1930), p. 218. Wilson identifies only one difference between this version and his original 1917 statement: in *Infantry Officer* he drops 'military' from the phrase, 'I am not protesting against the military conduct of the war' (Wilson, *Sassoon*, vol. 1, p. 374n.)
71. Sassoon, *Collected Poems*, p. 203.
72. Freud, 'Why War?', p. 357.
73. Ibid. p. 357.
74. Sassoon's terminology follows from Rivers, who makes no fundamental distinction between 'unconscious' and 'subconscious' (W. H. R. Rivers, *Instinct and the Unconscious*, 2nd edn (Cambridge: Cambridge University Press, 1924), p. 7).
75. Sassoon, *Diaries 1920–1922*, p. 236.
76. Sassoon, *Collected Poems*, pp. 85, 76.
77. Ibid. p. 187.
78. Ibid. p. 216.
79. Ibid. p. 217.
80. Ibid. p. 217.
81. Ibid. p. 217.
82. Ibid. p. 217.
83. Ibid. p. 212.
84. Ibid. p. 213.
85. Ibid. p. 226.
86. Ibid. p. 218.
87. Ibid. pp. 220, 221.
88. Corinthians 15: 51.
89. Sassoon, *Collected Poems*, p. 220.
90. Ibid. p. 221.
91. Ibid. p. 221.
92. Ibid. p. 221.
93. T. E. Lawrence, *The Letters of T.E. Lawrence*, ed. David Garnett (London: Cape, 1938), p. 835.
94. Ruth Bailey, 'Poems by Mr. Sassoon', rev. of *Vigils* by Siegfried Sassoon, *Times Literary Supplement*, 28 December 1935, p. 894.
95. A. C. Boyd, 'Echoes of the past', rev. of *Vigils* by Siegfried Sassoon, *London Mercury*, December 1935, pp. 226–7, p. 226.
96. T. E. Lawrence, *Letters*, p. 836.
97. George Buchanan, rev. of *The Road to Ruin* by Siegfried Sassoon, *Times Literary Supplement*, 15 March 1934, p. 190.
98. Richard Church, rev. of *The Road to Ruin* by Siegfried Sassoon, *Spectator*, 8 December 1933, p. 864. As well, the *London Mercury* criticized him for failing to 'bury the [First] war and its recriminations . . . It is time that Mr Sassoon left off his embittered war poems' (Yvonne Ffrench, rev. of *The Road to Ruin* by Siegfried Sassoon, *London Mercury*, January, 1934, p. 260).

99. John Stuart Roberts, *Siegfried Sassoon: 1886–1967* (London: Cohen, 1999), p. 249.
100. Stewart, *Unpublished Letters*, p. 225.
101. Quoted in Roberts, *Siegfried Sassoon*, p. 253.
102. Siegfried Sassoon to Geoffrey Keynes, letter, 12 December 1935, Papers of Siegfried Sassoon, Manuscript Department, Cambridge University Library.
103. Stewart, *Unpublished Letters*, p. 225.
104. Sassoon to Keynes, letter, 24 October 1933, Papers of Siegfried Sassoon, Manuscript Department, Cambridge University Library.
105. Ibid. 23 November 1933.
106. Ibid. 29 November 1933.
107. Edmund Blunden, *Cricket Country* (London: Imprint Society, 1945), p. 13.
108. Ibid. p. 15.
109. Ibid. pp. 45–6.
110. Sassoon to Keynes, letter, 12 August 1935, Papers of Siegfried Sassoon, Manuscript Department, Cambridge University Library.
111. Sassoon, *Sherston's Progress*, p. 57.
112. Sassoon, *Collected Poems*, p. 231.
113. Sassoon to Keynes, letter, 1 May 1939, Papers of Siegfried Sassoon, Manuscript Department, Cambridge University Library.
114. *Webster's New Unabridged Dictionary*, 1901 edn.
115. Stewart, *Unpublished Letters*, p. 256.
116. Siegfried Sassoon, *Letters to Max Beerbohm (with a few Answers)*, ed. Rupert Hart-Davis (London: Faber & Faber, 1986), p. 32.
117. Siegfried Sassoon, 'Theme and Variation', ms. 12 January 1935, Papers of Siegfried Sassoon, Manuscript Department, Cambridge University Library.
118. Siegfried Sassoon to Editor, *Lady Claire Magazine*, letter, 12 January 1935.
119. Sassoon to Keynes, letter, 23 December 1935, Papers of Siegfried Sassoon, Manuscript Department, Cambridge University Library.
120. Ibid. 23 December 1935.
121. Stewart, *Unpublished Letters*, p. 22.
122. Siegfried Sassoon, 'Educating Aunt Eudora', *Spectator*, 14 February 1936, pp. 250–1, p. 250.
123. Ibid. p. 251.
124. Sassoon, *Collected Poems*, p. 261.
125. Siegfried Sassoon, 'Foreword', in *The Collected Works of Isaac Rosenberg*, ed. Ian Parson (London: Chatto & Windus, 1979), p. ix.
126. For a thorough discussion of this lecture, see Michael Thorpe, *Siegfried Sassoon: A Critical Study* (Leiden: Universitaire Pers Leiden; London: Oxford University Press, 1966), pp. 181–206.
127. Siegfried Sassoon, *On Poetry* (Bristol: Arrowsmith, 1939), p. 11.
128. Ibid. p. 12.
129. Siegfried Sassoon, 'Aliveness in Literature', *Fortnightly Review*, November 1940, pp. 476–81, p. 480.
130. Siegfried Sassoon, '*The Dynasts* in Wartime', *Spectator*, 6 February 1942, pp. 127–8, p. 127.
131. Ibid. p. 127.
132. Ibid. p. 127.
133. Siegfried Sassoon to a correspondent identified only as Mr Hardcastle, letter, 29 October 1938, Sassoon Collection, Harry Ransom Humanities Research Center (HRHRC), University of Texas, Austin.
134. Sassoon, *Dynasts*, p. 128.

135. Thomas Hardy, *The Dynasts* (London: Macmillan, 1931), p. I.32.
136. Sassoon, *Dynasts*, p. 127.
137. Hardy, *The Dynasts*, p. III.347.
138. Sassoon, *Dynasts*, p. 128.
139. Ibid. p. 127.

4

WARTIME REVISITED: GHOSTS AND SPIRITS IN SASSOON'S PATRIOTIC VERSE OF THE SECOND WORLD WAR

Awake to the Nightmare: 3 September 1939

'We are therefore now back where we were in 1914.'

Sydney Cockerell, 3 September 1939[1]

When Chamberlain reluctantly declared war on 3 September 1939, Sassoon recorded in his diary: 'It all makes me wish that the July 1918 bullet had finished me. I can do nothing now except endure this nightmare.'[2] His crisis is evident not only in his likening of the new war to a nightmare, but also in his death-wish and the peculiar circumstances surrounding his last wound of the First World War; his near-encounter with death in July 1918 came from friendly fire, an absurd accident of war. The new war was no less full of absurd acts and incomprehensible events, prompting Paul Fussell to remark that 'blunders were almost the hallmark of Allied operations'; indeed, 'blunders, errors, and accidents [were] something very close to the essence' of the Second World War.[3] Edith Olivier observed that the outbreak of hostilities drove Sassoon further into his reclusive shell and released a flood of no longer repressible memories of his earlier war experience.[4] In Heytesbury House, domestic duties and the invasive war news on the wireless became overwhelming, and in a diary entry from late 1939 he noted that 'All I want to do is to forget – and forget – and have no arc-lights of practical mindedness turned on to my loathing of this Second Great War, by which I am being reduced to an impotent absurdity.'[5]

His old poem, 'Repression of War Experience', is particularly relevant to both his struggle to understand the new war and his intense desire to forget, and can be seen as a kind of model for his response to the 'Second Great War'. To begin with, the poem demonstrates the impossibility of repressing traumatic experience, which twenty-two years had perhaps dulled but not eliminated, and which was reawakened by the new war. In 'Repression of War Experience', as with so many of his poems, Sassoon is also concerned with the persistent and unpredictable incursion of the past into the present. Written at Weirleigh shortly before he was sent to Craiglockhart in July 1917,[6] the poem plays on contrasts between the peaceful setting of Sassoon's home and disturbing memories of war, and is rich in imagery of flight, darkness and light. In the Second World War, at Heytesbury, he was still oppressed by the contrast between his peaceful rural existence and the memories as well as the actuality of war. The guilt induced by the relative safety of his non-combatant role seems also to have provoked uncertainty about the relevance of autognostic poetry, which he continued to write during the war, though much of it is unpublished, and indeed unfinished. It must have been painful for Sassoon to imagine young soldiers seeing him as one of those 'horrible shapes in shrouds' he envisioned at Weirleigh in 1917, one of the 'old men who died / Slow, natural deaths'.[7] In any case, uncertainty about the relevance of his introspective poetry was exacerbated by the ongoing devastation of the renewed war. This uncertainty led to doubts about the value and meaning of life, about the strength of his nostalgic vision, and increasingly, in the late 1930s and 1940s, to his attempt to understand the absurdity of war within an unorthodox spiritual framework.

Edith Olivier's observation of Sassoon's withdrawal into his own memories of battle is confirmed by the first-hand account of Sydney Cockerell, who came to stay at Heytesbury House during the first months of the war. In contrast to the sense of desperation expressed in his diary, outwardly Sassoon reacted calmly to the declaration of war until a representative of the War Office came to Heytesbury a week later to warn him that the armed forces might requisition the house and grounds. He was distraught all afternoon, Cockerell records, and at tea exclaimed that Heytesbury meant everything to him, and if he was forced to give it up, he could not be held responsible for his actions. He stormed off to his room alone, utterly despondent. When he later learned that the chances of Heytesbury actually being requisitioned were small, Sassoon was calmed, though still reclusive and edgy. But his frantic reaction to the threat of being forced to leave his home and sanctuary indicates his attachment to this space redolent of the past which sequestered him from the present state of renewed war.[8]

He was harassed by the incomprehensibility of it all. In the view that war was absurd – especially this war, given the ravages of the previous war that was supposed to end all wars – Sassoon found a link between his experience as a soldier and his experience as a non-combatant, between his past and his present, but this link offered no clue to the reintegration of self and only intensified his need for meaning. The essence of war and its attendant puzzlements were distilled for Sassoon by the fate of his great Aunt Mozelle's house. Aunt Mozelle was his father's aunt, and the closest living connection to his wealthy Persian-Jewish ancestors. She lived for more than fifty years in 'the tidiest house imaginable', a place full of treasured belongings and irreplaceable mementoes of her life and family.[9] Sassoon suffered torments of bewilderment and anguish when this house of memories became a haphazard war casualty:

> Recently, a tank stopped in the road to do some repairs, and light-heartedly let off a tracer bullet, which went through Aunt Mozelle's front door and half demolished her drawing room – destroying, among other things, a complete set of my first editions which I'd given her at various times in the past 25 years.
>
> A German bomb – yes – but *why* one of our *own* projectiles in Auntie's drawing room?[10]

He had no answers to this question. '[The war] is a very bad business,' he had written to Blunden several months before, 'but when one gets behind the high-flown generalizations about the War and its purposes (apart from material self-preservation) it is usually the same heart-breaking story of private catastrophes.'[11]

Although he himself does not make the connection, the radical meaninglessness of the damage to his aunt's house by 'friendly fire' was similar to the meaninglessness of his final wound of the First World War, which he recalled in his diary on hearing the declaration of the new war against Germany, as I cited above. In *Sherston's Progress*, he describes how Sherston, returning from a raid in a self-congratulatory mood, removed his tin hat, stood up to have a final look at the German line, and was shot in the head. At first he thought he was 'a dying animal, on the verge of oblivion',[12] but soon returned to his trench on his own strength. His men looked at him with concern and relief,

> but the face of Sergeant Wickham was catastrophic . . . [For] it was he who had shot me . . . I was told afterwards that when he'd fired at me he rushed out shouting 'Surrender – you – !' Which only shows what a gallant man he was.[13]

Wickham was over-eager in following instructions given him by Sherston himself, and as Sassoon writes, 'The outcome was absurd, but logical.'[14] The wound proved nothing, contributed nothing to the ultimate victory; it was another example of the 'absurd logic' of war. Sassoon tried to cultivate an ironic fatalistic acceptance of such absurdities of war, but he was not always able to live up to such fortitude and poise against the accumulating effects of the new conflict.

THE LIMITS OF RECLUSION: PATRIOTISM AND THE REVIVAL OF THE PRE-PROTEST WAR POET

When the war broke out, his marriage had become a source of conflict and antagonism, and it was his enduring love for England, reinforced by especial passion for a pre-modern country life, that sustained Sassoon in the midst of catastrophe, and even helped him see the war as necessary and right, thereby counterpoising his sense of its 'absurdity'. He wrote to Blunden in the middle of the war: 'I firmly believe that there was no alternative to resisting the German effort – except surrender without resistance. We should have been next on Hitler's list for certain. The war was planned, prepared, and provoked by him. I regard this as beyond argument.' Still, he could not abide the distorted impressions of the German people shaped by propaganda and paraded by the local people he encountered: 'No one in Heytesbury Village thinks of Germans as human at all. They generalize them into monsters. The insular mentality is incurable.' Sassoon believed that the Nazi system was evil, that it caused the war: 'The "good" Germans were given no choice in the matter.' But regardless of all the finer points of 'unreal "high politics" ', the war had to be won: 'The mistakes which led to the war being "inevitable" seem at present irrelevant to what is merely a struggle for survival.'[15]

Sassoon was never a pacifist. His 'Soldier's Declaration' in 1917 was grounded in his view of the incompetence of politicians committed to a war of aggression that pointlessly sacrificed soldiers' lives. As he wrote to Christopher Hassall, 'For me it was a sort of crusade, based on my experience of the futility of war. But even I am obliged now to admit that pacifism is no sort of "proposition" in dealing with German aggression.'[16] And his association with the Peace Pledge Union in the 1930s was loose and sporadic.[17] While the Munich crisis in 1938 left him wondering 'whether [he] really could have come through another long war – unable even to do anything active or useful',[18] he accepted the potential necessity for England to take a stand against Hitler's Germany, although this acceptance was marked by distaste and anxiety:

> Well, those dictators are at us again; are we never to be allowed any respite from barbarism? I take refuge in playing the piano and reading anything rather than the newspaper, but the horror of it all always haunts one, and real peace of mind is as far away as heaven (if heaven there be).[19]

When the *Daily Sketch* newspaper telephoned Heytesbury to ask for 'a powerful article' on the situation in Europe, Sassoon was not interested: 'Here is my article: "B—y F—g awful" (Ten guineas a word).'[20] Sassoon did not want to think about a new war, but he did not oppose it. When it was finally declared, Sassoon clung to patriotism as a rare certainty in a chaotic sea of conflict. His personal writings, as well as some of his public pronouncements on the war (which he made reluctantly), testify to both his commitment to the war as a just cause and a dismayed sense of the 'evilness of the times'[21] that seemed to be making 'lunatics of us all'.[22]

This radical ambivalence in his feelings about the war made him seek resolution and meaning in a vision of war, history and life that looked to higher transcendental forces. Late in 1942, Sassoon was upset by a review in *Country Life* of E. L. Woodward's autobiography, *Short Journey*, which cited Woodward's modern assertion that 'the Christian religion . . . has no future'.[23] Perhaps surprisingly, given his spiritual development to that point, Sassoon was moved to defend religion and to uphold another nostalgic value: 'Can a better substitute be found? Religion seems to be the thing that people need more than anything else. Human beings *must* believe in something.'[24] At this time he expressed his imperative to believe 'in something' through his unwavering love of country, but this need now led him also to reject the modern 'materialist's' offering of technology and modern science as substitutions for religion: 'The spirit liveth – but not in machines and clever ideas.'[25] Sassoon's reactionary stance is another example of his commitment to a nostalgic societal fabric that predates the fuss and bother of material concerns. His own reliance on modern technology, not to mention the material interests attendant upon owning a fifty-two-room country house requiring a full-time staff of fifteen, demonstrate the inconsistency of his haughtily held position. Nevertheless, he associated this spirit with what he called 'aliveness' in literature, a sign of essential humanity which certainly pre-dates modernism. But his sense of the spirit not only embraced 'aliveness', it also transcended it. He struggled to find that spirit and even before his conversion he drew some consolation from figuring the war in spiritual terms. Though wary of seeing the battle against Hitler as a kind of 'holy war' in which God was automatically on 'our side',[26] he found the appeal to spiritual forces helpful in coping with the incomprehensibility of modern war.

Even before war had been declared, he invoked a conflation of art and spirituality to oppose the material brutality of war:

> Materialism can come here and ask me what use I am against a machine-gun or a highly organised propaganda system; but I still reply that no machine-gun can affect Blake's Songs of Innocence – or the essential truth and wisdom of Christ's words . . . The powers of darkness are in conflict with the powers of light always; but never so visibly as now. I acknowledge the superficial authority of materialism – in politics, and physiological and biological facts, and so on . . . But I maintain, with you, that the devils and angels are in conflict – above all that.[27]

To Cockerell, he wrote at the same time about the Munich crisis in a somewhat lighter vein: 'But the devil is active everywhere, and wins his easy victories by materialistic methods. "The spirit worketh secretly", as the scriptures say (or ought to, if they don't).'[28] And yet even as he rejected the scepticism and atheism of writers like Forster and Woodward, he was not moved by the conversion to Anglicanism of T. S. Eliot, whose modernist poetry he saw as at odds with the belated turn to Christianity.[29] For the time being, Sassoon's own idiosyncratic and loose transcendental framework provided him with some consolation about the disturbing material conditions of renewed modern war.

Civilian War Poet I: The War Poems

Compelled by honour and historical circumstance to revive his war poet self, but wary of disturbing the unsettling memories of traumatic experience, Sassoon wrote only a half-dozen poems treating the Second World War directly. The satiric edge and vitriolic protest of his earlier, more famous war poems were pushed aside by patriotic feelings. The love for England implicit in his autobiographical prose became explicit in his new war poetry.

Fearing that 'endorsing the war in silence' would drive him 'dotty', he wrote to Edward Marsh in May 1939, asking him to communicate to Churchill his interest in contributing his efforts in the event of war.[30] At the same time, he could not imagine what form these efforts might take, and, strangely for a man who thought of himself as a poet (and not just a poet of the 1914–18 war), he doubted his authority as a non-combatant to engage with the subject of war. On the twenty-fifth anniversary of the beginning of the First World War, the *Picture Post* asked him for an article. He was willing to contribute an article on poetry, but not on war.[31] And just as Dunn's request in 1926 for a prose contribution to a regimental history prompted Sassoon to write the poem 'A Footnote on the War', this request for an article prompted him to write a poem, 'August 4th, 1939',[32] which he chose not to publish. In the poem he speaks not as the 'war poet' but the 'autognostic poet', struggling to measure the impact on himself of the passage of time and the apparent repetition of history:

> To-day I'm old by five and twenty years
> Since 'War Declared' tolled tocsins to my ears:
> To-day, last thing at night, I face the fact
> That once again War's here in all but act, –

The prospect of a new war represents a kind of uncanny doubling on a historical level, a repetition writ large of the recurring traumatic residue of war experience that lingers in veterans like Sassoon. It leaves him desolate:

> Thus museful men alone at night, have wondered,
> While storms of history round their roof-tops thundered:
> Thus they have held their breath for what might come;
> And, hearing tyrants beat the distant drum,

> Held fast to their own faith amid the long
> And limitless malignancy of wrong.

Aligning himself with solitary ruminators of previous ages, Sassoon offers himself the possibility of shelter from the 'storms of history' in his 'own faith', which here remains unspecified except in its horror at the materialist 'tocsins of war' and its rejection of the claims of brute force: 'And thus, where Might has never proved its Right / Thought keeps one candle burning through the night.'

Soon after war was declared, Sassoon was surprised to hear from the Ministry of Information 'that they merely expect me "to continue to address the public through my accustomed channels"!'[33] He acknowledged that 'In any case I can't see myself writing a word about this war. There is nothing to be said – by civilians – except that we *must* fight Hitler to the last drop of someone else's blood.'[34] However, the dramatic losses in France in the spring of 1940 compelled him to write about the war in that spirit of defiant commitment. Finding his position as a 'civilian war poet' uncomfortable and false, he turned to the consolations he was already developing in this crisis: patriotism and grand, if vague, spirituality. He was to write eight poems in the years 1940–5 explicitly addressing the war, of which 'English Spirit' and 'Silent Service' are the best known. In these poems he expresses his devotion to the English cause, even when the war was going badly and his faith in the redemptive possibilities for the human race was profoundly shaken.

'The English Spirit' and 'Silent Service' were printed in the *Observer* in the last weeks before the fall of France and the evacuation of the British Expeditionary Force (BEF) from the battlegrounds where he had served in 1916–18. Sassoon admitted that the poems were 'deliberately . . . simple – even commonplace . . . written from a sense of duty; it seemed to be the only point of view I had any right to express.'[35] 'The English Spirit', composed on 19 May 1940, a point emphasized by the inclusion of the date at the end of the poem, conveys a note of resolute calm in the face of a military setback, which, in language drawn from his own service days, he likened to the 'laconic coolness of the company commander in a box-barrage'.[36] He appealed to the national tradition of 'coolness' under fire, fortitude in the face of 'the cultural crusade of Teuton tanks'.[37] In its title the poem conflates patriotism and a spiritual order. The first word of 'English Spirit' evokes 'Apollyon', the Satanic 'angel of the bottomless pit',[38] who '[has] decided' to wreak havoc on earth with his 'blind armaments'.[39] Sassoon transforms the monstrous locusts of Revelations into the destructive machinery of modern war threatening his countrymen, whom he calls on to draw strength from their traditional spiritual allies, to stand firm and together repel their diabolical enemy. England's spiritual strengths are identified (in what Sassoon felt were the poem's most emotionally resonant lines) as 'The ghosts of those who have wrought our English Past',[40] an image that may be drawn partly from his own ghosts, who had haunted him and invaded his sleep since the end of his war. Now there is no sense that their deaths were futile; in the phrase 'our English Past' these ghosts are endowed with a transcendent patriotic purpose, elevated to the stature of angels, able to intervene in the material fray and do battle above it against Apollyon.

Sassoon's attitude in this poem, so at odds with fashionable literary tastes, nevertheless accords with contemporary governmentally sanctioned views of the national crisis. John Masefield, the poet laureate, discovered the same 'spirit' behind the 'success' at Dunkirk. The apparently unstoppable enemy, who had made short work of the Belgians and French, failed to encircle and capture the BEF: 'he came up against the spirit of this Nation, which, when roused, will do great things.'[41] And Churchill, too, had come to see his nation's struggle in transcendental terms. He later wrote of becoming

> conscious of a kind of uplifted detachment from human and personal affairs. The glory of Old England, peace-loving and ill-prepared as she was, but instant and fearless at the call of honour, thrilled my being and seemed to lift our fate to those spheres far removed from earthly facts and physical sensation.[42]

Besides the invocation of a spiritual sphere, Churchill's appeal to 'Old England' suggests the breadth of appeal of Sassoon's rural England found in his prose autobiographies.

'Silent Service', written at about the same time, begins with the patriotic proclamation: 'Now, multifold, let Britain's patient power / Be proven within us for the world to see.'[43] In this poem also, forces of evil, embodied by 'Daemons in dark',[44] are clearly arrayed against forces of good, supported by 'A kneeling angel holding faith's front-line'.[45] Angels exist for Sassoon as both inner visions and spiritual entities, and as symbols in his poetry they represent his desire to look for meaning beyond the chaos of material existence.[46] In 'Silent Service', evil and good operate both 'within us' and also above us, on a spiritual plane.

Writing poems motivated by patriotic feeling and duty gave Sassoon some trouble. Biblical allusions served to impress upon his readers the magnitude of the upcoming struggle, but he remarked to Blunden that he worried about inflating the significance of the material agents. Linking Hitler to Apollyon, for example, granted the humourless 'blind fanatic and egomaniac' too much distinction.[47] He also told Cockerell that

> The last line of 'The English Spirit' was a problem. ['The cultural crusade of Teuton tanks'[48]] I decided on under-emphasis and irony, as the alternative seemed to be a less effective display of resounding rhetoric. The poem is, perhaps, over-condensed, but you will see that it begins

> in an ironic tone of voice, becomes deeply felt in lines 3–6, and ends laconically (which is more characteristic of B.E.F. mentality than fine phrases?) . . . I wanted to make it a plain statement of our resolve to remain undaunted.[49]

At the same time he was aware of an element of grandiosity in the poem, and wrote to Beerbohm: 'I hope I haven't overdone the "grand style" note, and that it may hearten a few people – shattered with anxiety and strain as they must be.'[50] The troops must be rallied and the civilians too; 'there isn't much left to say, is there, except "Endure all that is required of us, and rely on Winston's inspiring leadership" – surely a heroic episode in our "island story".'[51] The discouraging war news had curtailed his cricket and riding, but anxious as he was about the war, his abiding love of the countryside invigorated his patriotic dedication: 'I shall go for a walk "with earth's defended freedom in my eyes," [a paraphrase of line 8 of 'Silent Service'] I suppose – whistling "Rule Britannia" while I plod.'[52] He was adjusting to the role of civilian war poet he had earlier discussed for himself.

Not everyone was swept up by patriotic zeal and rhetoric. Already in 1940 Stephen Spender found it 'lamentable that the fine poet of the last war should write in the manner of the Sunday newspapers',[53] and later critics have been similarly disappointed that a man who had made his poetic reputation protesting against the madness and suffering of war should write patriotic verse. In *Heroes' Twilight*, for example, Bergonzi singles out 'Silent Service' as a particularly damning effort, a blatant contradiction of all of Sassoon's most powerful and meaningful poetry from the First World War. He excuses Sassoon the feelings that inspired the poem, but not for having written it.[54] But there were extra-literary factors at play in Sassoon's poetry during the war. The Ministry of Information's request that he contribute to the war effort does not justify uninspired poetry, but it does offer insight into the pressure Sassoon was under to contribute something to his country's cause.

At some point in 1941 he wrote 'Air Activity in 1940',[55] in which he seeks out meaning in the devastation wrought by the air battles over Britain, focusing not on the imminence of victory but upon the cost of war. The metaphor of 'The drone of a bombing-plane / Is the moan of a world in pain' is in distinct contrast with the patriotic confidence of 'Silent Service'. He even expresses misgivings here about the outcome of the transcendent dimension of the airborne struggle: even if 'for machineried-man / All goes according to plan', 'Angelhood' in Heaven observes the droning aeroplanes in the skies with 'heavy heart'. Invoking Churchill's stirring tribute to the RAF fighter pilots of the Battle of Britain, Sassoon writes, 'Thus, for the many and few, / Only the method is new,' grounding his poem in the specific historical moment which he also sees as part of a cycle leading back into history, including, of course, the First World War.

Early in 1944 he returned to the poem, changing the title first to 'The 1940 Atmosphere' then to 'The Armageddon Atmosphere'. Sassoon's recollection of the feeling of impending doom in 1941, when the outcome of the war was in doubt and his faith in intervening spirits wavered, was understandably troubling and 'Air Activity in 1940' was never published.

'Go, Words, on Winds of War', his next published war poem after 'Silent Service', appeared in the *Spectator* in April 1943. Written in response to newspaper accounts of Nazi atrocities, which he described as 'devil's work',[56] it was meant to be a way of 'dealing with Germany's responsibility for the war, feeling that everyone ought to try and contribute something against the inevitable post-war assertions that they were basely "attacked" by the British and French!'[57] In four alexandrine quatrains and a final couplet, the poem combines the specific vocabulary of the conflict – 'the Stuka squadron', 'the Reich', 'armoured columns' – with archaisms like 'adjure', 'ruthful' and 'wherefore'.[58] Although he chose not to reprint this 'poor little verse exercise',[59] 'Go, Words, on Winds of War' is yet another example not only of Sassoon's patriotism but also of his increasing spirituality. 'Recording angels' oversee the earthly fray where 'the bombed city burns, the sinking ship explodes' and 'the souls of men are lost.'[60] This angelic perspective is explicit in attributing the blame for the war: '*One fact we understand. This feud was German-planned.*'[61] As in the crisis poems of 1940, Sassoon strove as a civilian war poet to maintain this front of patriotic certainty.

As V-E Day approached, the *Observer* telephoned Sassoon 'soliciting a poem on the end of the war. I had felt quite incapable of any such thing, but managed to drudge out a dozen lines.'[62] 'To Some who say Production won the War'[63] conveyed the general relief that it was at last over, as well as his desire to focus the nation's gratitude on the servicemen, 'ardent or afraid', who in their 'fortitude prevailed' against 'foul aggression and its creed of crime'.[64] Victory proved the validity of his patriotism. What had been at stake was not merely political or territorial, but the very 'soul of man assailed' by a devilish foe.

It is fitting that Sassoon saw the end of the Second World War as inseparable from the First. He wrote the unpublished poem '1914–1945', which chronicles in four balladic stanzas of irregular fourteeners a condensed history of the world wars, emphasizing with the first image the nostalgic pre-1914 world: 'From a world that seems now half Elysian with peace long unbroken, / Young men went to war in their ardour, untried and untaught.'[65] Their ardour and resolve for future peace was unwrought through the 'confused economics and [blind] governments' of the interwar years, so a new generation was called upon to oppose renewed aggression: 'Through this the strength of England reinvigorated rose.' Perhaps now, after millions have perished, peace will be secured, as it was not in 1918, but 'the sequel no one knows.' This is the poem's final phrase, underscoring its sober tone wary of celebration, uncertain of a brighter future. While Sassoon had celebrated the prospect of a kind of social revolution after the First World War, when he had taken up the literary editorship of the socialist *Daily Herald* and composed his widely anthologized 'Everyone Sang', this ebullient mood could not be recreated in 1945. A kind of social revolution had indeed taken place with the defeat of Churchill at the hands of a Labour government. But Sassoon's socialist sympathies had long ago eroded, and a Labour government amounted to a further threat to the hierarchical vision of an Elysian English rural life he lovingly represented in prose and poetry, and sought to embody in Heytesbury House. The war had ended but what was left? The awkward metre and syntax of '1914–1945' reinforce the realization that the war did not end in a victory to be celebrated, but a deliverance to be accepted.

As Sassoon learned of the extent of the war's cruelty and devastation, his faith in spiritual intervention on behalf of the enemies and victims of the Nazis was shaken. 'Belsen',[66] which he never published, was triggered by reports of Bergen-Belsen, which had been liberated by British troops in April 1945. At first, he was reduced to 'mental flatness' by the burden of imagining 'the Unthinkable, the Unspeakable, and even the *Unfeelable*',[67] and did not approach this oppressive subject for months. Coinciding with the trial of the SS leaders of Bergen-Belsen, which was widely reported in the British media in the autumn of 1945,[68] Sassoon attempted to address his doubts about human salvation:

> What is the appropriate attitude of mind
> From which to absorb this ultimate pollution?
> *Unthinkable*, we think, compassion-blind;
> *Unutterable*, we say, stunned to confusion.
> But how to live it down? How to redeem
> The heart of humankind – that maniac face
> Marred by abominations? How undream
> Gas chambers and the torturer's ghoul grimace?[69]

The 'problem' raised through the repetition of four unanswerable questions, which hang heavily in the octave, is only answered by the sestet's indefinite certainty: 'Something has happened to the human soul.' In the final line of the first draft, he had situated this crisis 'in Germany', but amended this perspective to say that the questions it raised 'cannot be humanly' or 'judicially' solved. He is beginning to move beyond simply indicting one nation, as in '*This feud was German-planned*' from 'Go, Words, on Winds of War', to questioning his stubborn faith in human nature and in the authority and benevolence of higher powers. As he wrote to Tomlinson, '[can] human nature . . . escape responsibility by calling [the camps] an epidemic of national dementia?'[70] There is in 'Belsen' only the faint possibility of redemption through its form, which invokes love, the traditional subject of the sonnet form, as a potential source 'to redeem / The heart of humankind'. But he was unable to finish the poem, and its unfinished state reflects his helplessness in answering the questions that he posed about human nature and about moral and spiritual life.

In 'Litany of the Lost', published in the *Observer* in November 1945, Sassoon is able to moderate his despair while he invokes the moral desolation left by the death camps and the atomic bombs exploded over Hiroshima and Nagasaki. The poem expresses his dismay at the 'breaking of belief in human good',[71] and seems to ask: if the war was won, was the soul lost? Lamenting the 'slavedom of mankind to the machine', he fears that even the angelic forces have fallen and fused with the material world: 'Aeroplane angels, crashed from glory and grace'.[72] Yet the form of the poem – a litany – suggests by its ecclesiastical associations that despite the 'marvellous monkey innovations' of the material world,[73] there is still the possibility of redemption, as the refrain of the people prays: '*Deliver us from ourselves.*'[74]

The war's bleak aftermath stirred in Sassoon, and many others, a crisis of faith in the beliefs that had sustained him through the uncertainty of the conflict. While his nostalgic love of English country life and pastimes, culture and literature was undiminished, he seems to have realized that patriotism could not exonerate or protect him from the evils of war that tainted all human endeavour. The 'English Spirit' of the 1940 war poems is powerless before what 'has happened to the human soul'. The looming questions he poses in 'Belsen' indicate a level of despair apparently beyond the grasp of spiritual intervention. And yet 'Litany of the Lost' indicates the prospect of a new direction, by hinting at the possibility of redemption and faith in the spiritual realm to restore order to chaotic material existence. Before the end of the Second World War and this new prospect, Sassoon had looked not to the future for order, but to the past, transformed by his nostalgic vision.

Notes

1. Sydney Cockerell stayed at Heytesbury for almost two months at the beginning of the War. Cockerell's unpublished diary, among the Cockerell Papers at the British Library, provides a detailed record of his two extended visits with Sassoon during the Second World War. I refer to these diary entries in the notes by date.
2. Quoted in Joha Stuart Roberts, *Siegfried Sassoon: 1886–1967* (London: Cohen, 1999), p. 257.
3. Paul Fussell, *Wartime: Understanding and Behaviour in the Second World War* (New York: Oxford University Press, 1989), pp. 21, 26.
4. Edith Olivier, *From Her Journals: 1924–48*, ed. Penelope Middelboe (London: Weidenfeld & Nicolson, 1989), p. 221.
5. Quoted in Roberts, *Siegfried Sassoon*, pp. 277–8.
6. Siegfried Sassoon, *The War Poems*, ed. Rupert Hart-Davis (London: Faber, 1983), p. 85n.
7. Siegfried Sassoon, *Collected Poems 1908–1956* (London: Faber & Faber, 1961), p. 90.

8. Insights into Sassoon's activities during the early days of war come from Sydney Carlyle Cockerell's unpublished diary, 5, 10 September 1939.
9. Siegfried Sassoon to Geoffrey Keynes, letter, 4 December 1943, Papers of Siegfried Sassoon, Manuscript Department, Cambridge University Library.
10. Ibid. 4 December 1943.
11. Siegfried Sassoon to Edmund Blunden, letter, 1 May 1943, Sassoon Collection, Harry Ransom Humanities Research Center (HRHRC), University of Texas, Austin.
12. Siegfried Sassoon, *Sherston's Progress* (London: Faber & Faber, 1983), p. 143.
13. Ibid. p. 143.
14. Ibid. p. 144.
15. Siegfried Sassoon to Edmund Blunden, letter, 18 April 1943, Papers of Siegfried Sassoon, Manuscripts Department, Cambridge University Library.
16. Siegfried Sassoon to Christopher Hassall, letter, 2 March 1940, Papers of Siegfried Sassoon, Manuscripts Department, Cambridge University Library.
17. Sassoon did not respond to the question posed by Auden, Spender and others in the *Left Review* and published in *Authors Take Sides in the Spanish Civil War* (1937). Two of his close friends and correspondents did respond; H. M. Tomlinson was 'For' foreign intervention against Franco's fascism, while Edmund Blunden, following his pacifist principles, was 'Against'. In 1940, in response to the *Observer*'s publication of new poems by Sassoon that supported the war, the secretary of the Peace Pledge Union (PPU) made 'a friendly inquiry' about his position, and his association with the Union came to a discreet conclusion (Roberts, *Siegfried Sassoon*, p. 276). Occasionally, J. C. Dunn intervened in an attempt to recruit him to the PPU cause. Sassoon once informed Blunden that 'Dr. Dunn has sent me eleven foolscap pages to prove that I am at fault in suggesting that the war was planned by Germany. He fairly rubs it in with his historical facts' (Sassoon to Blunden, letter, Cambridge University Library, 18 April 1943). Sassoon remained unconvinced and patriotic.
18. Siegfried Sassoon to a correspondent identified only as Mr Hardcastle, letter, 2 October 1938, Sassoon Collection, Harry Ransom Humanities Research Center, (HRHRC) University of Texas, Austin.
19. Sassoon to Keynes, letter, 14 April 1939.
20. Ibid. 1 May 1939.
21. Ibid. 19 September 1939.
22. Siegfried Sassoon, '*The Dynasts* in Wartime', *Spectator*, 6 February 1942, pp. 127–8, 127.
23. Howard Springs, rev. of *Short Journey* by E. L. Woodward, *Country Life*, 16 October 1942, pp. 762–3.
24. Sassoon to Hardcastle, letter, 20 November 1942.
25. Ibid. 20 November 1942.
26. Siegfried Sassoon, quoted in James F. Stewart, *A Descriptive Account of Unpublished Letters of Siegfried Sassoon in the University of Texas Collection*, diss, University of Texas, Austin (Ann Arbor, MI: UMI, 1972), p. 37.
27. Sassoon to Hardcastle, letter, 28 October 1938.
28. Viola Meynell (ed.), *Friends of a Lifetime: Letters to Sydney Carlyle Cockerell* (London: Cape, 1940), p. 61.
29. Stewart, *Unpublished Letters*, p. 28.
30. Quoted in Roberts, *Siegfried Sassoon*, p. 274.
31. Stewart, *Unpublished Letters*, p. 36.
32. Siegfried Sassoon, 'August 4th, 1939', in 'ms. notebook', Hart-Davis Section, Papers of Siegfried Sassoon, Manuscript Department, Cambridge University Library, 17 April 1944.

33. Sassoon to Keynes, letter, 18 September 1939.
34. Ibid. 18 September 1939.
35. Viola Meynell, *The Best of Friends: Further Letters to Sydney Carlyle Cockerell* (London: Hart-Davis, 1956), p. 78.
36. Sassoon, quoted in Stewart, *Unpublished Letters*, p. 246.
37. Sassoon, *Collected Poems*, p. 256.
38. Revelations 9: 7–12.
39. Sassoon, *Collected Poems*, p. 256.
40. Sassoon, *Collected Poems*, p. 256.
41. John Masefield, *The Nine Days Wonder: The Operation Dynamo* (London: Heinemann, 1941), p. 54.
42. Winston Churchill, *The Gathering Storm*, vol. 1 of *The Second World War* (Boston: Houghton, 1948), p. 409.
43. Sassoon, *Collected Poems*, p. 257.
44. Ibid. p. 257.
45. Ibid. p. 257.
46. Sassoon appears to have believed in the actual presence of angels. According to Felicitas Corrigan, Sassoon's friend and chronicler of his spiritual journey, 'Angels may be a pretty poetic device – or they may not. Sassoon really believed in angels' (Felicitas Corrigan, 'Introduction', in Sassoon, *Siegfried Sassoon: Poet's Pilgrimage* (London: Gollancz, 1973), p. 27). In later life he recounted that, when falling asleep, his mind would be filled with visions of angels (Corrigan, 'Introduction', p. 29), suggesting that visions 'within us' could confirm the existence of a transcendent reality and instil faith.
47. Sassoon, quoted in Stewart, *Unpublished Letters*, pp. 40, 244.
48. Sassoon, *Collected Poems*, p. 256.
49. Siegfried Sassoon to Sydney Carlyle Cockerell, letter, 22 June 1940, Sassoon Collection, Harry Ransom Humanities Research Center (HRHRC), University of Texas, Austin.
50. Siegfried Sassoon, *Letters to Max Beerbohm (with a few Answers)*, ed. Rupert Hart-Davis (London: Faber, 1986), p. 85.
51. Sassoon to Cockerell, letter, HRHRC, 22 June 1940.
52. Ibid. 22 June 1940.
53. Stephen Spender, 'Poets of Two Wars', rev. of *Rhymed Ruminations* by Siegfried Sassoon and *The Trumpet and other Poems* by Edward Thomas, *New Statesman and Nation*, 7 December 1940, p. 570.
54. Bernard Bergonzi, *Heroes' Twilight*, 2nd edn (London: Macmilla, 1980), p. 105.
55. Siegfried Sassoon, 'Air Activity in 1940', in 'ms. notebook', Hart-Davis Section, Papers of Siegfried Sassoon, Manuscript Department, Cambridge University Library, 29 February 1944.
56. Sassoon, quoted in Stewart, *Unpublished Letters*, p. 261.
57. Sassoon to Cockerell, letter, HRHRC, 24 March 1943.
58. Siegfried Sassoon, 'Go, Words, on Winds of War', *Spectator*, 2 April 1943, p. 313.
59. Sassoon, quoted in Stewart, *Unpublished Letters*, p. 261.
60. Sassoon, 'Go, Words', p. 313.
61. Ibid. p. 313.
62. Meynell, *Best of Friends*, p. 154.
63. This poem, not reprinted, was published in the *Observer*, 6 May 1945, and is also in the notebook of poems in the Hart-Davis Section, Papers of Siegfried Sassoon, Manuscript Department, Cambridge University Library.
64. He had previously referred to the Nazi regime as a 'creed of crime' in 'On Edington Hill', written in 1935 and published in *Rhymed Ruminations*.

65. Siegfried Sassoon, '1914–1945', ms., Hart-Davis Section, Papers of Siegfried Sassoon, Manuscript Department, Cambridge University Library, June 1945.
66. Siegfried Sassoon, 'The Problem of Belsen', in 'ms. notebook', Hart-Davis Section, Papers of Siegfried Sassoon, Manuscript Department, Cambridge University Library, 2 October 1945.
67. Sassoon, quoted in Stewart, *Unpublished Letters*, p. 271.
68. Joanne Reilly, *Belsen: The Liberation of a Concentration Camp* (London: Routledge, 1998), p. 39.
69. Sassoon, 'The Problem of Belsen', 2 October 1945.
70. Sassoon, quoted in Stewart, *Unpublished Letters*, p. 272.
71. Sassoon, *Collected Poems*, p. 205.
72. Ibid. p. 205.
73. Ibid. p. 205.
74. Ibid. p. 204.

5

LOOK BACK TO 'GLADNESS': NOSTALGIA AND SASSOON'S PERSONAL POEMS, 1940–5

Rhymed Ruminations (1940)

Though moved to contribute to the war effort with his patriotic verse, Sassoon continued with the work of autognosis and the poetry of his private self throughout the war. Amidst the anxieties and distractions of wartime, much of his autognostic creative energy was directed to the composition of his prose memoirs, and since before the war began, he had been beset with nagging doubts about his poetic ability. By 1939 he had come to consider his poems in which he sought to express his true or inner self as 'essentially private communications'.[1] Choosing and arranging poems for *Rhymed Ruminations*, his only volume of new verse published during the war, he worried about the discrepancy between his autognostic approach and contemporary modernist tastes.[2] In the war years he endured long spells of poetic inactivity, though he was by no means completely silent, writing more poetry than has been generally realized, most of it unpublished. The manuscripts containing this work – about forty poems – are marked by signs of his crisis of confidence; many lines are crossed out, there are scribbled amendments and convoluted additions, leaving the impression that he lacked the creative energy to complete this work or the confidence to see it published. When he considered a second wartime volume in 1944, he imagined a collection of only sixteen poems,[3] a number soon reduced to twelve, and even then he doubted their cohesiveness as a sequence.[4] And yet, in spite of all this doubt, he continued to write poetry.

While his relative isolation in the Wiltshire countryside insulated him from the war, in many of his personal poems he returned to concerns earlier addressed in 'Repression of War Experience'. They deal with the interconnectedness of past and present, peace and conflict, repeatedly using imagery of flight, darkness and light to bring his private experience into focus. Written mainly before September 1939, the poems in *Rhymed Ruminations* (1940) are clouded by war looming on the horizon, which disturbs the traumatic residue of the war in which he had served as a young man. 'Thoughts in 1932' sets the tone for much of the collection. On horseback in the woods, the poet considers with contentment the pastoral splendour of the day, while contrasting that present with various eras of the past as so many levels of an archaeological dig: 'the Black Thirties', 'the late Victorians', 'pre-Roman' travellers. Then the sound of warplanes manœuvring above Stonehenge catches his attention, and his mind is drawn up and thrown fearfully to the future:

> Cities, I thought, will wait them in the night
> When airmen, with high-minded motives, fight
> To save Futurity. In years to come
> Poor panic-stricken hordes will hear that hum,
> And Fear will be synonymous with Flight.[5]

Like the moth in 'Repression of War Experience', whose power of flight brought it too near the 'scorch[ing] . . . liquid flame',[6] the humming warplane is linked to fear. The poem's juxtaposition of the present moment with past epochs creates a sense of historical connectedness and continuity. The poet's imagination constructs a bridge between past and present, overcoming a gap that haunted and preoccupied him all his adult life.

The past in *Rhymed Ruminations* is invoked archaeologically and personally. In 'Thoughts in 1932', 'On Edington Hill', '878–1935', 'A Remembered Queen', 'Prehistoric Burials' and 'Antiquities', Sassoon traces relics of previous eras or ages in the landscape. In 'On Edington Hill', 'the downlink barrows' at night mark the mounds where King Alfred marched to fight off the invading Danes.[7] Informed by 'historians', the poet notes that Alfred's Christian righteousness was instrumental in beating back 'in the old skull-shattering way . . . the powers of darkness', and wonders if 'today's historians' will be able to report similar victory over menacing forces in Nazi uniforms.[8] In the final stanza, 'dawn breaks where tribes once fought with flints' and a white owl flits past.[9] The 'flint' is emblematic of a distant era and a simpler mode of warfare, while the owl, 'whose instincts are as old as time', both bridges and deepens the millennial gap, for like the barrows, it would have been as clearly visible to Alfred as it is to the poet in 1935, the year given after the final line.[10] But the owl 'on silent wing' also provides a stark contrast to the 'aeroplanes' with their power to 'bomb[] to bits' the poet and his age.[11] The owl's silent and harmless flight suggests the supremacy of the natural motion of birds and the harmony of nature, implying a nostalgic reading of the English countryside that sustains and consoles amidst the onslaught of modernity.

'878–1935' functions in a similar way, though here the appeal of the past is darker. What is noteworthy about this poem is the manner in which Sassoon's own personal past becomes entangled with the historic past. Looking back again to the era of Alfred (and implicitly his own war experiences), he writes:

> Then, it was quite correct to hack and hew the Dane,
> And to be levied for a war was life's event.

But at once he recollects his own situation as a retired combatant:

> Now in a world of books I try to live content,
> And hear uneasily the droning aeroplane.[12]

He does not 'envy those who fought at Eathundun',[13] for as he 'levied' himself for war in the summer of 1914, he learned too well that the brutality ('hack and hew') of war can shape and grip one's memories irrevocably. The life of 'some dim ninth-century thane' was bleak, but, he asks, is not the life of a passive observer of the mechanized nature of modern war even more 'insane'?[14]

Rhymed Ruminations also contains poems in which the immediacy of the past is invoked not archaeologically, but through personal encounters with art, as well as ghosts in visions or dreams. In his 1938 poem '"A View of Old Exeter"', Sassoon conveys the power of the eponymous painting to connect 'the past's provincial peace' to the viewer, particularly the privileged viewer of the painting who 'bought it cheap' fifteen years ago and has longingly eyed it often since.[15] The poet is swept into the nostalgic scene depicted by artist J. B. Pyne and sighs at the loss of 'That simpler world from which we've been evicted'.[16] The ease of the 'slow-paced fifties' is not available to the 'air-raid-worried mind' of the present except through Pyne's 'affectionate recording'.[17] But of course, Pyne's pastoral recording forgets as much as it recalls of the 1850s; the disastrous Battle of Balaclava in the Crimean War, immortalized by Tennyson's 'Charge of the Light Brigade', to take one example, belies Pyne's 'slow-paced' or 'simpler' past. As Sassoon's speaker contemplates the painting, he feels transfixed and then transported by the poem's last line: 'For time has changed this "View" into a Vision'.[18] It is a vision of double nostalgia: first Pyne's, then Sassoon's.

'Tragitones' records the unpredictable influence of ghostly presences on Sassoon's moods:

> I have not sought these quietened cadences,
> These tragitones, these stilled interior themes,
> These vistas where imagined presences
> Lead me away from life, – loved ghosts or dreams?[19]

These ghosts come unbidden to him from the unconscious, released as 'imagined presences' through the mechanism of dreams, either sleeping or waking. And these ghosts lead him away from active engagement with quotidian life into the vistas of recollected experience, which is pleasant if they are benign and can enliven his nostalgic ruminations, but disturbing if they are revenants from his traumatic memories. In 'Repression of War Experience', the speaker observes that 'there must be crowds of ghosts among the trees' of his garden, 'horrible shapes in shrouds'.[20] In 'Tragitones' and all of *Rhymed Ruminations*, Sassoon is able to distance himself from the malevolent ghosts, but the atmosphere of war lurks in the background, just as it does in 'Repression of War Experience'.

Published in the middle of the Battle of Britain, *Rhymed Ruminations* was generally well received, even as reviewers noted Sassoon's preoccupation with the past. Richard Church in the *Spectator*, focusing on 'the nostalgic' vision that also characterizes Sassoon's autobiographical prose, found evidence in the poetry 'that the fissure in Mr Sassoon's personality [from his First World War experience] still is only partially closed'.[21] The *Times Literary Supplement* noted the commingling of past and present throughout the poems which endowed Sassoon's nostalgia with 'more than an easeful refuge'.[22] Sensitive as ever, Sassoon seized upon notes of reservation in the reception of this volume and expressed renewed doubts about the currency of his autognostic poetics:

> I feel that these poems are the end of a chapter for me. If I ever produce another volume of verse it will have to be less personal and more innovative in technique. The trouble is that a poem like 'Old Exeter' seems scarcely worth writing where 20 times as many people would read it if it were in prose![23]

And indeed, the robust sales of his prose volumes and the poor sales of his new poems contributed to a curbing of poetic activity; manuscript evidence suggests that in the next two years he wrote fewer than half a dozen poems, and his next book of poetry was not published until 1950. But *Rhymed Ruminations* was clearly not the end of a chapter and innovative verse does not characterize his nostalgic poetry of the 1940s.

Civilian War Poet II: Wartime Sanctuary and the Limited Consolation of the English Countryside

In the guardedly optimistic days following D-Day and the long-awaited establishment of a Second Front, Sassoon told Geoffrey Keynes about plans for a forthcoming slim volume of poetry 'of about sixteen pages, when conditions are less decivilized and "enemy actionized"'.[24] But even this modest plan proved unrealistic. Soon after D-Day he was shaken by the news of his friend Rex

Whistler's death in the fighting near Caen,[25] which he described in his diary as 'the worst pain I have felt since the war began. I somehow felt he would be killed.'[26] In 'The Hardened Heart', a poem printed in the *Observer* in August 1944, he bemoans the loss of youth's innocence to the heart-numbing knowledge of 'the ugly facts of night' and the sense 'That life beloved had lied'.[27] The events of the war, especially his personal loss and the dissolution of his marriage, may have all contributed to his change of plans for a new collection:

> I have only got about a dozen printable [poems], and am not sure that they would make a very good sequence. Would prefer to wait a bit longer, and hope that a few new lyrics may turn up when the oppression of this destructive war is over.[28]

All the same, despite being weighed down by anxiety and depression, which lasted well after 1945, Sassoon did manage to write more than forty lyrics during the war – a greater number than appeared in any single volume since *The Old Huntsman* (1917) – mainly in 1943 and 1944, before receiving the news of Whistler's death.

The act of writing poetry, when 'Head, hand and heart unite to make me whole again,' was a means of gaining 'sanctuary from [the] foiled unrest' of domestic and international strife.[29] He valued his isolation at Heytesbury even as it contributed to his sense of detachment from the experience of war, which was once so profoundly integral to his poetry. While many of his Second World War poems bracket off the war without wholly denying its existence and pursue the poet's sustaining engagement with the English countryside, they often recall a characteristic technique of his First World War poetry that made him famous: an ironic *volte* at the poem's conclusion, or 'end[ing] with a fortissimo line', as Sassoon put it[30] – a formal reflection of an acute sense of contrast at the heart of his war experience. As well, the troubled negotiation between past and present that runs through many of these 1940s poems finds expression in imagery that echoes 'Repression of War Experience': the interplay of candlelight and darkness, the layered topography of a haunted past, and the redemptive potential of flight.

In this poetry, in contrast to the orientation of his patriotic verse, Sassoon does not invoke patriotism or spiritual intervention to make sense of war and his frustrating role in it. He states in 'A Wartime Remonstrance' that 'Contrast promotes an active mind,'[31] but even an active mind is not capable of understanding fully the divide between his personal experience and the war raging round him. His rural isolation is ultimately 'beyond all knowing', though he returns repeatedly to the enigmatic contrast at the heart of his Second World War experience: 'War daunts fancy in the wild-rosed lane'[32];'the scene of sylvan quiet was strange with war's unrest.'[33] Few poems from this period are not animated by this enigma, either in explicit or implicit terms.

In 'Fourth Winter', which captures Sassoon's sense of bewilderment at his isolated situation, he recalls thinking shortly before the declaration of war that if war came, he would return to 'ardent acts with reawakened mind'.[34] Yet four winters later, he finds himself riding through leafless wooded lanes, 'a landscape figure still', and realizes that 'throughout this war I've done what looks like nil.' While the poem ends with the poet consoled and strengthened by the landscape, which not only surrounds but includes him and even augurs the end of the war, an underlying despondency is clear in his unfulfilled yearning to return to the 'ardent acts' of his First World War experience.

Indeed, all the poems concerned with his feeling of isolation from the events of war express that wistfulness or lament the absurdity of his being 'out of it'. But at least he knows he is not alone. 'Middle-aged . . . bedulled and dumb', like others of his generation listening to war news on the wireless, the poet is

> too old to be engaged
> In this unpictureable fight.
> Perils and pains for us are staged
> In quiet rooms, by log-fire's light.[35]

In 'Getting Queer in Wartime', the too-old speaker moves from the protected warmth of his fire-lit room, where war news is channelled through the modern wireless, to the rustic splendours of his parkland, a movement from passivity to limited action. The natural world awakens body memories of combat the speaker does not consciously register. A 'much-memoried man' potters about on his land,

> Stopping to slash at nettles with his stick,
> He stares awhile on auburn shoals of sundown –
> 'Day's elegy, sad beyond Salisbury Plain,'
> He murmurs, for the moment grown poetic.
> Snails crunch beneath his footsteps. Here and there
> He halts to shake them off a mountain ash.[36]

The slashing, crunching and shaking of his rustic movements evoke the experience of combat this 'much-memoried man' carries about with him, recalling his life as a soldier and at the same time his distance from that past self. Confined to 'stay-at-home internment', he is also far removed from the present 'infernal war', leaving him chafing at his enforced passivity. Feeling 'obsolete' and 'Dotty, perhaps', he concludes sarcastically, 'But anyhow I'm harmless.'

The term 'dotty', of course, recalls his jocular name for Craiglockhart back in 1917, which he used then to help distance himself from that 'live museum of neuroses'.[37] Here the term allows him similarly to manage his 'queer' sense of obsolescence. 'Dotty' allows him to articulate his anxiety over the effect of isolation on his mental stability, yet the articulation in its wry self-awareness helps him keep the dottiness at bay. And while feeling 'harmless' was not without its comfort for Sassoon, it marks a stark contrast to his role in the First World War, when he was active and engaged. Yes, he became known as 'Mad Jack' and lusted to kill, and was immersed in trauma. But he was also endowed with sufficient agency to protest publicly against his government's war aims, which sent him into the institution he called 'Dottyville'. His use of 'dotty' in this poem from the Second World War seems to convey a rueful recognition of his present impotence and the guilt attending his inactivity and relative safety.

'Queer' is another important word in Sassoon's lexicon. Odd, strange, peculiar, eccentric, are all denoted in this poem, but 'queer' has also a pathological sense: 'not in a normal condition . . . giddy, faint, or ill'.[38] Indeed, Sassoon spent the entire war and the years leading up to it feeling 'not in the normal condition', at odds with modernity, removed from the active world of combat by age, placed on the periphery of the London-based literary culture by choice. In *The Old Century*, the first volume of his autobiography, there is the oft-quoted confession of his 'queer craving to revisit the past and give the modern world the slip',[39] which explicitly invokes an aspect of his nostalgia. Early in *Siegfried's Journey* there is also a curious passage purportedly from his First World War diary that seems to add both immediacy and ironic distance to the portrayal of his youthful self and 'that queer hankering for extinction which I can't explain'.[40] The dominance of what Freud called a 'parasitic double' in driving the soldier to threaten his own safety had waned for Sassoon in the Second World War with his enforced passivity. But in 'Getting Queer in Wartime' its after-effects linger in the imagery of the hitherto passive tree-talking old walker's violent attack upon the nettles, a present substitute for the past Germans who had killed his beloved comrades.

'Queer' was in the 1930s also acquiring its slang meaning of homosexual. During the 1920s and 1930s Sassoon was deeply involved not just in a series of love affairs with men, but also in a kind of privileged homosexual community that weekended in country houses and took extensive motoring tours of the Continent.[41] But once he broke with Stephen Tennant, married Hester Gatty and acquired Heytesbury House, he effectively withdrew from this community. Added to his literary and military isolation during the war is this further sense of seclusion. 'A man, with no one of his sort to talk to', he writes in the final stanza of 'Getting Queer in Wartime'. The word 'queer' thus relates to both his experience as a combatant and now his being a removed observer of life and war, a duality which resonates in the title of this poem and is affirmed in its final line. 'Dotty, perhaps' returns Sassoon and his readers to his confinement at Craiglockhart, while 'but anyhow I'm harmless' takes us back to his present rural isolation.

The Encroaching War: Trauma and Detachment

Many of these Second World War poems focus on the tension between the personal benefits and costs of his isolation. Paul Fussell has observed that the Sherston memoirs are structured by Sassoon's 'binary vision', founded upon a series of contrasts between the pastoral beauties of Sherston's 'weald of youth' and the French and Flemish countryside mired in war.[42] Such a binary vision is also at work in these later poems in the series of contrasts between the relative security of his bucolic life and the ravages of war in the world beyond. It is particularly clear in 'The Contrast'.[43] Jogging along a 'dozy summer road' on horseback, Sassoon observes the blossoming dog rose, a singing finch and, high above, an aeroplane, which he typically associates with bombardments, but the pastoral setting counters the menacing associations as he notes that the plane is 'out to do no harm'. However, when he leaves the peaceful scene, he remembers at once the war in Libya 'and friends in foundered tanks / And havoc for my heart beyond all knowing'. As often in his earlier poems, satirical and lyric, the final lines here provide an arresting turn to sharpen a contrast, in this case between the peace he enjoys in his immediate circumstances and the world at war. The consoling power of the natural world is brought into doubt, undermined by the ruin of war. In 'On Scratchbury Camp',[44] one of the few poems published at the time, Sassoon looks for continuity in the natural world to offset the shocks and uncertainties of war. The apparently timeless landscape and the sky seem to offer him the nostalgic assurance of such continuity. Even though the pasture has been transformed into a runway for the 'fighter-squadron' droning overhead, he tells himself that this militarization of the natural world is merely a modern version of 'war's imperious wing', which once also manned the 'fosse' with 'bronze and flint-head spear'[45] but has left little sign of its intrusion. The land will also survive modern warfare, even its aerial scourge, as it survived Bronze Age battles. Compared with Sassoon's unpublished work from these years, this confidence seems momentary and fragile. In 'A Country Character', written in the summer of 1944, after a portion of his park had been transformed into a temporary base for troops massing for the Normandy invasion, he interrogates himself as a 'self-contained Soliloquist', wondering what he has accomplished 'by keeping calm while war convulsed mankind'.[46] His answer is that he has observed closely the natural beauty of his land for five years of changing seasons while 'his mind resumed its memoried monotone . . . [and] evad[ed] the shock of history grown insane'. The 'self-contained' poet constructs the 'beloved and known' paths of Heytesbury as nostalgic barriers to protect against the insane pressures of history, but the poem's final phrase – 'the advent of the aeroplane' – reveals the anxiety that undercuts his confidence in this defence.

In the daytime, usually in the afternoons, Sassoon sought consolation in his pastoral surroundings, but his writing was done late at night. Nocturnal contemplation and rumination is a common feature of his Second World War poems. In 'First and Last Delight', 'Star-sown space and gloom defying, / Must haunt his clocked and candled nights.'[47] Flickering candlelight illuminates the pages of his notebook; he imagines how from afar the window of his room offers a precarious beacon in the night's darkness. But just as often the 'unfriending night' feels oppressive and gloomy, threatening to drown the light of his candle and his hope.[48] In 'Fourth Winter', Sassoon recounts a late afternoon ride 'in wartime lanes, alone with leafless trees', and imagines how different the same ride would be when the war is over: 'I'll feel grateful riding home toward night, / For cottage windows unafraid to show a light'[49] because blackout measures would be lifted. His faith in the continuity of the natural world, though at times shaken during the war, often led him to imagining how the personal and geographic devastation of wars in the past had been overcome. Time, dulled by the war, 'fares on' like Sassoon jogging on horseback 'along this empty road', as others did before him. Casting his mind back he imagines 'when surly barons blundered by with visored eyes, / To Scottish wars they went, or far Crusades' and then places himself in the lineage of English fighters:

> No baron I; and my crusading's done.
> Once was enough for me. And then I prayed
> That betterment for earth might be begun.[50]

In 1940 he described his protest against the war in 1917 as a 'sort of crusade, based on [his] experience of the futility of war' against German militarism.[51] But his prayers for improvements in the world after his war went unanswered. The darkened cottages and his awareness of 'lives lost, and souls that mourn' remind him that once was not enough for history. Still he rides on. The historically layered path he treads offers no insight, but prompts him to pray again, this time with seemly modesty and realism: 'I ride into the year / With nothing in my head but "Peace make haste."'

Looking to the distant past for insight was a nostalgic strategy encouraged by E. M. Forster during a visit to Heytesbury in the summer of 1942. Forster advised Sassoon to study Roman history around AD 400 and the works of Ausonius for 'parallels and portents',[52] perhaps seeing in Ausonius a figure whose life had distinct parallels to Sassoon's.[53] His response to Forster's advice was 'A Post-Ausonian Poet [A.D. 410]', in which he retreats into the Roman past and imagines 'a man sit[ting] at a table with a light', contemplating the motivation of poets: 'he has much – though few the words – to write.'[54] The '[A.D. 410]' of the title is the year of the sack of Rome, well after Ausonius' death, implying that the distant post-Ausonian poet is an archetypal figure of the poet in a time of crisis. The precise identity of this poet is left ambiguous; he is at once a Roman observer and Sassoon himself. The poem brings out the 'parallels and portents' that assist Sassoon in contextualizing his own situation, and yet a feeling of anxiety afflicts both the distant poet and Sassoon, arising from analogous national emergencies. London had not fallen but it was under threat, and the British Empire was on the verge of collapse.

That distant poet, alone in the dark night with his candle, a beacon of light, 'wonder[s] why poets put themselves on paper' in the face of the violence of history. Words that make sense of the destruction of a great civilization are difficult to find:

> Outside, where plane-trees hush the garden gloom,
> A distant glare foretells the Visigoth
> Advancing, in accordance with his plan
> To slaughter or enslave unbarbarous man.[55]

Nevertheless, the poet struggles with 'his ultimate lines', noticing that above his candle, 'Attracted by the flame, a dancing moth / Beats softly on the ceiling of the room.' The ancient poet may fear that his struggle for the right words is as futile as the moth's struggle towards the light reflected on the ceiling, because 'soon death will toll a tocsin to his ears' as he is overwhelmed by exterior 'storms of History'. The ring of the tocsin (a military warning sounded by a bell) will drown out the sound of the trapped moth's wings, and 'carnage' and 'death' will announce the conclusion of 'The Silver Age'. But the poem ends on a hopeful note: 'Museful men . . . [cling to] their own faith' in words against the violence of 'power politics', as 'thought keeps one candle burning through the night.'[56]

The final stanza of 'A Post-Ausonian Poet [A.D. 410]' is borrowed virtually word for word from 'August 4th, 1939',[57] which provides an explicit parallel between the present English crisis and the fall of the Roman Empire. Like 'Fourth Winter', where he connects his experience in the 1940s explicitly to his 'crusading' in 1917, Sassoon's historical view of the distant past in 'A Post-Ausonian Poet' passes through the prism of his experience of the First World War by symbolic allusion to the moth that flits about in 'Repression of War Experience':

> Now light the candles; one; two; there's a moth;
> What silly beggars they are to blunder in
> And scorch their wings with glory, liquid flame –[58]

Sassoon's poetic persona is withdrawn from battle, as if from a flame, scorched by his experience. As it was for Sassoon's post-Ausonian poet twenty-five years later, 'the words' to express himself are few and the 'big, dizzy moth . . . [that] bumps and flutters . . . on the ceiling' serves as an objective correlative for the speaker's state of mind, which bumps senselessly against the onslaught of history.[59]

The significance Sassoon found in the symbolic capability of candlelight to reflect experience is further demonstrated in 'Cleaning the Candelabrum', also written in the first half of 1943.[60] Taking apart and polishing his six-branched candle-holder, his mind moves from the present to his own past, and then to thoughts about the history of the seventeenth-century candelabrum that has held the light that 'illuminated . . . much vista'd history, many vanished lives'.[61] The lives it conjures up for Sassoon are civilized, decorous, aware of the storms of history but protected from them, as he imagines two spinsters from Jane Austen's 'cosmos' conferring 'volubly about Napoleon / And what was worn at the Assembly Hall'.[62] Sassoon cannot wholly condemn an age when war was sufficiently distant and confined to rank conversationally with fashion gossip. Such associations help him enjoy nostalgic comforts of the 'period atmosphere' in the midst of wartime anxieties. The modern 'million-volted glare' of 'mankind's advancement'[63] is to candlelight what the aeroplane is to the moth, and though it may shed more light than a candle, or six candles, it generates only foreboding about the future and washes out the shadows of the past.

'A 1940 Memory',[64] also written in the relatively fertile period of early 1943, expresses again Sassoon's clinging to the natural world and its imagery. 'Disconsolate' at the 'direful' war news, his mind was arrested and eased by a 'Clouded Yellow butterfly'.[65] Like the recurrent candle in his poetry, the butterfly is a powerful symbol of the transformative potential of nature, which he uses even in his own prose autobiography, which I will discuss in greater detail in the following chapters. In the concluding scene of *The Old Century*, written in 1938, a butterfly makes an important symbolic appearance. On his twenty-first birthday, Sassoon is alone in his studio at Weirleigh, his childhood home, contemplating the room's book-lined walls, extensive views and his aspirations as a writer. The studio was once his father's, and as he tries to imagine what memories of his father it still contains, he is interrupted by 'the flutterings of a butterfly' entangled in the window dressing of the skylight.[66] When he manages to extract the intruder, he realizes that the 'loftiest [entomological] ambition of my childhood had been belated realized. I had caught a Camberwell Beauty.'[67] But the belated triumph reminds him of the separation of his parents and the subsequent death of his father – 'sad events which had so impressed themselves on my mind'.[68] He resists the sad memories through the trope of metamorphosis:

> Perhaps the Camberwell Beauty had flown across the English channel to remind me of the foreign countries to which my father had always said he would take me. Perhaps it *was* my father.[69]

When he tries to show his prize to his mother, who had been in the lower studio, she 'had disappeared'.[70] Reminiscent of the poignant scenes early in *The Old Century* when his father's rare visits compelled his mother to absent herself, his father's spirit, embodied in the Camberwell Beauty, still seems to keep his mother away, although her studio is suffused with her ghostly presence, evoked by the sights and smells of her paints and canvases. He finds it 'rather strange' that this elusive creature that he had so coveted as a boy should appear on his twenty-first birthday[71] – his 'coming of age', as he says[72] – as if to mark his own metamorphosis from child into adult. His symbolic interpretations of the butterfly in this episode – at once himself, his childhood ambition and his father – fuse together to enrich our understanding of his development. In the Camberwell Beauty he glimpses a mirage, rooted in childhood longing, of his own transformation into the man he imagined his father to have been. But that butterfly, a portent of hope and change, is freighted too with the loss of the father, the burden of early trauma rooted in the troubled relationship of his parents.

The 'Clouded Yellow butterfly' in 'A 1940 Memory' shares the symbolic specificity of *The Old Century*'s, but it is not as exotic as the Camberwell Beauty; it is an English species, which adds to its symbolic function of reclamation as a reminder of past joys and better times to come:

> From those appalled and personal throes
> Time will dissolve the pain, one knows;
> And days when direful news was heard
> Be indistinct, unreal, and blurred.[73]

Just as the associated imagery of candle and candlestick is benign and reassuring on the surface, but accompanied by not always tacit reminders of surrounding and often threatening darkness, so too can the redemptive butterfly be shadowed by melancholic associations. The dark underside of this potentially positive image is especially the case when one considers the moth, the exotic butterfly's ordinary variant. It is clearly an emblem of a mind on the verge of crisis in 'Repression of War Experience' and 'A Post-Ausonian Poet', in which the poet pursues his compulsive search for the right word, even though he knows that his civilized world is about to collapse around him. Thus, this recurrent redemptive and liberative imagery shows the nostalgic appeal of traditional symbology, in which past systems of order can act as balms to present chaos while also revealing its limitations. In wartime, trauma always intrudes. In the final stanza, the memory of 'that slow loitering butterfly', he realizes, 'will faithfully recur' each time he passes along that path,[74] but the facade of solace is cracked by the trochee that begins the final line, sounding a slightly ominous note, as the poet does not merely watch but 'Stalk[s] that slow loitering butterfly'.[75] It may not be too forced to hear in the word 'stalking' echoes of Sassoon's pursuit of German soldiers in the no man's land of the First World War, and this military association undermines the gladness ushered in by his apparently simple and comforting '1940 Memory'.

The compulsive return to the theme of contrast between a private nostalgic paradise and the world at war in many of his poems from the Second World

War leaves an impression of foreboding. He fears that the present war and his past traumatic memories will inevitably intrude upon his carefully nurtured, if sometimes guiltily enjoyed, refuge. During this war, Sassoon found in writing poetry 'the anodyne of dreams in love with death'[76]; that is, the anodyne of dreams, impressions and memories saturated with war. The degree to which his memories of the past were shaped by trauma is evident in the narcissistic and nostalgic patterns that characterize his prose autobiographies, on which he was also intermittently working during this period of personal and international anxiety.

Notes

1. Siegfried Sassoon to Geoffrey Keynes, letter, 1 May 1939, Papers of Siegfried Sassoon, Manuscript Department, Cambridge University Library.
2. Ibid. 14 April 1939.
3. Ibid. 28 June 1944.
4. Ibid. 15 August 1944.
5. Siegfried Sassoon, *Collected Poems: 1908–1956* (London: Faber & Faber, 1961), p. 232.
6. Ibid. p. 89.
7. Ibid. p. 235.
8. Ibid. p. 236.
9. Ibid. p. 236.
10. Ibid. p. 236.
11. Ibid. p. 236.
12. Ibid. p. 237.
13. Ibid. p. 237.
14. Ibid. p. 237.
15. Ibid. p. 242.
16. Ibid. p. 242.
17. Ibid. pp. 242–3.
18. Ibid. p. 243.
19. Ibid. p. 248.
20. Ibid. pp. 89–90.
21. Richard Church, 'Looking back', rev. of *Rhymed Ruminations* by Siegfried Sassoon, *Spectator*, 15 November 1940, p. 508.
22. H. Fausset, 'Mr. Sassoon: Peace remembered', rev. of *Rhymed Ruminations* by Siegfried Sassoon, *Times Literary Supplement*, 2 November 1940, p. 558.
23. Siegfried Sassoon to Sydney Carlyle Cockerell, letter, 17 December 1940, Sassoon Collection, Harry Ransom Humanities Research Center (HRHRC), University of Texas, Austin.
24. Sassoon to Keynes, letter, 28 June 1944.
25. Laurence Whistler, *The Laughter and the Urn: The Life of Rex Whistler* (London: Weidenfeld & Nicolson, 1985), p. 285.
26. John Stuart Roberts, *Siegfried Sassoon: 1886–1967* (London: Cohen, 1999), p. 286.
27. Sassoon, *Collected Poems*, p. 265.
28. Sassoon to Keynes, letter, 15 August 1944.
29. Siegfried Sassoon, 'Nirvana', in 'ms. notebook', Hart-Davis Section, Papers of Siegfried Sassoon, Manuscript Department, Cambridge University Library, 17 April 1944.

30. Quoted in Dennis Silk, *Siegfried Sassoon* (Tisbury, Wilt.: Compton Russell, 1975), p. 23.
31. Siegfried Sassoon, 'A Wartime Remonstrance', in 'ms. notebook', Hart-Davis Section, Papers of Siegfried Sassoon, Manuscript Department, Cambridge University Library, 28 September 1942.
32. Siegfried Sassoon, 'A Private Peace', in 'ms. notebook', Hart-Davis Section, Papers of Siegfried Sassoon, Manuscript Department, Cambridge University Library, 16–18 May 1944.
33. Siegfried Sassoon, 'A Personal Path', in 'ms. notebook', Hart-Davis Section, Papers of Siegfried Sassoon, Manuscript Department, Cambridge University Library, 26 July 1943.
34. Siegfried Sassoon, 'Fourth Winter', in 'ms. notebook', Hart-Davis Section, Papers of Siegfried Sassoon, Manuscript Department, Cambridge University Library, 18–26 January 1943.
35. Siegfried Sassoon, 'Out of It', in 'ms. notebook', Hart-Davis Section, Papers of Siegfried Sassoon, Manuscript Department, Cambridge University Library, 5 February 1943.
36. Siegfried Sassoon, 'Getting Queer in Wartime', in 'ms. notebook', Hart-Davis Section, Papers of Siegfried Sassoon, Manuscript Department, Cambridge University Library, 29 April 1943.
37. Siegfried Sassoon, *Sherston's Progress* (London: Faber & Faber, 1983), p. 12.
38. 'Queer', *Shorter Oxford English Dictionary*, 2 vols (Oxford: Oxford University Press, 1944).
39. Siegfried Sassoon, *The Old Century* (London: Faber & Faber, 1938), p. 128.
40. Siegfried Sassoon, *Siegfried's Journey: 1916–1920* (London: Faber & Faber, 1945), p. 42.
41. For a discussion of Sassoon's homosexuality, see Jean Moorcroft Wilson, *Siegfried Sassoon: The Journey from the Trenches: A Biography 1918–1967*), vol. 2 (New York: Routledge, 2003).
42. Paul Fussell, *The Great War and Modern Memory* (New York: Oxford University Press), p. 90.
43. Siegfried Sassoon, 'The Contrast', in 'ms. notebook', Hart-Davis Section, Papers of Siegfried Sassoon, Manuscript Department, Cambridge University Library, 18 June 1942.
44. First published in *Country Life*, 25 June 1943, 'On Scratchbury Camp' was also selected for *The Best Poems of 1943* (1944) and reprinted in Siegfried Sassoon, *Emblems of Experience* (Cambridge: Rampant Lions, 1951).
45. Sassoon, *Collected Poems*, p. 279.
46. Siegfried Sassoon, 'A Country Character', in 'ms. notebook', Hart-Davis Section, Papers of Siegfried Sassoon, Manuscript Department, Cambridge University Library, 4 July 1944.
47. Siegfried Sassoon, 'First and Last Delight', in 'ms. notebook', Hart-Davis Section, Papers of Siegfried Sassoon, Manuscript Department, Cambridge University Library, 19 March 1943.
48. Siegfried Sassoon, 'The Solution', in 'ms. notebook', Hart-Davis Section, Papers of Siegfried Sassoon, Manuscript Department, Cambridge University Library, 27 August 1943.
49. Siegfried Sassoon, 'Fourth Winter', in 'ms. notebook', Hart-Davis Section, Papers of Siegfried Sassoon, Manuscript Department, Cambridge University Library, 18–26 January 1943.
50. Ibid. 18–26 January 1943.

51. Siegfried Sassoon to Christopher Hassall, letter, 2 March 1940, Papers of Siegfried Sassoon, Manuscripts Department, Cambridge University Library.
52. Quoted in Stewart, *Unpublished Letters*, p. 255.
53. Ausonius was tutor to the young Emperor Gratian in the last half of the fourth century and was commissioned to celebrate with epigrams or epistles of verse some of the spectacular Roman victories in the Germanic wars near the Danube in AD 368–9 (Hugh G. Evelyn White, 'Introduction', in Decimus Magnus Ausonius, *Ausonius with an English Translation*, trans. Hugh G. Evelyn White (London: Heinemann, 1919), pp. ix–x). By the end of this decade, Ausonius retired to the country and dabbled in literary pursuits (White, 'Introduction', p. xii).
54. Siegfried Sassoon, 'A Post-Ausonian Poet [A.D. 410]', in 'ms. notebook', Hart-Davis Section, Papers of Siegfried Sassoon, Manuscript Department, Cambridge University Library, 22 January 1943.
55. Ibid. 22 January 1943.
56. Ibid. 22 January 1943.
57. 'August 4th, 1939' and 'A Post-Ausonian Poet [A.D. 410]' appear on facing pages of the manuscript notebook, and the last two quatrains of the earlier poem are duplicated in the final stanza of 'A Post-Ausonian Poet [A.D. 410]'.
58. Sassoon, *Collected Poems*, p. 89.
59. Ibid. p. 89.
60. 'Cleaning the Candelabrum' was later published in the *Listener*, May 1944, and collected in Sassoon, *Emblems of Experience* (1951), as well as Sassoon, *Collected Poems: 1908–1956*, p. 282.
61. Sassoon, *Collected Poems*, p. 282.
62. Ibid. p. 282.
63. Ibid. p. 282.
64. 'A 1940 Memory' was published in the *Observer*, 12 July 1943, and later collected in Siegfried Sassoon, *Common Chords* (Stanford Dingley: Mill House, 1950), as well as Sassoon, *Collected Poems: 1908–1956*, p. 266.
65. Sassoon, *Collected Poems*, p. 266.
66. Sassoon, *The Old Century*, p. 279.
67. Ibid. p. 279.
68. Ibid. p. 281.
69. Ibid. p. 283. Given its association with Sassoon's deceased father, it is symbolically felicitous that the Camberwell Beauty is also known in North America as the Mourning Cloak. See David Carter, *Butterflies and Moths of Britain and Europe* (London: Heinemann, 1982), p. 78.
70. Sassoon, *The Old Century*, p. 284.
71. Ibid. p. 280.
72. Ibid. p. 276.
73. Sassoon, *Collected Poems*, p. 266.
74. Ibid. p. 266.
75. Ibid. p. 266.
76. Siegfried Sassoon, 'Nirvana', in 'ms. notebook', Hart-Davis Section, Papers of Siegfried Sassoon, Manuscript Department, Cambridge University Library, 17 April 1944.

6

NARCISSISM AND AUTOGNOSIS: SASSOON, 1936–42

Narcissism and Autobiography

There is little doubt that Sassoon, judging by his own admission and the observations of his friends,[1] was throughout his life narcissistic and self-absorbed, and that this motivated and shaped his autobiographical project. In his version of autognosis, which was never as rigorous and disciplined as Rivers might have encouraged, Sassoon's response to literary tradition was as important as any systematic, psychoanalytic self-scrutiny. When he had completed his trilogy of semi-fictionalized memoirs, he turned almost immediately to autobiography, a genre clearly suited to his preoccupations. Having participated in the great wave of war books in the late 1920s with the Sherston memoirs, Sassoon's choice of genre in 1936 demonstrates that, despite his contrarian aesthetic claims, his work kept up, if not always precisely in step, with prevailing literary tastes.

In the late 1930s autobiography was a popular form for serious contemporary and modernist writers. In *Blasting and Bombardiering* (1937), a late inclusion in the war book phenomenon, Wyndham Lewis draws together key moments in his vorticist and military past in this construction of self. Younger writers with no army experience to draw from focused on their early and formative interactions with another key English institution, the public school. Cyril Connolly's *Enemies of Promise* (1938), for example, attends to the scarring and ideologically oppressive imprint of his school days upon his self-understanding. Like Orwell's later 'Such, Such were the Joys' (1947),

Connolly's cutting reconstructions of the cruelty of the school system and his suffering within it are sceptical rather than nostalgic, and are in some ways reminiscent of Joyce's earlier *Portrait of the Artist as a Young Man* (1916), adapting the malice of the Irish Catholic school to the English public schools. Wary of the conservative English values enshrined in an uninterrogated smoothing-over of the past, Connolly and Orwell are distinctly aware that the contemporary situation cannot be given the slip, as Sassoon sought to do. Sassoon's autobiographical reconstruction of the past is very different in so far as he focuses on a childhood outside of his experience of his English public school, and is pointedly nostalgic, not sceptical in its tacit endorsement of conservative English values and class hierarchies. However, each of these autobiographers has in common the strategy of opposing the hostile and disorienting world they encounter with the construction of an integrated self.[2]

In a contemporary world of fearful possibilities, the prospective return to devastating modern war and renewed anxieties of fragmentation, autobiography has the potential to provide the solace of elusive and illusory unity. Virginia Woolf rejected this solace, acknowledging that any identity is inseparable from its representation. In her final autobiographical sketches, on which she was working in the early years of the Second World War, she pursued a diffuse rather than a unified subjectivity.[3] In this way, Woolf was exceptional. The romantic self, given autobiographical form most forcefully by Rousseau and Wordsworth, persists in the modern period despite the disdain voiced by Hulme, Eliot, Pound and others. The romantic self endures, 'called back to life again as a nostalgic revenant', as Linda Anderson has it.[4] A romantic conception of self underlies the autobiographical work of Lewis, Connolly and Orwell. And Sassoon's autobiographical quest for his 'true self' is a quest for a unified, romantic construction of self founded upon his engagement with literary and cultural traditions, past and contemporary. Sassoon's work follows the literary path trod by Wordsworth, Pater and Proust, whose influence I discuss in the next chapter.

Sassoon was guided in the literary recreation of his past by the writing of Pater, whose chief appeal he describes in *The Weald of Youth* (1942) as the ability to evoke an 'atmosphere of life treated as "an act of recollection," subdued to the stately movement and lulling cadences of his style'.[5] Sassoon acknowledges that the narcissism and nostalgia underlying *The Old Century* (1938) and *The Weald of Youth* are informed and shaped by Pater when he writes that 'The reclusive tendency in my nature found in [Pater] its cloister and its abbey-church.'[6] Graham Hough argues for the 'psychological inevitabil[ity]' and the historical justification of Pater's nostalgia, his 'longing for home as a place enclosed and sealed against the turbulence of the outside world' that 'boil[ed] up' in the Boer War.[7] Similarly, Sassoon's own 'withdrawal' and nostalgic, self-absorbed temperament had their roots in historical 'turbulence', although he himself associated Pater only with the ideal of sheltered seclusion. Paterian echoes in Sassoon's prose comprise a part of his nostalgia for 'home' – a place enclosed from the incursions of the mechanical and violent modern world – and have as much to do with the present from which he recoils as the past that comforts and consoles. Adapting from Proust some of the techniques of revisiting sites and emotional states of home, Sassoon constructs in his autobiographies a modern romantic self that is 'forever casting and recasting itself' as a form of self-reflection.[8] Wordsworth, whose 'egotistical sublime' Keats had admired already in 1818,[9] worked on *The Prelude; or The Growth of a Poet's Mind* throughout most of his life and once said that 'it is a thing unprecedented in literary history that a man should write at such length about himself.'[10] Rousseau may have trumped Wordsworth here, but there is certainly no shortage of antecedents. Spender described '*The Prelude* [as] the first great *Recherche du temps perdu*',[11] and each in different ways provides literary models for Sassoon's narcissistic inclinations that reach far back into his past and gave shape to his autobiography.

Despite such impressive exemplars, Sassoon's focus in his poetry and memoirs on his past and the growth of his poetic self was – and continues to be – regarded with reservations. The first volumes of his openly personal autobiographies were dismissed as belated, nostalgic, self-indulgent and historically irrelevant to a world on the brink of war. But taking into account the influence of Rivers, one can see the prominence of nostalgia and narcissism in *The Old Century* and *The Weald of Youth* as especially interesting because it manifests a literary nostalgia that combines the Victorianist tradition of his youth that he championed and the modernist tradition that he hated but could not escape. The third volume, *Siegfried's Journey* (1945), is less interesting in this respect because Sassoon altered his approach to concentrate on a catalogue of famous people he encountered during his critical heyday, 1916–20. Though he might have bristled at the thought, he seems to have followed the dictates of his estranged friend Robert Graves on the necessary 'ingredients' of a popular memoir: 'People like reading about poets. I put in a lot of poets [in *Goodbye to All That*] . . . And they like hearing about T. E. Lawrence, because he is supposed to be a mystery man.'[12] Sassoon 'put in' both of these 'ingredients', and *Siegfried's Journey* has been much more popular than *The Old Century* and *The Weald of Youth*, though it was by far his least favourite book of the three.[13] These volumes, then, are deeply relevant to the historically anxious years of the late 1930s and early 1940s, not in spite of his nostalgic and narcissistic inclinations but because of them.

Narcissism and Autognosis

Sassoon was still working on the proofs of *Sherston's Progress* when he began what he described as 'a parallel portrait of myself (as a poet), which will allow me more imaginative freedom – (my indoor self, as it were – Sherston being my "outdoor" self) . . . I have done about 25,000 words already – about childhood.'[14] He regarded Rivers as 'the solution' to the Sherston memoirs, and Rivers was, through the force of his character more than the influence of his ideas, also the solution to this new self-portrait. In *The Old Century*, Sassoon was able to follow Rivers's 'autognostic' course in prose by tracing the conditions by which his inner self was produced back to his earliest remembered past.[15] Sassoon claimed that he wished quite consciously to convey in *The Old Century* his 'real life',[16] and his past as it shaped his 'real state of mind'. And yet, at the same time, his powerful nostalgic outlook persistently narrowed and limited the memories available for his reconstruction of a childhood and youth.

Like nostalgia, narcissism has been pathologized by psychological writers as a regressive condition,[17] and like nostalgia, it can inform the autobiographical impulse of literary expression. Rivers, Sassoon's inspirational guide to self-understanding, identified the tendency to regress to an early stage of development as an example of the widespread biological phenomenon of 'devolution' postulated by Hughlings Jackson, who claimed that a diseased organism 'tends to retrace the steps through which it has passed in its development'.[18] In *Beyond the Pleasure Principle*, Freud hypothesized the ultimate theory of regression with the death drive, in which the organism strives to return to its inanimate origins. Rivers found aspects of Hughlings Jackson's theory of general biological regression in his patients suffering from traumatic experiences of war, citing symptoms such as the excessive desire for solitude and inability to mix with others, extreme emotional response, and like Freud's uncanny, the blurring of reality with imagination.[19] The common ground Rivers saw in all of these symptoms was a withdrawal from the dangers associated with the present, or the recent traumatic past, to a safer bastion in the distance, which he linked with a regression to childhood or infancy.

In the mid-1930s, the appearance of Sassoon's first and only child produced an uncanny double that returned him to the imaginative space and time of his own childhood. It is fitting that this child shares the same Christian name as his alter ego from the George Sherston memoirs, only recently completed when he was born. In 'Meeting and Parting', a poem addressed to his son, Sassoon begins: 'Myself reborn; I look into your eyes.'[20] He wrote to Ruth and Henry Head: 'How I wish you could have seen him an hour after he was born. The likeness to me was quite extraordinary . . . It was as though I saw myself on September 8, 1886': that is, on the date of his own birth.[21] And to Max Beerbohm he wrote: 'I must tell you that little George is very like his papa. He has the same face.'[22] Identification with his son is a consistent theme in his letters of the period of the composition of *The Old Century*, which was begun shortly before George's birthday. George seems to have unwittingly performed the function of a mirror in whose reflection Sassoon glimpsed a reanimation of his own childhood.

NARCISSUS AND *THE OLD CENTURY*

Sassoon begins the story of his life with a lush visual image that realizes his intention to present 'Emotion drawn at its experience', like water drawn from a well:

> Prelude
>
> Far off in earliest-remembered childhood I can overhear myself repeating the words 'Watercress Well.' I am kneeling by an old stone well-head; my mother is standing beside me and we are looking into the water. My mother tells me that it is 'a very deep-rising spring'; but I do not want to be told anything about it, even by her. I want nothing at all except to be gazing at the water which bubbles so wonderfully up out of the earth, and to dip my fingers in it and scatter the glittering drops . . . The well reflects the empty sky; I can see myself in it, rather obscurely, when I am not watching the bubbles climbing up in the middle of the crystal-clear water.
>
> Many a half-hour's pilgrimage we made from our house to Watercress Well, which, after having been one of my 'favourite places to go to,' now becomes a symbol of life itself in an opaque and yet transparent beginning. From that so intensely remembered source all my journeyings now seem to have started. If I were to go back and look for it I might find that it has vanished; but in my thoughts it is for ever the same. Around and above it whisper the woodland branches; time's wavering shadows are falling across the glade; but there will be no sunset for that pictured afternoon. Light as a leaf, a robin drops down and decides to have a drink. I look again; the robin is not there. The well-head is alone with its secret energy of life.[23]

Freud wrote about the significance of autobiographical beginnings. Discussing Goethe's recollection of his childhood, Freud observed that 'the very recollection to which the patient gives precedence, which he relates first, with which he introduces the story of his life, proves to be the most important, the very one that holds the key to the secret pages of his mind.'[24] Sassoon's prelude is similarly important for its foregrounding of the image of narcissism, which is significant and characteristic of his poetry and prose of this period, as well as indicative of the nostalgic conception of self associated with his own wartime experiences.

Shortly before he began writing *The Old Century*, his poem 'Metamorphosis' appeared in *The Best Poems of 1935* (its very appearance there offering further evidence that he was not as marginalized as he and his later critics purported). It is a poem permeated with a nostalgia similar to his prelude: 'In a quaint narrow age, remote from this, / Sat Sandys translating Metamorphosis.'[25] Sassoon revels in George Sandys's 1632 translation of Ovid and its pleasingly 'obsolete' scholarship, which included the myth of Narcissus, the setting unmistakably invoked in Sassoon's prelude. Sandys recounts how Narcissus at the silver waters of the pool

> againe upon his Image gaz'd;
> Teares on the troubled water circles rais'd,
> The motion much obscured the fleeting shade.[26]

The water of Sandys's Narcissus is obscured by his tears shed from the unslaked yearning to embrace his image. The water of Sassoon's childhood is obscured by 'water circles raised' not from falling tears, but from the depths of the well-head, which he calls 'the secret energy of life'[27] and figures symbolically as the unconscious. Like Narcissus at the water's edge, Sassoon is both fascinated by the reflection and troubled by the elusiveness of the image. His mother is established as a kind of Echo figure, integral to bringing the Narcissus to the pool in the first place but disregarded by him, despite her love. Sassoon is troubled by the unconscious energies that bubble forth and disrupt the integrity of the reflected image of his past self. A similar image recurs in his poem 'Eyes', from *Rhymed Ruminations* (1940), which begins 'Narcissus youth has looked at life and seen / In the strange mirror only his own stare.'[28] Sassoon contrasts this youthful concern for the self only with 'Prophetic age', which is able to 'read' in others 'the intensely sphered reflection of his own' journey toward knowledge.[29] Here the older remembering self has learned through experience to 'read' or gaze upon others as if their function was to reflect his self-image. It is an intensely solipsistic perspective conveyed in 'Eyes', one that acknowledges the deferential role of others, and more generally, the environment, in shaping and reflecting back the development of the experienced self, which is still the centre of the narcissistic gaze.

Narcissism also suggests a theoretical context that invokes his traumatic experiences during the First World War. While Freud postulated a latent 'primary narcissism in everyone',[30] other Freudians forged a link between narcissism and the traumatic impact of frontline service. At the first International Psychoanalytic Congress in 1918, Freud's keenest supporters participated in a Symposium on 'Psychoanalysis and the War Neurosis'. Sandor Ferenczi asserted that, like the traumatic neuroses of peacetime, war neuroses often produced symptoms of 'increased ego-sensitiveness' which he associated with narcissism:

> This over-sensitiveness arises from the fact that in consequence of the shock, which has been experienced once or repeatedly, the interest and sexual hunger (libido) of the patients is withdrawn from the object into the ego . . . [and] degenerates into a kind of infantile narcissism.[31]

Such backward-reaching tendencies were reiterated at the Symposium by Karl Abraham, who attested that 'the trauma acts on the sexuality of many persons in the sense that it gives the impulse to a regressive alteration which endeavours to reach narcissism.'[32] I raise the contemporary psychoanalytic connections between neuroses, traumatic neuroses and narcissism to situate Sassoon's self-reflecting inclinations within a pathological framework appropriate to his experience: a framework that seeks, as Sassoon sought, to understand the effects of the past on the present. Rather than precisely diagnosing Sassoon's narcissistic inclinations as primary narcissism or secondary narcissism, which is both impossible at this stage and of limited critical value, my point is to draw out the general regressive tendencies of narcissism in Sassoon's autobiographical project, to emphasize the connection between the 'consequence of the shock' of his own war experience and his intense absorption with past incarnations of self.

Contemporary descriptions of Sassoon's military exploits in the First World War pre-figure the central narcissistic image of the prelude to *The Old Century*. In the early days of the Battle of the Somme, Sassoon went for a walk in the war-torn countryside during a lull in fighting:

> I'd found comfort for a while in being something like my old solitary self – leaning over a rough wooden bridge to gaze down into the dark-green swaying glooms of the narrow river full of weeds –[33]

Less than three weeks after the most devastating losses ever suffered by the British army, Sassoon was able to 'gaze down' into water, like Narcissus, but he found beyond the weeds the reassurance of his 'old solitary self', where Narcissus found only an unbridgeable gap. This innocent self, which yields solitary comforts unavailable to the experienced infantry officer then dominating Sassoon's character, could be reached through self-reflection. Lady Ottoline Morrell, who met and befriended Sassoon in 1917, confided to her diary:

> Siegfried is terribly self-centred, and it seems almost as if when he does a valiant action, such as [his protest against the continuation of the War], that he watches himself doing it, as he would look into a mirror.[34]

The image Morrell invokes, if taken a little further, supports my argument about the sustaining presence of a past self. In the mirror, Sassoon measures his actions in the tumultuous world of modern war against the calming stability of a reflected image he can associate with an authentic and whole self of the past, like the 'old solitary self' from the Somme bridge. This fascination with his own image, then, is linked indirectly to his traumatic experiences and is not without its dangers. He acknowledged in his diary entry from February 1918 an awareness of his narcissistic tendency: 'I am too deep in myself.'[35] The withdrawal of interest in the external world, according to Ferenczi, corresponds with an increase in the sensitivity of ego characteristic of a pathological narcissism.[36] Even after the war Sassoon's interests were 'dammed up' in his ego in a manner that buttressed his solipsism and enforced a social reclusiveness.

However, articulating the voice of childhood in *The Old Century* allowed Sassoon to express a deep-seated narcissistic impulse while bypassing its potential source in the psychological disturbances of his war experience. Nevertheless, the impact of his trauma is profoundly impressed upon *The Old Century*, in part by the vitality of narcissism that animates the narrative. The genuine affection the aggrieved and experienced Sassoon brings to the recreation of his younger self instils in the narrative an emotional warmth that dispels much of the melancholy integral to his childhood experience: the separation of his parents, the death of his father, his own life-threatening illness. Towards the end of *The Old Century* he discloses his method: 'All human beings desire to be glad. I prefer to remember my own gladness and good luck.'[37] He fixes his gaze upon the well-head of his innocent past and insists ('too much') upon his fascination with the calming reflection. However, the presence of his war trauma and ill-luck in this 'parallel portrait of myself (as a poet)' declares itself by its conspicuous absence, revealing unwittingly the inherent obscuration of intensely circumscribed self-reflection. His narcissistic tendencies, then, are not merely modes of fanciful escapism that isolate Sassoon from the world around him; they are rooted in a profoundly modern experience, his traumatic encounters in the First World War. Just as the lingering political fall-out from the war pushed European culture back into the abyss of historical disaster, the lingering effects of the war unsettled Sassoon and found expression in the narcissism that preoccupied his writing. The narcissistic aspects of *The Old Century* are both a legacy of his survival of traumatic experience and a compensatory strategy to assuage its unbearable cost. In this way, Sassoon's narcissism is an aspect of his nostalgia.

Sassoon's nostalgic aspirations for *The Old Century* are self-conscious and purposefully constructed, as he described in a notebook in 1937:

> What I want [in *The Old Century*] is – not the recovery of facts so much as the recovery of *feeling* – the emotion of experiencing things which evoked aliveness and intensity of expectation and illusion – Emotion drawn at its experience. The nostalgic quality must be sustained – Everyone will know that the nostalgia is in the remembering voice – not in the experiences as they *really were*. Memory set to music – The narrator is eloquent; transfiguring his past – his lost youth. *Flatness* may be the truth of realism, but it is not true to the magic of remembering one's youth eloquently and poetically, as I am doing.[38]

While Freud insisted that 'the only way of returning home is through recognition of early childhood trauma',[39] Sassoon resisted this dark vision. He sought to recover only the comforting feelings of returning home, not the facts. He had earlier shirked off childhood trauma in *Memoirs of a Fox-Hunting Man* by establishing Sherston as a sporting orphan who does not remember 'eloquently or poetically', or factually, his early life, thereby occluding tensions arising from sibling rivalries, his separated parents and the early death of his father. By transforming his mother-figure into the benign but distant Aunt Evelyn, Sassoon further insulates Sherston from the anxieties of the family romance. For Sherston, trauma arises from war, not childhood. The war trauma he recounted in the Sherston memoirs effectively displaces the need to revisit childhood trauma in his poetically remembered autobiography, and in this way his return home in *The Old Century* is realized through occluding childhood trauma in a cloud of gladness.

Nostalgia: Disease and Antidote

The Old Century was published in September 1938, during the anxious days of the Munich crisis, and was generally well received. Not surprisingly, Edmund Blunden called it 'a composition of delicate but decisive order, a performance governed by a faith in the fine art of writing';[40] the *Times Literary Supplement* seized upon what Sassoon described as his 'artfully artless way'[41] and found the deceptively simple reminiscences 'in their fashion nearly perfect'.[42] David Garnett described it as a book 'soaked in beauty and in the spirit of peace' which gained poignancy when placed in the context of Sassoon's earlier writing on the memories of war.[43] But the 'superior intellectuals' were not impressed,[44] which was disappointing, if not unexpected to Sassoon. In the *Spectator*, Graham Greene praised as poignant and effective the melancholy early scenes of the death of Sassoon's father, but considered the second half of the book mere 'poetical reconstruction in fictional form': not real autobiography and therefore not an accurate portrayal of the period it purports to recreate.[45] Malcolm Muggeridge called *The Old Century* 'an anaemic fairy story – something belonging to a remote past and with no bearing on the so ominous present'.[46] In his later study of Sassoon, Thorpe identifies the 'nostalgic spirit' that animates *The Old Century* and *The Weald of Youth*, suggesting that the nostalgia is not merely escapist, but rooted in the 'mad fevers' of the Second World War, though he does not pursue the intriguing implications of his insight.[47] More recently, *The Old Century* is typically read as quaint and beautiful in its way, but anachronistic,[48] and incomplete as a self-portrait because it fails to fulfil its stated intentions.[49] Sassoon's 'queer craving to revisit the past and give the modern world the slip' has left the book damned by faint praise.[50]

The book may look back to 'a remote past'; it may be nostalgic, escapist and egocentric, as critics have charged. But far from having 'no bearing on the so ominous present', Sassoon's 'queer cravings to revisit the past' are integrally related to his own immediate present, to his fear of the impending war and to his 'inescapable and unforgettable' frontline experience, which gives specific force to those fears. He fixes his gaze upon the well-head of his innocent past and is not frustrated like Narcissus, but fascinated by the calming reflection. While 'superior intellectuals' saw his self-absorption as a flaw, he saw this narcissistic inclination as the cornerstone of his autobiography's 'nostalgic quality [that] must be sustained'. The point, Sassoon implies, is not merely to afford fanciful escapism, but to offer himself and his readers a vivid reminder of the goodness of life to counter the bleakness of a present embroiled in crisis.

Sassoon's choice of diction when describing the purpose of his 'nostalgic reminiscences' is revealing: 'I wrote *The Old Century* as an antidote to the times we live in.'[51] And in retrospect, less than a year from his death in 1967, he explained that 'I wrote it as a mental release from Hitler and Mussolini – (and the war that seemed to me almost a certainty.) And I designed it as an anodyne for my fellow sufferers'.[52] As 'fellow sufferers' emphasizes, 'antidote' and 'anodyne' both have obvious pathological associations. Sassoon saw 'the times we live in' as overrun and unbalanced by scientific and technological 'advances', and oppressive to the sensitive human soul. He contrasted the dubious 'progress' of the contemporary world to the innocence of childhood, and wondered if maturing to adulthood was some 'form of malignant dementia'.[53] He related past to present, like the relation of happiness and well-being to the sufferings of modern war, through the metaphor of medication and disease.

Sassoon's expressions of nostalgia seem to derive both from eighteenth-century medical discourse (which saw nostalgia as curable, if properly treated) and from the mystification of Romantic yearning, which rendered it as essentially incurable, for from a Kantian perspective, it is the vitality and innocence of childhood that we long for, not the 'actual place' associated with it.[54] Sassoon's yearning to return home was also a yearning for place, which is exemplified in the significance of the act of revisiting specific homes from his childhood and youth in the evocation of his past in *The Old Century* and *The Weald of Youth*, and he defiantly regarded these yearnings as 'instructive adherence[s] to sanity in a (superficially) mad world'.[55]

Thus when, in the spring of 1939, Sassoon found himself anxious about the German takeover of Danzig and the Polish corridor crisis, he was also developing a means to protect his 'sanity':[56] 'The sequel to *The Old Century* . . . is in my head and will give me no peace until it is on paper.'[57] He was unable to begin the sequel until after war was declared, and in late October 1939 he announced that he was 'Back again in the old drudgery of prose-ing, I feel more than ever that it demands every bit of my vitality. One dreads and yet loves it.'[58] As in *The Old Century*, he linked his return to the past directly to the bleak present:

> I have 'at long last' made another beginning, and Volume Two is now seven days old (and not yet christened). It was the War that did it, I think. The newspapers just drove me away from 1939; and how happy I've been during my six days revisitation of 1909 . . . I have resumed operations on the delectable treadmill of nostalgic reminiscence.[59]

The 'dread' of this revisitation may well have stemmed from the dynamics of the process of recollection. While he deliberately sought to focus on happy memories, the danger of stirring up painful ones could never have been far from his consciousness. As he writes in *The Old Century*: 'I prefer to remember my own gladness and good luck, and to forget, whenever I can, those moods and minor events which made me low-spirited and unresponsive.'[60] The phrase 'whenever I can' makes clear his awareness of the contingent nature of extracting only 'delectable' memories from all that there was to be encountered on the journey to revisit the past. But as the morass of war widened, the need for nostalgia increased, while its demands on Sassoon intensified: 'The delight of being back again in that other world of transmuted memory is like coming to life again after – not being very much alive!'[61] By the end of November 1939 he had completed more than 18,000 words of

> *The Weald of Youth* – my new book of nostalgic and breezy reminiscences of 1908–1914 . . . There are passages in it which will, as I hope for Heaven, console you momentarily for the age we exist in. Too tired to continue, I am now transcribing.[62]

When the barbarism and cruelty of 'total war' became apparent to Sassoon, he began to lose faith in the civilizing potential of his autobiographical project: 'Writing a book about "nothing much happening thirty years ago" isn't easy!' he once confided to Keynes.[63] He was stalled for more than a year, and when he resumed writing in February 1941, he found the work very draining; by April he felt that he had 'altogether slaved myself to [another] standstill' writing and rewriting the manuscript.[64] He even admitted to Tomlinson that he had 'cracked up' from the strain and again questioned the relevance of his 'tame autobiographical writing' in a mad world driving him to the brink of madness, 'or at least eccentricity'.[65] Writing made him feel 'rather tired in the head' and he added that 'I don't think I shall ever have the nerve to write another prose book!'[66] But by Christmas 1941, when the Americans had joined the Allied cause and the outlook on the war had decidedly improved, Sassoon once again returned to *The Weald of Youth*, this time with new confidence in himself and what he was doing. At the end of January 1942, he wrote to Max Beerbohm about the page proofs he was sending:

> You will probably find it rather a relief to be reading a book about 'practically nothing happening' in 1909–1914. One's daily reading of the

> world's news is so consistently violent that one really does long for a day when nothing has happened.[67]

The friends who read the book first were impressed and, of course, he himself was pleased and relieved, for he said, '[it] was written with blood and sweat, with the deliberate purpose of providing mental relief to my kind readers.'[68] In *Siegfried's Journey: 1916–1920*, the volume that followed this taxing writing experience, he was unable to sustain his nostalgic vision, in part, I suggest, because his memories of that period of his life were not so easily reconstructed into the pleasant diversion of 'practically nothing happening'.

While the world of Sassoon's childhood in Kent was 'irrevocably severed' from the days of rearmament and appeasement, not to mention civilian bombing, his nostalgic inclinations formed indeed a kind of 'strategy of survival'. Sassoon insisted that this exquisite recreation of self was no mere 'fairy story' rooted in a time long past; it had 'its work' to do in the immediate present: '*The Old C[entury]* . . . is a reassurance, for decent people, that decency still exists – . . . In its artfully artless way, my book will do its work.'[69] Utility is found not simply in childhood, but in his own childhood and in the act of looking back from present chaos into that past, to be reminded that clarity and order could be imposed on the past and could exist again, or at least could be imagined to exist again. Sassoon believed *The Old Century* to be 'an instructive adherence to sanity in a (superficially) mad world'.[70] Praise he received from readers, especially soldiers in the field, validated the utility of his nostalgic introspection for the antidotal benefit of others. In *The Old Century* and *The Weald of Youth*, Sassoon fashioned from his narcissism and nostalgia literary work with which, finally, he was greatly satisfied: 'I think that the two books (really one book) are – in this way – an almost flawless achievement.'[71] Together, these two volumes create what Robert J. Lifton would call Sassoon's 'golden age',[72] a period implicitly related to the trauma he sought to repress. Lifton reiterates Rivers's notion of regression by observing that the survivor of war trauma 'must look backward as well as forward in time. His tendency to claim a personal "golden age" *prior* to the death encounter can, it is true, distort, but may also serve as a source of life-sustaining imagery now so desperately required.'[73] Sassoon saw that his own 'life-sustaining imagery' had a positive, assuaging literary and cultural function. His self-absorbed nostalgia, through an uncanny ironic inversion, is a disease become antidote, a vaccination of the present with the past. Far from evading the contingencies of the historical moment, Sassoon's later writing was immersed in the wellspring of those contingencies, and is deeply relevant to and engaged with the concerns of the modern world on the brink of disaster – not in spite of, but precisely because of its unique deployment of narcissism and nostalgia.

NOTES

1. Sassoon's friends, Ottoline Morrell, Olivier, Cockerell, Keynes and Ackerley, have all remarked on Sassoon's self-absorption and backward-looking preoccupations. See Ottoline Morrell, *Ottoline at Garsington: Memoirs of Lady Ottoline Morrell, 1915–1918*, ed. Robert Gathorne Hardy (London: Faber, 1974); Edith Olivier, *From Her Journals: 1924–48*, ed. Penelope Middelboe (London: Weidenfeld & Nicolson, 1989); Sydney Cockerell, 'Diaries', in Cockerell Papers, British Library, London; Geoffrey Keynes, *The Gates of Memory* (Oxford: Clarendon, 1981); J. R. Ackerley, My *Sister and Myself: The Diaries of J. R. Ackerley*, ed. Francis King (London: Hutchinson, 1982).
2. Regenia Gagnier, *Subjectivities: A History of Self-Representation in Britain, 1832–1920* (Oxford: Oxford University Press, 1991), p. 229.
3. Linda Anderson, *Autobiography* (London: Routledge, 2001), p. 96.
4. Ibid. p. 59.
5. Siegfried Sassoon, *The Weald of Youth* (London: Faber, 1942), p. 33. Michael Thorpe likens the 'carefully worked' and 'elevated quality' of Sassoon's prose to the prose of Pater (Michael Thorpe, *Siegfried Sassoon: A Critical Study* (Leiden: Universitaire Pers Leiden; London: Oxford University Press, 1966), p. 87). See also Paul Moeyes, *Siegfried Sassoon: Scorched Glory: A Critical Study* (New York: St Martin's, 1997), pp. 201–5.
6. Sassoon, *The Weald of Youth*, p. 33.
7. Graham Hough, 'The Paterian temperament', in *The Last Romantics* (London: Duckworth, 1949), pp. 166–74, p. 173.
8. Anderson, *Autobiography*, p. 53.
9. John Keats to Richard Woodhouse, letter, 27 October 1818, in Maurice Forman (ed.), *The Letters of John Keats*, 2nd edn (Oxford: Oxford University Press, 1935), p. 227.
10. In the letter to George Beaumont, Wordsworth goes on to justify himself: 'It is not self-conceit . . . but real humility . . . I was unprepared to treat any more arduous subject and diffident of my own powers' (William Wordsworth to George Beaumont, letter, 1 May 1805, in Ernest de Selincourt (ed.), *The Letters of William and Dorothy Wordsworth*, 2nd edn, vol. 1 (Oxford: Clarendon, 1967), p. 536). By masking self-indulgence with diffidence, Wordsworth serves as a model for Sassoon's own quiet defence of casting and recasting of his own past experience into literary form.
11. Stephen Spender, *The Struggle of the Modern* (Berkeley, CA: University of California Press, 1963), p. 33.
12. Quoted in Paul Fussell, *The Great War and Modern Memory* (New York: Oxford University Press), p. 205.
13. See Siegfried Sassoon, *Letters to a Critic*, ed. Michael Thorpe (Nettlestead, Kent: Bridge, Conachar, 1976).
14. Siegfried Sassoon to Ellis Roberts, letter, 9 September 1936, Sassoon Collection, Harry Ransom Humanities Research Center (HRHRC), University of Texas, Austin.
15. See W. H. R. Rivers, 'Psycho-Therapeutics', in James Hastings (ed.), *Encyclopedia of Religion and Ethics*, vol. 10 (New York: Scribner's, n.d.), p. 437, as I have discussed in Chapters 2 and 3.
16. Siegfried Sassoon, quoted in James F. Stewart, *A Descriptive Account of Unpublished Letters of Siegfried Sassoon in the University of Texas Collection*, diss., University of Texas, Austin (Ann Arbor, MI: UMI, 1972), p. 235.
17. Besides Rivers (in *Instinct and the Unconscious*), who cites Hughlings Jackson's influence, see Freud ('On narcissism: an introduction', in James Strachey (trans.)

and Angela Richards (ed.), *On Metapsychology* (London: Penguin, 1991), pp. 59–97; 'A childhood recollection from *Dichtung und Wahrheit*', in James Strachey (trans.) and Albert Dickson (ed.), *Art and Literature* (London: Penguin, 1991); *Beyond the Pleasure Principle*, in James Strachey (trans.) and Angela Richards (ed.), *On Metapsychology* (London: Penguin, 1991), pp. 269–338); and Abram Kardiner and Herbert Spiegel, *War Stress and Neurotic Illness* (New York: Hoeber, 1947). All identify narcissistic and nostalgic tendencies as symptoms common to regressive neuroses. Ferenczi et al. focus on narcissism and war neuroses (Sandor Ferenczi, Karl Abraham, Ernst Simmel and Ernest Jones, *Psycho-Analysis and the War Neuroses* (London: International Psychoanalytical Press, 1921)).

18. W. H. R. Rivers, *Instinct and the Unconscious*, 2nd edn (Cambridge: Cambridge University Press, 1924), p. 148.
19. Ibid. pp. 149–54.
20. Siegfried Sassoon, *Collected Poems: 1908–1956* (London: Faber & Faber, 1961), p. 251.
21. Sassoon to Ruth and Henry Head, letter, 3 November 1936, Sassoon Collection, Harry Ransom Humanities Research Center (HRHRC), University of Texas, Austin.
22. Sassoon, *Letters to Max Beerbohm*, ed. Rupert Hart-Davis (London: Faber & Faber), 1986, p. 30.
23. Siegfried Sassoon, *The Old Century* (London: Faber & Faber), pp. 11–12.
24. Sigmund Freud, 'A childhood recollection', p. 325.
25. Sassoon, *Collected Poems*, p. 243.
26. George Sandys, *Ovid's Metamorphosis: Englished, Mythologized, and Represented in Figures*, ed. Karl Hulley and Stanley Vandersall (Lincoln: University of Nebraska Press, 1970), p. 140.
27. Sassoon, *The Old Century*, p. 12.
28. Sassoon, *Collected Poems*, p. 257.
29. Ibid. p. 257.
30. Freud, 'On narcissism', p. 80.
31. Ferenczi et al., *Psycho-Analysis and the War Neuroses*, p. 18.
32. Ibid. p. 23.
33. Siegfried Sassoon, *Diaries 1915–1918*, ed. Rupert Hart-Davis (London: Faber & Faber, 1983), p. 96.
34. Morrell, *Ottoline at Garsington*, p. 183.
35. Sassoon, *Diaries 1915–1918*, p. 217.
36. Ferenczi et al., p. 18.
37. Sassoon, *The Old Century*, p. 233.
38. Unpublished notes from Sassoon's 1937 Rapallo diary, held at Harry Ransom Humanities Research Center, University of Texas (HRHRC), Austin. Most of the Rapallo diary was published in *Letters to Max Beerbohm* (1986).
39. Quoted in Svetlana Boym, *The Future of Nostalgia* (New York: Basic, 2001), p. 54.
40. Edmund Blunden, 'Siegfried Sassoon – early years', rev. of *The Old Century* by Siegfried Sassoon, *London Mercury*, October 1938, pp. 570–2, p. 570.
41. Siegfried Sassoon to Hardcastle, letter, 29 October 1938, Sassoon Collection, Harry Ransom Humanities Research Center, University of Texas, Austin.
42. Cyril Falls, 'Education of a poet: Mr. Sassoon's first years', rev. of *The Old Century* by Siegfried Sassoon, *Times Literary Supplement*, 24 September 1938, p. 615.
43. David Garnett, rev. of *The Old Century* by Siegfried Sassoon, *New Statesman and Nation*, 17 September 1938, p. 418.
44. Sassoon to Keynes, letter, 23 December 1935.
45. Graham Greene, 'A lost Arcadia', rev. of *The Old Century* by Siegfried Sassoon, *Spectator*, 16 September 1938, p. 449.

46. Malcolm Muggeridge, 'Poet's memories: Mr Siegfried Sassoon's autobiography', in the *Daily Telegraph*, 20 September 1938.
47. John Stuart Roberts, *Siegfried Sassoon: 1886–1967* (London: Cohen, 1999), pp. 132, 227.
48. Sanford Sternlicht, *Siegfried Sassoon* (New York: Twayne, 1993), p. 95.
49. Paul Moeyes, *Siegfried Sassoon*, p. 198; Roberts, *Siegfried Sassoon*, p. 266.
50. Sassoon, *The Old Century*, p. 128. See, for example, Thorpe (*Siegfried Sassoon*, p. 132), Fussell (*Great War*, p. 92), Moeyes (*Siegfried Sassoon*, p. 208), Roberts (*Siegfried Sassoon*, p. 267), all of whom cite this line.
51. Sassoon to Hardcastle, letter, 2 October 1938.
52. Siegfried Sassoon, *Letters to a Critic*, ed. Michael Thorpe (Nettlestead, Kent: Bridge, Conachar, 1976), p. 20.
53. Sassoon to Keynes, letter, 18 November 1938.
54. Jean Starobinski, 'The idea of nostalgia', *Diogenes*, 54, 1966, pp. 81–103, p. 94.
55. Sassoon to Hardcastle, letter, 29 October 1938.
56. Quoted in Stewart, *Unpublished Letters*, p. 35.
57. Sassoon to Keynes, letter, 28 April 1939.
58. Sassoon quoted in Viola Meynell (ed.), *The Best of Friends: Further Letters to Sydney Carlyle Cockerell* (London: Hart-Davis, 1956), p. 74.
59. Sassoon, *Letters to Max Beerbohm*, pp. 80–1.
60. Sassoon, *The Old Century*, p. 233.
61. Sassoon, *Letters to Max Beerbohm*, p. 81.
62. Ibid. p. 83.
63. Sassoon to Keynes, letter, 1 April 1941.
64. Ibid. 1 April 1941.
65. Quoted in Stewart, *Unpublished Letters*, p. 249.
66. Sassoon to Keynes, letter, 1 April 1941. He had embarked upon *The Old Century* in the middle 1930s, when he required an 'antidote' to the contemporary situation, and he began working on *The Weald of Youth* with similar motivations after the fall of Poland, breaking off writing for the first time just before the Fall of France. He did not resume writing until the short-lived British victories in Libya in early 1941, and broke off again with news of British losses to Rommel's army. The war was going badly and so was his project to escape from it into the past.
67. Sassoon, *Letters to Max Beerbohm*, p. 90.
68. Siegfried Sassoon to Sydney Carlyle Cockerell, letter, 24 August 1942, Sassoon Collection, Harry Ransom Humanities Research Center (HRHRC), University of Texas, Austin.
69. Sassoon to Hardcastle, letter, 29 October 1938.
70. Ibid. 29 October 1938.
71. Sassoon to Keynes, letter, 6 October 1942.
72. Robert J. Lifton is now seen as a pioneering figure in trauma studies (Robert J. Lifton, *The Broken Connection* (New York: Simon & Schuster, 1979), p. 178).
73. Ibid. p. 178.

7

LIMINAL MOMENTS, UNCANNY SPACES: SASSOON'S AUTOBIOGRAPHY AND THE MODERN SUBJECT

The Threshold

At crucial points in his autobiographical project, Sassoon recounts physically returning to specific sites of his past, which generate recurring symbols and tropes of longing and provoke fascinating, uncanny collisions between present and prior selves.

On the verge of such confrontations, often announced by the image of a threshold, Sassoon apprehends a spatial and temporal gap, a liminal moment of heightened perception of subjectivity. I contend that Sassoon's engagement with these uncanny spaces, at once distantly familiar and strangely new, demonstrates fissures in his pseudo-Victorian model of aesthetics that reveal an unexpected affinity for the modernist preoccupation with representing fragmented subjectivity.

Once again, Rivers offers a personal and psychological context for two rich literary symbols prevalent in Sassoon's autobiographical writing: the unconscious configured as a room, and the stairway as a means to gain access to its threshold. In *Instinct and the Unconscious*, Rivers describes in uncharacteristically vivid visual detail an interior space remembered from childhood, observing that he has 'a more definite knowledge of the topography of the house I left at the age of five than of any of the many I have lived in since'.[1] He attributes this fact to the innately visual nature of childhood mental development, a quality subsumed by the formation of his abstract, scientific way of thinking. In the course of his exploration of this recollected domestic space, Rivers discovers that his knowledge of the house was limited to certain areas, and some rooms he could no longer visualize at all:

> So far as I remember the house had three floors. I can remember, and even now image fairly vividly, every room, passage and doorway of the ground-floor. I can in imagination go downstairs into a kitchen in a basement and I can go upstairs towards the upper floor, but when I reach the top of the stairs I come to the absolutely unknown, an unknown far more complete than is the case with any house occupied more recently.[2]

The completeness of the 'unknown' intrigues and fascinates him: 'For more than two years I have been attempting, by means which have succeeded in evoking other early experience, to penetrate into the mysterious unknown of the upper storey.'[3] But he cannot 'explain the completeness of the blank left by the memories of the upper storey' through any rational discourse,[4] finally attributing this phenomenon of blankness to a migration of experience from his conscious mind to the unconscious. He comes to consider the conscious mind's 'suppression' of experience into the unconscious characteristic of both childhood experience and the conditions of war:

> [Early life] is especially apt to afford occasions for experiences to become unconscious, but the passing of experience into the unconscious may happen at any age, and its occurrence has been brought to notice very widely by the experience of war. One of the most frequent features of the nervous disturbances of war has been the complete blotting out of the memories of certain events, the obliteration usually extending considerably beyond the event which furnished its special occasion.[5]

The image of Rivers facing 'the absolutely unknown' at the top of the stairs in his childhood home conveys his own suppression of an 'especially unpleasant event' in a richly literary way that resonates in Sassoon's interwar and Second World War autobiographical writings.

Henry Head, who had become a 'father-figure' to Sassoon after Rivers's death, was impressed by the psychological acuity of the central trope of 'A Short Story', an uncollected poem published in *Country Life* in February 1926, when for the first time since shortly after the Armistice Sassoon addressed his lingering experience of trauma. A narrative of twenty-two lines in mixed metre, the poem begins at four in the morning with a young woman knocking at the door of her visiting uncle's room; he is her only connection with her happy childhood in Kent. His visit has been precipitated by a crisis in her married life that severed her physically and psychologically from the blooming gardens of her childhood and youth. She waits on the threshold to 'the door of the top-floor room' to gain through this uncle the 'dahlia-guarded gates of long ago' and the 'days all happy and lost to sight'.[6] Head was 'delighted' by this poem and admired the economy of its narrative and the subtle expression of 'emotional stress'.[7] He liked particularly 'the selection of a moment outside the door of a room as its central point. Psychologically, you are certainly right . . . I hope you will be able to do more work on these lines which, except for some of Hardy's poems, strikes a new vein.'[8] Both the poet and the young woman in the poem were entranced by the aura of innocence of their Kentish childhood; both experienced some kind of trauma as adults that has severed them from this past. The moment at the doorway of a mysterious upper room represents a reaching out to an unconscious aspect of self that offers the possibility of insight into the nature of the rupture between the past and present, and of a return to either the pleasures of the distant past which compel the journey to that room in the first place, or the torments of the more recent traumatized past, which provoke a hesitation at the door. It is a moment rich with symbolic potential, as Head implied, a liminal moment of heightened psychological significance.

The moment of hesitation at the doorway functions as a recurring trope in Sassoon's autobiographical writing. Such moments often represent a reaching out to a past self that offers the fleeting possibility of insight into the nature of the rupture between the past and present. Threshold moments represent conflicted opportunities. First there is the sought-after opportunity to recollect the pleasures of the distant past, which motivates the journey to the memory-laden space behind the door. At the same time, the doorway represents the distinct possibility of reliving the torments of the more recent traumatized past, which provokes a hesitation before the door. Though new for Sassoon, such tropes have a rich lineage, including many of his English contemporaries; examples of imagining physical spaces as rooms of uncharted unconscious are prevalent in writers like Hardy, Edward Thomas, E. M. Forster and Virginia Woolf. Henri Lefebvre describes the door as 'Transitional, symbolic and functional, [an] object . . . [that] serves to bring a space, the space of a "room," say, . . . to an end . . . the threshold . . . of an entrance is another transitional object, one which has traditionally enjoyed an almost ritual significance.'[9] In Sassoon's writing the door functions as both symbol and point of transition. Liminal moments at the doorway awaken the kind of 'almost ritual significance' that Gaston Bachelard articulates in the *Poetics of Space*: 'How concrete everything becomes in the world of the spirit when an object, a mere door, can give images of hesitation, temptation, desire, security, welcome and respect. If one were to give an account of all the doors one has closed and opened, of all the doors one would like to re-open, one would have to tell the story of one's entire life.'[10] By physically returning to key spaces in his past, Sassoon is able to 're-open' those doors precisely in order to 'tell the story of his entire life', including those parts once concealed and inaccessible behind closed doors.

Sassoon's negotiation of spatial and temporal returns marks the chief way his highly subjective and seemingly anachronistic literary aesthetic participates in the literary modernism of his contemporaries. The thematic end to which Sassoon manipulates his imagery of domestic space is perhaps most closely connected to the mode of Marcel Proust, whose *Swann's Way* in Scott-Moncrieff's translation Sassoon had read several times by 1925, finding it 'one of the most stimulating books' he had encountered in recent years.[11] Reminiscences, especially those surrounding the imagery of domestic space, function in Sassoon's autobiographical project in a Proust-like fashion, allowing him to plumb the depths of the self, to tell in Bachelard's terms, 'the story of one's entire life'.

INTERIORS

In 'Farewell to a Room' in *The Heart's Journey* (1928), Sassoon combines his efforts to articulate his true self with the notion of the liminal moment that Head encouraged him to explore. The poem begins on the threshold:

> Room, while I stand outside you in the gloom,
> Your tranquil-toned interior, void of me,
> Seems part of my own self, which I can see.[12]

From the doorway, he observes that the room, of which he is a part, 'has housed so much / Nor hand, nor eye, nor intellect could touch –';[13] it has housed, in other words, the unconscious. He calls this space 'Cell',[14] and in his address to it he contends that

> Could I condense five winters in one thought,
> Then might I know my unknown self and tell
> What our confederate silences have wrought.[15]

Rivers had attributed to the unconscious the ability to condense many meanings and experiences into a single image or thought.[16] But in this case, the poet seems to stand outside the unconscious, lacking the power to 'condense' five years of experience, and cannot 'know my unknown self' – or selves – beyond the threshold. In coaxing meaning from a spatial representation of the unconscious Sassoon is, like Rivers, unsuccessful in recollecting his childhood home.

The idea of identity as a confederation of selves is configured in the imagery of domestic interiors in 'Past and Present',[17] which Sassoon considered 'one of my best and most characteristic poems':[18]

> My past has gone to bed. Upstairs in clockless rooms
> My past is fast asleep. But mindsight reillumes
> Here in my ruminant head the days where dust lies deep.[19]

The upstairs room is dark and ill-equipped to measure time, which invokes the unconscious, that timeless space where the past rests.[20] Through 'mindsight' the poet illuminates the dusty past at the centre of the unconscious, stirring the hollow 'inhabitants' of the 'rooms': 'Sleep-walkers empty-eyed com[ing] strangely down the stairs. / They are my selves.'[21] These selves that the poet beholds are endowed with the virtues and foibles of youth: pride, passion, vehement dedication. To the 'brooding' middle-aged poet they betoken a lost innocence and unworldliness: 'I know not when they died, / Those ignorant selves,'[22] but he does know that time and mutability – the 'dust' that lies deep in the room they inhabit – separate him from lost vitality. 'Dwindling, they disappear,'[23] 'ignorant' of their transformation into the older, 'ruminant' self that now wistfully observes them. Sassoon is content to conjure up these past selves, noting their multiplicity, but he offers no attempt to explain their fleeting reappearance from the upstairs rooms, nor the gulf that separates the present self from the values they represent.

In *The Old Century*, which he began not long after the publication of 'Past and Present', Sassoon remains concerned with the recovery of the past, and in the Edingthorpe chapter (Book I, Chapter 8) invokes precisely the imagery and location of 'My past has gone to bed.' His friends praised it as 'miraculous', and Sassoon himself considered it 'one of the best things I ever wrote'.[24] The passage begins before Sassoon reaches the Norfolk rectory that his mother used to rent for part of the summer, with him imagining 'by some chronological miracle my 1937 self' returning in the summer of 1897, when Sassoon would have been almost 11, to the house in Kent where he was born:[25]

> Waiting outside the front door . . . [r]inging the bell and asking to be allowed to walk in and have a look at one's past! All the world would like to do that, for the sense of the past is strong in us – as strong as our awareness of the irredeemable errors in it.[26]

Once again, there is a moment of striking psychological tension upon the threshold, as Sassoon considers the past and 'the irredeemable errors in it'.

The reclamation of childhood joys is not an easy task, and in contemplating the Edingthorpe rectory Sassoon records a frustration similar to Rivers's in his attempt to remember the upper rooms of his childhood home:

> To transfer myself to Edingthorpe should have been scarcely the work of a moment. But when I tried to do so, mind-sight was unable to recreate the place. It had been a transient experience, and for many years I had almost forgotten about it . . . Edingthorpe gradually became a memory which haunted my mind, but I couldn't see it at all distinctly.[27]

He then decides simply 'to transfer myself back there in my motor car';[28] perhaps seeing the place again will help him penetrate the deep, dim region of his mind where this aspect of his past has sunk. Sassoon notes no irony in the modern mode of transport that propels his nostalgic voyage. The 'chronological miracle' of venturing back forty years is managed by a modern journey over space, as the mature man revisits a site of childhood, after the manner of Proust, though with a crucial difference. Proust writes in the last volume of *Recherche*:

> I was distressed to see how little I relived my early years. I found the Vivonne [river] narrow and ugly alongside the towpath. Not that I noticed any great physical discrepancies from what I remembered. But, separated as I was by a whole lifetime from places I now happened to be passing through again, there was lacking between them and me that contiguity from which is born, even before we have perceived it, the immediate, delicious, and total deflagration of memory.[29]

Whereas Marcel finds disappointment in his return's incapacity to deflagrate, to 'flame up' his memory, Sassoon savours a kind of immediacy when he reaches the Rectory at Edingthorpe: 'My memory of the house had been like an old photograph, obsolete and empty. But when I leant my elbows on the front gate I saw a fragment of 1897 quite clearly.'[30] While the outcomes differ, the older Marcel and the older Sassoon share the same hopeful expectations of spatial contiguity that cannot be realized.

The imaginative return to the past proves full of psychological complications of regret and longing for impossible change in Sassoon:

> In mind-sight we return: but even if in more than mind-sight we could somehow be there in the actuality of outlived experience, we should be strangers, invisible, and powerless to avert so much as the overwinding of a clock . . . Not by one faintest whisper could we safeguard our vanished self while he gaily or sullenly created the sorrow and bitterness of after days.[31]

Sassoon resorts, not for the first time in his memoirs, to the terms and images from his poems: 'mind-sight', past selves as 'strangers', and the persistent wistful fantasizing about what is recognized as impossible – seizing the past and altering it. But in this passage, as in his entire autobiographical project – poems, prose, diaries and letters – there is yearning for the ever-elusive but potentially redemptive Proustian regaining of lost time, which by the 1930s had become for Sassoon identical with his quest for self-knowledge and mastery.

During his return to Edingthorpe, the mature Sassoon catches a glimpse of his younger self as a boy, but before doing so he visits the village churchyard and pauses before its small war memorial: 'Here, surely was the gate to the past toward which I had made this pilgrimage.'[32] The gravestone of a young lance-corporal proclaims the devastating battles that preceded Sassoon's own service in France: 'Mons, Le Cateau, The Marne, The Aisne, The First Battle of

Ypres'.[33] The date of the soldier's death reminds Sassoon of his brother Hamo, who also died in the autumn of 1915. He recalls a scene from childhood in which his mother had warned Hamo, '"Don't let the donkeys eat the laurels."'[34] This recollection is followed by a Freudian free association typical of the unconscious: 'Laurels and donkeys. The donkeys who made the Great War were generous with their laurels, I thought.'[35] But he curtails this line of bitter reflection and, proceeding along the well-remembered path, 'encounters' his 'vanished' incarnation reading H. G. Wells's *The Invisible Man* under the shade of a tree. This youthful self, he notes, 'knows nothing of [his older self]' or the 'delusions and discontents' he must yet muddle through, nor of the war and the 'war-memorial' in the village churchyard.[36]

Unlike the poem 'Past and Present', where the source of the gulf that divides the older from the younger self is implicit, here the war is openly invoked through the image of the 'war-memorial'. The structure of this scene, with its site of commemoration and compelling invitation to remember the war dead, provides a model of Sassoon's method of recuperating his past. It is an uncanny model. Expanding Freud's observations of the double, Nicholas Royle describes the uncanny as 'a sense of ourselves as double, split, at odds with ourselves'.[37] To gain imaginative access to enchanted childhood and youth (an idealized version of the past, as he readily admits), he must first acknowledge the 'unforgettable and inescapable' existence of his memories of war experience. That is, he must acknowledge the uncanny splitting of his fragmented subjectivity and grapple with the temporal contiguity of idealizing and traumatizing memories. Avoidance of those painful memories will not really spare him, for the specific traumas not explicitly recognized will only distort his sense of both the present and the past. Having in effect acknowledged and honoured these memories by engaging with the war-memorial, he is able to imagine how his present self might explain the confluence of past and present incarnations to his childhood self, mystified by his 'resuscitation' from the past into his future: 'the word resuscitation . . . means "to imbue one's past life with saturations of subsequent experience."'[38] The bland term 'subsequent experience' belies the physical and psychological hardships of his ineluctable involvement in the war and its aftermaths.

In 'Past and Present' he had written of his past selves' unawareness of him as he is now – 'Me they do not foresee'.[39] In the Edingthorpe chapter of *The Old Century*, he writes of his childhood self in the same language:

> Me he does not foresee, with my queer craving to revisit the past and give the modern world the slip. Thus we are together – the boy I like to be remembering and the man he might have liked to be with, could he but have known me, his completed self.[40]

This sense of completion and integration is absent in the poem, where 'Sleepwalkers empty-eyed come strangely down the stairs' while the present self can only 'brood', watching them dwindle and disappear, unable to forge a connection.[41] In the Edingthorpe passage, the boy and the man 'are together', at least for the moment, united by the man's willingness to admit into the scene his troubling and formative experience in spite of his desire to 'give the modern world the slip'. The fundamental difficulty in his project of self-expression, which both blocked and inspired his 'revisiting' of past scenes, was his complicity through experience and history in the modern world he so longed to escape. He is modern in so far as he is shaped by his experience of modern war and its traumatizing consequences. Only through the deliberate effort to retrieve the distant peaceful past by returning to its surviving sites or spaces, bypassing the lingering after-effects of the intervening traumatic years, could he combat the sense of modern fragmentation and hope to feel reunited with his younger selves. But he could do so only sporadically.

Sassoon concludes the Edingthorpe chapter by recounting how he turned back and, opening a door in the kitchen-garden wall, sat down, like his younger self, by a lime tree and allowed his mind to wander. The resuscitation of his past at Edingthorpe has run its course: 'The house didn't seem to have much to say to me now.'[42] But the house, with its upper storeys, interior spaces and thresholds, remained a resonant metaphor for him. Driven by a potent mix of nostalgia and hope, Sassoon returns in his Second World War writings to the trope of the threshold, with its promise of recovering the past and the rueful recognition of the elusive and ephemeral nature of this recovery.

Atop the Stairs

The Weald of Youth, begun in the autumn of 1939 within weeks of the declaration of war, offers another poignant example of how the liminal moment, combined with the return to a remembered location, serves the process of self-recovery. The setting involves Sassoon's rooms in the Raymond Buildings, Gray's Inn, in central London, which he rented in the months before the beginning of the First World War, and features two key moments of return: one in the hot summer of 1914 before war was declared, and the other in the autumn of 1941. Originally found for him in 1914 by Edward Marsh, then editor of *Georgian Poetry* and private secretary to Winston Churchill, these rooms at the top of a winding staircase represented the aesthetic inner poetic self Sassoon was trying to cultivate. Decorated beyond his means but furnished sparsely, this carefully designed space was meant to foster his poetic aspirations, but it failed to comfort or inspire. A scene from the book's opening chapter foreshadows the significance of these two heightened moments of return to Sassoon's vexing rooms on the top floor of the Raymond Buildings, a space at once full of promise and frustration.

Sassoon describes his 1907 meeting with the magazine editor T. W. H. Crosland to discuss the prospect of his first substantial poetic publication:

> there I was, sprucely but soberly dressed, climbing the steep stairs to the unexpectedly poky office of the liveliest of the literary weeklies. Climbing also, I hoped, toward poetic reputation.[43]

At the top of the stairs he experiences a liminal moment, as he pauses before the doorway to Crosland's office then 'blunder[s]' in, tripping over the hidden step.[44] His interview seemed at first a 'veritable triumph', as he had nine sonnets accepted, but ultimately it became a kind of blunder, as not all of the poems were printed and the promised payment never materialized.[45] Seven years later, Sassoon's poetic career is not much advanced. He describes how he settled into his new rooms at Gray's Inn after the most successful hunting season of his life, having placated, he hoped, the needs of his 'outdoor self'. Once again he focuses on climbing stairs, this time to his own rooms:

> Latch-key in hand, I went briskly up the twisty stone stairway to the fourth floor of 1 Raymond Buildings. It was my first night there, so I stood for a moment looking at my name, painted in neat letters above the outer door, the solidity of which I observed with proprietary satisfaction.[46]

After pausing at the doorway, he crosses the threshold and 'survey[s] the interior',[47] which he fondly connects with his aspirations for his 'poetic self' and with the unconscious, where he believed the creative energies mysteriously resided.[48] Then he notes a fine 'rosewood clock . . . more expensive than I had intended' that tells the time in 'melodious chime[s]', recalling him to the realities of conscious life, routine and discipline. Sassoon's interest in the materiality of the world, and its grim and gritty details which would so animate his later war poetry, was, before the war, a distraction from his insubstantial fantasy of poetry effortlessly flowing from his pen, inspired by the elegance of his interior décor. The letters on the outer door promised solidity, but the rich potential of the tasteful interior was not to be realized. Within three months of moving in, Sassoon joined the army and the First World War began.

The second key moment of return to the Raymond Buildings narrated in *The Weald of Youth* takes place during the Second World War. While completing the first draft, Sassoon visited London in the autumn of 1941 for the first time since the war began. He had by this time almost finished writing about the London of his youth and the unrealized expectations of his residence at Gray's Inn. Worried by reports of bomb damage in the late summer air raids,[49] he returned to check on the state of that place which still meant much to him. Noting the heavy military traffic on Theobald's Road, over which his old rooms looked, he approached them with trepidation:[50]

> it was not until the autumn of 1941 that I again climbed the stairs to my former flat. I then discovered that mutability had done its work with Germanic thoroughness. The solid outer door remained, but the interior

> had vanished. My top-floor rooms were the only part of Raymond Buildings which had been completely destroyed.[51]

Twenty-seven years after he took possession of the rooms, he again climbed the winding stairs, only to experience a genuinely shocking version of his recurrent moment upon the threshold; 'the interior had vanished' and with it the tangible link to the past. Though these rooms were sites of frustration, Sassoon had invested them with his youthful, if ineffectual, poetic aspirations. These rooms were beloved because so redolent of this prior self, innocent of the fragmenting experience of modern war. They were destroyed not by Sassoon's return and a discrepancy of expectations, but by the return of modern war and its reiteration of traumatic, fragmenting experience. The innocent pre-war self Sassoon sought in his physical return to the Raymond Buildings had vanished, become as inaccessible as the destroyed apartment once so connected to his innocent aspirations.

Revisiting spaces of personal significance was important to Sassoon. Perhaps this contiguity could enkindle a flaming up of memory and offer a glimpse, however fleeting, of that quasi-mystical experience of time regained. In his 'miraculous' vision at Edingthorpe in 1937, the past unrolled before him like a legible scroll: 'how easily it showed myself as I once was'.[52] He found the village less changed than he was, and saw no one to distract him as he wandered about, 'open to the past and its harmonious vibrations'.[53] On his last visit to Gray's Inn in 1941 he wandered about a site transformed inharmoniously by war. After discovering his destroyed rooms, he descended the stairs, hoping the gardens might offer a more solid link to the past and to his self within that past. There he found debris accumulated in the grounds. The contents of private interior spaces – solicitors' offices – were scattered among the wreckage of aerial bombardments in the public space of the gardens. An apparently random discovery adds resonance to what he had written in the manuscript of his book shortly before coming to London:

> Pottering sadly around Gray's Inn gardens I picked up a much damaged but decipherable legal document – one of many which were lying about among the ruins of burnt-out offices. I was surprised to find that it referred to the will of a man named Sparrow; for I had already written the passage in which I have compared myself to one of those birds. Why that name, of all others? I wondered.[54]

Sassoon's question is answered by a kind of syllogism. Sassoon is a sparrow; sparrow is the name on the will; therefore, Sassoon is linked to a legal document concerned with mortality and one's legacy. Comparing himself to a bird invokes the obvious symbolism of freedom, but in the context of this discovery the symbol is ironically undercut and serves to reinforce the pervasiveness of mortality. While Gray's Inn does not resuscitate the past as Edingthorpe did, it does trigger a psychological illumination. In his elegant but creatively barren rooms in the Raymond Buildings, the young Sassoon was ignorant of mortality and incapable of writing. The older Sassoon realizes symbolically through his discovery that experience and encounters with mortality are necessary aspects of a fuller sense of subjectivity. This realization he reluctantly accepts. It is noteworthy that Sassoon compares himself not simply to a will document but to a 'much damaged' document: one might say a document fragmented by the experience of modern war, much as Sassoon was.

In ' "The Uncanny" ', Freud cites Schelling's famous definition of the term; it is the disturbing experience of 'something which ought to have remained hidden but has come to light'.[55] In Sassoon's autobiographies, Edingthorpe village of 1897 and his rooms in the Raymond Buildings of 1914 are in precisely this way uncanny spaces. They are uncanny because they invoke subjectivity as split, double, at odds with itself, and reify the unsettling realization that a return can only confirm the breach with past incarnations of self. The trauma of war ought to remain hidden, but as the war memorial at Edingthorpe and the destroyed apartment in the Raymond Buildings attest, it is ever lurking, poised to emerge into the light.

Constructing the Mature 'Sassoon'

The passage in *The Weald of Youth* in which Sassoon refers to himself as a sparrow occurs in his account of a chance meeting in the London Zoo on a summer day in 1914 before the declaration of war. Helen Wirgman, an old friend of the Thornycrofts, comes in *The Weald of Youth* to represent the matured, knowledgeable self Sassoon desires to be. That day at the zoo, following an afternoon concert, he brings 'Wirgie' back with him for tea at Gray's Inn – his very first guest there. He complains about lacking the power to improve himself, and these complaints plunge Wirgie into dejection, which drives him into a deeper and safer interior space – the kitchen – to 'wash-up' and avoid her:[56]

> And after that I see her sitting alone and silent; alone with her inscrutable cognizance and understanding, in comparison with which I knew no more about life than a sparrow in Gray's Inn gardens.[57]

From the vantage point of 1941, Sassoon sees in Wirgie qualities he could not see before the world wars – the sad knowledge of experience that he has gained through all he has endured since 1914, especially the Western Front and his own survival into the new war. The older Sassoon – the recollecting autobiographer – establishes Wirgie as a mirror into which his younger self could have gazed, had he the gumption to confirm the elder self's vision of experience to come: 'She could have told me of change and recurrence; but I should not have understood [then].'[58] While the mature Wirgie has understood the inevitability of change and recurrence through her thoughtful and quiet experience of life, Sassoon's understanding would come through the traumatic shock of modern war and its ensuing recurrence, both psychological and historical, which distorts but does not erase Wirgie's relevance. The strength of his desire to see continuity between the lessons of Wirgie's maturity and his own is the strength of his nostalgic desire to forge connections with his pre-1914 life.

Sassoon recalls her attempt in 1914, while he was hidden in the kitchen washing up, to rebut his self-absorbed and short-sighted negativism about the possibility of self-development, but only now does he understand what, he believes, she had understood already:

> I can infer from that then half-audible monologue that she was testifying – to an unheeding audience of her vanished selves – the inexpressible futility of explaining to the young those things which they will never find out until they have discovered the truth by knocking their heads against it.[59]

The striking similarity of language between his depiction of Wirgie and his writing about himself and his search for self-understanding that I have discussed – expressed in terms of his many 'vanished selves' – is further evidence of her role in the narrative as a representative of, and model for, his mature self. He can understand retrospectively that aspects of herself had, like his rooms at Gray's Inn, vanished from sight beneath the accumulation of life experience, but not without leaving significant traces.

A postcard from Wirgie the next day failed still to communicate to the young Sassoon what he was not ready yet to absorb. She had written:

> Someone – I can't remember who – said that we see clearly a second time through the spectacles of experience. My own experience is that half one's life is spent in trying to understand things and the other half in trying to make people understand what one has learnt.[60]

By emphasizing the optics of experience, as it were, these words are Proustian, but 'the wisdom of this message was wasted on me,'[61] Sassoon writes, noting that at the time his main reaction was admiration of Wirgie's handwriting. Only now, with his own vision enhanced by experience, can he properly endeavour to understand the lessons of his own life as he understands what she had tried to tell him about the process. His fondness for returning to familiar places after many years, for brooding over the past and apparently needing to tell it again in different modes, shows his determination 'to see clearly', as Wirgie had, paraphrasing Ibsen, 'a second time through the spectacles of experience'.[62] It is important too that this wisdom, so crucial to his personal development, is seen to come from Wirgie, a friend firmly rooted in his personal and emotional life, and not directly from Ibsen's philosophical position; he is moved by and trusts knowledge gained through the emotions more than through the intellect.

Ghosts of Selves Past

Time and experience, which could potentially foster the self-understanding that led to growth, wisdom and maturity, also led to an accumulation of past selves that haunted Sassoon's present. In the sonnet 'While Reading a Ghost Story', which was inspired by his reading of James's *The Turn of the Screw*, he shifts the liminal moment from doorstep to a window sill and illustrates the persistence of his haunting. In his room at midnight, the poet seeks relief from a tense, anxious mood and throws open a window. Outside, 'nothing monstrous' moves, 'nothing mars.'[63] The book he has been reading lies open, its theme ringing through his head: '*Corrupt revisitation by the dead*'.[64] Emphasized by italics, the line fuses the anxiety evoked by James's story and the capacity for anxiety rooted in the poet/reader's own traumatic experiences; for has not he himself been frequently revisited by the dead?[65] The sonnet's sestet can be read as a conflated vision responding to both James's story and Sassoon's own haunted past, each readily configured in images of domestic space:

> Old houses have their secrets. Passions haunt them.
> When day's celestials go, abhorred ones taunt them.
> Inside our habitation darkness dwells.[66]

'Old houses' can refer to Bly or to Heytesbury House, but most importantly it refers to the body that houses the unconscious – 'our habitation' in which 'darkness dwells' – and it is the power of literary and emotional fusion suggested by this conflation that moves him to open a window and seek relief, escape, refreshment. With his mood tainted by the darkness of the book he was reading, the poet cannot bear to enlist these 'abhorred' spirits within himself, even fleetingly, to advance his quest for self-knowledge.

Similarly, in 'Sanctuary', a poem written shortly after the end of the Second World War, Sassoon invokes the imagery of domestic space to depict the intensity of a past he cannot accommodate:

> I shall find the door –
> Somewhere across the labyrinth of my mind –
> Where fool events can follow me no more
> And everyday attritions fall behind.
> Freed from these dullard meddlings with my brain,
> I shall wake again.[67]

The future tense that runs through this stanza in effect creates the pause on the threshold, enforcing a mode of contemplation over action. The 'fool events' and treacheries, from which he will contrive to escape, presumably refer to his traumatic past as well as the quotidian tumults of married life, which were causing him profound distress at the time.[68] From these, the 'invisible door' – a kind of spiritual gateway to a 'sanctuaried place' full of love – will release him. Invoking ideas of confession, absolution and redemption, he realizes that 'sanctuary' is gained not by fleeing the self, but by passing through 'my shriven self'. The goal to 'rediscover / The lost commander of my life' (or in the earlier draft, 'the lost companion of my past') reflects the change in his desire to accommodate his past self – to be reconciled with it and feel completed – to his desire to be accepted in the secure love of God. But as yet, with Europe finally at peace, though in ruins, his domestic life in crisis, the anticipated sanctuary of spiritual afterlife is animated by longing, not secured by faith.

Certainly, working his way into his past enabled Sassoon to endow his life with a sense of meaning. As he put it in March 1943 in an unpublished poem, 'A Rejection of Reality':

> These moments I remember – near my fortieth year –
> When first it struck me that, to make such aspects last,
> One must contrive to see the present as the past
> And steal a march on memory while disclosure's clear.[69]

Again, he seems to be looking for what Proust saw as 'something which, common to both past and present, is far more essential than either',[70] an elusive, quasi-mystical experience fusing the contemplative intensity of recollections with the immediacy of present sensations. But Sassoon's search for such experience is here presented differently. 'Such aspects' refers to experiences of contentment emerging only haphazardly and fleetingly from the unconscious, sources of his nostalgic vision, which are often preceded and followed by much that is 'hateful and repellent'. What we can see in the title of the poem, taken together with the awkward phrase 'while disclosure's clear', is a persistent, uneasy uncertainty and ambivalence about the nature of reality; the factual, historical, everyday life in which one is inescapably immersed is contrasted with the 'buried life' that flashes out in epiphanies that disclose what may indeed be deeper truth. By experiencing the present as in fact 'always already' – always in the process of becoming the past – Sassoon takes its ordinariness for granted while remaining open to its 'aspects' that are normally recognized as significant only with the passage of time: through both the mysterious workings of the unconscious and consciously nostalgic reconstructions. To 'steal a march on memory' is to try to exert some mastery over both memory and the unconscious – some mastery over one's life and its meaning.

Although the desire for such mastery may lie behind his increasingly reclusive way of life during and after the war, Sassoon complained that mastery remained elusive:

> The unrevealed processes of memory are mysterious. Neither unconscious selection nor uncontrolled hazardry can be held responsible for one's recovery of some moment which emerges – actual as ever – in contrast to the generalized indistinctness wherefrom one elaborates the annals of personal experience.[71]

It proved harder than he expressed in 'A Rejection of Reality' to 'steal a march on memory'. But the sketches of his many returns to the past indicate that he was often surprisingly successful at encouraging memories to emerge – 'actual as ever' – especially by revisiting places that time had confirmed as significant.

Sassoon's moment at the top of the stairs at 1 Raymond Buildings, Gray's Inn, in the autumn of 1941 marked a turning point in his autobiographical writing. His shock at finding destroyed the interior that he remembered with affection, as well as regret and disappointment, was deep and lasting. In *Siegfried's Journey*, which he began not long after completing *The Weald of Youth*, there is a distinct change in his approach to the past. The full title, *Siegfried's Journey: 1916–1920*, marks a gap in the chronological continuity of the autobiographies. *The Weald of Youth* ended with his decision on 31 July 1914 to enlist; *Siegfried's Journey* opens 'at the beginning of August 1916'.[72] Elided in this gap is his initiation into military service and the 'hideous realism of the war-zone',[73] some of his most harrowing experiences of war and death, including the Battle of the Somme and his discovery that he was capable of feeling 'the lust to kill'.[74] Referring from the vantage point of the Second World War to his earlier treatment of these experiences in the guise of George Sherston (in *Memoirs of an Infantry Officer*), Sassoon is 'thankful not to be obliged to drag my mind through th[ose] details again'.[75] This unwillingness to reiterate his memories of that disturbing time marks what he called his turn to 'reporting' not 'recreating' the past.[76] Sketches of famous personalities he encountered during the period of his own popular acclaim replace the vibrant and intense exploration of the past and the self-consciousness of recollection that distinguish the first two volumes.

His interest in his interiority, the contours and nuances of his inner self, vanishes in *Siegfried's Journey*. 'Inexactitude worries me very much!' he wrote to Cockerell, 'and memory, though mother of the muses, has a naughty way of inventing and supporting things to suit it with barefaced effrontery!'[77] The recreation of the emotional significance of experience and its contributions to the development of the inner, intensely alive (if not always visible) self that sustains *The Old Century* and *The Weald of Youth* is conspicuously lacking in *Siegfried's Journey*. Quickly he passes over his energetic post-Armistice party-going as 'long-vanished activities' and 'indigestible experience', which now makes him 'positively dizzy to contemplate'.[78] Even Weirleigh – the enchanted heart of the early sections of *The Old Century* and the rural counterbalance to his rooms at Gray's Inn – failed to spark any creative, or recreative, inspiration. Now it 'had become a repository for my defunct pre-war self. Its unlively atmosphere oppressed me.'[79] The trouble is that this past is no longer a golden age of pre-war, rural order, no longer susceptible to nostalgic reconstruction. This age has been shattered by the trauma of modern war; it is defunct.

The absence of ruminative self-scrutiny characteristic of the first two volumes in *Siegfried's Journey* contributes to its failure to realize his intent to 'analyse and investigate the inner history of a course of action' undertaken by a past self from the supposedly objective vantage point of the present.[80] Though this failed intention applies to the book as a whole, the 'course of action' to which he refers specifically in the phrase quoted above is the very particular drama of his public protest of the war that led him to Craiglockhart and his fateful and profoundly transforming encounter with Rivers. By 1944, Sassoon was not inclined to revisit that complex sequence of events, and was simply content to assert again that he 'never regretted' any of his actions, not even his decision in the end to rejoin his regiment at the front.[81] His 'inner history' at this stage is neglected while he recalls encounters with Arnold Bennett, H. G. Wells and Wilfred Owen, and emphasizes their responses to his protest rather than the impact of the crisis on himself. While he was struggling to write this third volume of autobiography, he wrote 'Valediction to Dead Youth', apparently an ironic retort to Owen's acclaimed 'Anthem for Doomed Youth', which he had described in *Siegfried's Journey*, noting his minor editorial role in its composition at Craiglockhart:[82]

> To Youth – that booby trapp'd idealist –
> I say good-bye with minimum regret,
> Observing how infallibly he missed
> The gist of good, and mocked at truths unmet.
> . . .
> Lie down, my lad, among exploded schemes,
> And till the Day of Judgement hold your tongue.
> With due indulgence for your nimbus'd dreams,
> I breathe relief that I'm no longer young.[83]

The final line confirms Sassoon's identification of his youthful self with the 'booby-trapp'd idealist', and his relief is only matched by his confidence in youth's demise: 'I, too, am tolerant of your hot-head haste / (And can afford to be, since you're so dead).' As in the prose narrative of *Siegfried's Journey*, he seems to have lost interest in recapturing and engaging with a 'defunct' self – a vanished interior – and the history of his protest. The hot-headed fusilier, and the war poems that brought him fame and turmoil, no longer represent a threshold that must be passed through before entering into a more innocent, nostalgic vision of his pre-war past, as he did in *The Old Century* and *The Weald of*

Youth. Very little nostalgic potential can be wrung from this idealistic, deluded and defunct martial self, and Sassoon found it easier to bid it farewell, with 'minimum regret'.

Notes

1. W. H. R. Rivers, *Instinct and the Unconscious*, 2nd edn (Cambridge: Cambridge University Press, 1924), pp. 11–12. This passage from Rivers's book figures prominently in the second novel of Pat Barker's *Ghost Road* trilogy (Pat Barker, *The Eye in the Door* (New York: Penguin, 1993), pp. 137–42). She suggests that the 'unknown' of this scene is a veil that masks a profoundly repressed childhood trauma, which is in keeping with Rivers's own insights about repression, though he did not explicitly direct these insights toward this vividly recollected blankness.
2. Rivers, *Instinct*, p. 12.
3. Ibid. p. 12.
4. Ibid. p. 13.
5. Ibid. p. 14.
6. Siegfried Sassoon, 'A Short Story', *Country Life*, 20 February 1926, p. 264.
7. Henry Head to Siegfried Sassoon, letter, 8 March 1926, Papers of Siegfried Sassoon, Manuscript Department, Cambridge University Library.
8. Ibid. 8 March 1926.
9. Henri Lefebvre, *The Production of Space*, trans. Donald Nicholson-Smith (Oxford: Blackwell, 1991) pp. 209–10.
10. Gaston Bachelard, *The Poetics of Space*, trans. Maria Jolas (Boston: Beacon Hill, 1994), p. 224.
11. See Siegfried Sassoon, *Diaries 1923–1925*, ed. Rupert Hart-Davis (London: Faber & Faber, 1985), p. 301. It is unclear how many subsequent volumes of *Remembrance of Things Past* Sassoon read, but his own approach to the past is consistent with Proust's quest for 'a fragment of time in its pure state' sought by resurrecting the past through fusing recollection with the immediacy of the present, which could lead also to the elusive glimpse of 'his true self' (Marcel Proust, *In Search of Lost Time: Time Regained*, vol. 6, trans. Andreas Mayor, T. Kilmartin, D. J. Enright (New York: Modern Library, 2003), p. 264). This process of recollection, as Roger Shattuck remarks, can offer a 'glimpse of "the essence of things" . . . represent a rudimentary form of true spiritual experience' (Roger Shattuck, *Proust's Way* (New York: Norton, 2000), p. 111). Perhaps surprisingly, Sassoon does not seem to have suffered any anxiety of influence or been intimidated by attempting to write in a mode whose pinnacle Proust had attained already. He once noted with disdain Arnold Bennett's dismissive reaction to Forster's unpublished novel (*Maurice*): ' "That subject has already been done once and for all by a man named PROUST," ' to which Sassoon took umbrage, observing 'How can a subject be done "once and for all"?' (Siegfried Sassoon, *Diaries 1920–1922*, ed. Rupert Hart-Davis (London: Faber & Faber, 1981), p. 129).
12. Siegfried Sassoon, *Collected Poems: 1908–1956* (London: Faber & Faber, 1961), p. 179.
13. Ibid. p. 179.
14. The monastic associations of 'cell' in 'Farewell to a Room' have been seized upon by Paul Moeyes, who situates it as a precursor to the theme of religious journey that runs through Sassoon's later poetry (Paul Moeyes, *Siegfried Sassoon: Scorched Glory: A Critical Study* (New York: St Martin's, 1997), p. 121). But a 'cell' is also the constitutive unit of all organic life, and as such, invokes the idea of the poet's own self as organic, with the unconscious as the 'unknown' part. This association

is reinforced by the aural proximity of 'cell' and 'self', a point especially relevant to a poet who took such pleasure in the sound of words (Siegfried Sassoon, *The Weald of Youth* (London: Faber & Faber, 1942), p. 112).

15. Sassoon, *Collected Poems*, p. 179.
16. W. H. R. Rivers, *Conflict and Dream*, ed. George Elliot Smith (London: Kegan Paul, 1923), p. 19.
17. Sassoon, *Collected Poems*, p. 213.
18. Siegfried Sassoon to David Wright, letter, 26 November 1952, Sassoon Collection, Harry Ransom Humanities Research Center (HRHRC), University of Texas, Austin.
19. Sassoon, *Collected Poems*, p. 213.
20. Freud called the 'unconscious mental processes timeless . . . the idea of time cannot be applied to them' (Freud, *Beyond the Pleasure Principle*, in James Strachey (trans.) and Angela Richards (ed.), *On Metapsychology* (London: Penguin, 1991), pp. 269–338, p. 299).
21. Sassoon, *Collected Poems*, p. 213.
22. Ibid. p. 213.
23. Ibid. p. 213.
24. Sassoon, *Letters to a Critic*, ed. Michael Thorpe (Nettlestead, Kent: Bridge, Conachar, 1976), p. 14.
25. Siegfried Sassoon, *The Old Century* (London: Faber & Faber, 1938), p. 116.
26. Ibid. p. 117.
27. Ibid. pp. 118–19.
28. Ibid. p. 119.
29. Proust, *Time Regained*, p. 2.
30. Sassoon, *The Old Century*, p. 122.
31. Ibid. p. 117.
32. Ibid. p. 126.
33. Ibid. p. 125.
34. Ibid. p. 126.
35. Ibid. p. 127.
36. Ibid. p. 128.
37. Nicholas Royle, *The Uncanny* (New York: Routledge, 2003), p. 6.
38. Sassoon, *The Old Century*, p. 129.
39. Sassoon, *Collected Poems*, p. 213.
40. Sassoon, *The Old Century*, pp. 128–9.
41. Sassoon, *Collected Poems*, p. 213.
42. Sassoon, *The Old Century*, p. 129.
43. Sassoon, *The Weald of Youth*, p. 10.
44. Ibid. p. 10.
45. Ibid. p. 13.
46. Ibid. p. 201.
47. Ibid. p. 201.
48. In his public poetry lecture, Sassoon situates the source of 'poetry of inventive genius' in the unconscious, 'which as far as I can make out, knows a lot more than the conscious [mind]!' (Siegfried Sassoon, *On Poetry* (Bristol: Arrowsmith, 1939), p. 7.)
49. Siegfried Sassoon to Sydney Carlyle Cockerell, letter, 8 September 1941, Sassoon Collection, Harry Ransom Humanities Research Center (HRHRC), University of Texas, Austin.
50. James F. Stewart, *A Descriptive Account of Unpublished Letters of Siegfried Sassoon in the University of Texas Collection*, diss, University of Texas, Austin (Ann Arbor, MI: UMI, 1972), pp. 253–4.

51. Sassoon, *The Weald of Youth*, p. 247.
52. Sassoon, *The Old Century*, p. 128.
53. Ibid. p. 123.
54. Sassoon, *The Weald of Youth*, pp. 247–8.
55. Quoted in Sigmund Freud, 'The "uncanny" ', in James Strachey (trans.) and Albert Dickson (ed.), *Art and Literature* (London: Penguin, 1991), pp. 335–76, p. 364.
56. Sassoon, *The Weald of Youth*, p. 245.
57. Ibid. p. 246.
58. Ibid. p. 242.
59. Ibid. pp. 245–6.
60. Quoted in Sassoon, *The Weald of Youth*, p. 246.
61. Sassoon, *The Weald of Youth*, p. 246.
62. In a note on a typescript that formed an early basis for *The Old Century*, Sassoon wrote: 'Half one's life is spent in trying to understand things; the other half is spent in trying to make other people understand what one has learned from life' (Sassoon, 'Preliminary Notes for Early Recollections', ts., 7 September 1936, Papers of Siegfried Sassoon, Manuscript Department, Cambridge University Library). That these words appear almost verbatim five years later in *The Weald of Youth* in the guise of a postcard from Wirgie reaffirms the function of Wirgie as a representative of Sassoon's older self.
63. Sassoon, *Collected Poems*, p. 235.
64. Ibid. p. 235. Sassoon's unpublished letters make clear that he was reading James's fiction, letters and diaries intensely during the early years of the Second World War, and was impressed by the affective power of James's ghost story. 'Corrupt revisitation of the dead' is not an exact line from *The Turn of the Screw*, but it does capture in a phrase James's intentions for the story, cited in his notebook on 12 January 1895, which involve 'corrupt . . . servants [who] die . . . [and] return to haunt the house and children' (Henry James, 'A Notebook Entry', in Deborah Esch and Jonathan Warren (eds), *The Turn of the Screw* (New York: Norton, 1999), p. 112).
65. In his final years, he admitted to Thorpe that his war experiences had haunted his dreams throughout his life (Siegfried Sassoon, *Letters to a Critic*, ed. Michael Thorpe (Nettlestead, Kent: Bridge, Conachar, 1976) p. 14).
66. Sassoon, *Collected Poems*, p. 235.
67. Siegfried Sassoon, 'Sanctuary', in 'ms. notebook', Hart-Davis Section, Papers of Siegfried Sassoon, Manuscript Department, Cambridge University Library, 24 November 1945.
68. John Stuart Roberts, *Siegfried Sassoon: 1886–1967* (London: Cohen, 1999), p. 280.
69. Siegfried Sassoon, 'A Rejection of Reality', in 'ms. notebook', Hart-Davis Section, Papers of Siegfried Sassoon, Manuscript Department, Cambridge University Library, 9–10 March 1943.
70. Proust, *Time Regained*, p. 263.
71. Sassoon, *The Weald of Youth*, p. 103.
72. Siegfried Sassoon, *Siegfried's Journey: 1916–1920* (London: Faber & Faber, 1945), p. 5.
73. Siegfried Sassoon, *Diaries 1915–1918*, ed. Rupert Hart-Davis (London: Faber & Faber, 1983), p. 22.
74. Ibid. p. 52.
75. Sassoon, *Siegfried's Journey*, p. 55.
76. Quoted in Stewart, *Unpublished Letters*, p. 268.
77. Sassoon to Cockerell, letter, 15 November 1944, Papers of Siegfried Sassoon, Manuscript Department, Cambridge University Library.

78. Sassoon, *Siegfried's Journey*, p. 105.
79. Ibid. p. 118.
80. Ibid. p. 55.
81. Ibid. p. 55.
82. Ibid. pp. 59–60.
83. Siegfried Sassoon, 'Valediction to Dead Youth', in 'ms. notebook', Hart-Davis Section, Papers of Siegfried Sassoon, Manuscript Department, Cambridge University Library, 26–27 June 1944.

CONCLUSION

Clearly, the composition of *Siegfried's Journey* was a fraught experience that left Sassoon exhausted. In 1946 he agreed to write about the life of another man – George Meredith – as a relief from the travails of literary autognosis.[1] Though he began the work with characteristic diffidence,[2] he completed *Meredith* in manuscript almost on schedule, in August 1947. In his approach to Meredith, it is interesting to note the same heightened awareness of the multiplicity and elusiveness of self that marks his autobiographical writing. He felt 'confronted', he writes, 'by the protesting presence of Meredith' warning him of the impossibility of knowing an author in any personal way through his works and a few scraps of letters, through the veil of 'posthumous opacity'.[3] 'You can see *through* me', the spectre of Meredith tells him, 'but you will never see *into* me,'[4] as it disappears in another variation of Sassoon's liminal moment: 'Bowing with a sort of elaborate courtesy, he vanishes' like aspects of Sassoon's own interiority that pass beyond the limits of his vision at key moments of self-scrutiny in his autobiography.[5] '[Meredith's] career, however, remains' in the material solidity of the books that 'crowd' the shelves of Sassoon's library,[6] something like the surviving solid door at the top of the stairs at 1 Raymond Buildings in 1941 that discloses an emptiness.

The success of *Meredith* in 1948[7] did not have the energizing effects for which Sassoon had hoped. He complained that his 'emotional apparatus had gone flat' and he was unable to get back to his autobiographical project beyond glancing at his notes and diaries from the 1920s.[8] J. R. Ackerley, who visited

Heytesbury House for a fortnight in the summer of 1949, found Sassoon wrapped up in himself: 'Siegfried is sweet, kind, loquacious, absent-minded, lonely, dreadfully self-centred . . . [He talks] always about himself, his life, his past fame, his present neglect, his unhappy marriage, his passionate love for his son. It is all intensely subjective.'[9] And yet, several months later, Sassoon declined to give a talk for the BBC on the theme of 'I speak for myself,'[10] saying that he did not have anything to say on the subject.[11]

Nevertheless, within a week of Armistice Day 1949, he began to write a fourth volume of autobiography, perhaps seeking another nostalgic antidote from his past to assuage his present malaise. He opens this sequel by invoking *Siegfried's Journey*'s concluding image of a man standing in Trafalgar Square in 1920, at a crossroads in his life: 'That man was, of course, myself . . . [but] the distance between us has widened in more than years . . . he has dropped out of my life.'[12] He felt he was confronting 'a stranger . . . an insubstantial representative of a vanished generation'.[13] He could muster little empathy for this vanished past self: 'It seems that I, his successor, have outlived our former intimacy. And I am not sure that I want to revive my relationship with him.'[14] This uncertainty contrasts sharply with the nostalgic reconnections with his earlier versions of past selves in *The Old Century* and *The Weald of Youth*: 'In previous volumes . . . I enjoyed exploring the past and creating a plausible semblance of my vanished selves.'[15] But the self that had survived the First World War now seemed to repel the older, self-consciously enervated writing self that had survived two wars. The weary veteran survivor was unable to summon the confidence, interest or energy to engage fully with his damaged post-war 'selves' that did not have the benefit of golden age reflections.

But he persisted with the challenge, calling up another stair-climbing, liminal moment at his rooms on Tufton Street, his home from 1920 to 1925: 'Going upstairs again, I stood for while, contemplating the lighted interior of my room through the doorway.'[16] Once again he turns domestic space into an expression of his interior life, and uses it to evoke his sense of the multiplicity of selves, even referring to 'my private self' in the third person:

> the room in which one lives and does one's concentrated thinking is something more than cubic feet of space. Unknown to others, it can become saturated by the presence of its occupant and permeated by the intensity of his mind-working solitudes. And that cell-like room was indeed to be, for several years, the hermitage of my private self . . . It represented the part of me which I had always instinctively tried to keep separate. In that room I should be a single-minded poet . . . Wherever I went, I should leave my private self behind in that room, in whose confederate silences, through many a night-time, he had sought to discover and develop such talents as were his, and to understand and express the finer elements of his being.[17]

This is ground he had already covered in the poem 'Farewell to a Room' (which he wrote back in December 1925 when actually leaving Tufton Street), using very similar language ('cell-like room', 'confederate silences', for example). These rooms served for Sassoon the same function as his rooms at the Raymond Buildings before the war, and they too have now become inaccessible. Twenty-three years on, recollection and imagination could not revive the distant self these still-standing rooms were meant to nurture and inspire.

Early in 1950, he set aside this fourth volume, fearing that accounts of his visits with Thomas Hardy at Max Gate and his association with Edmund Gosse might seem 'trivial and gossipy'.[18] When he tried to resume it in the autumn of 1951, he worked in a haphazard manner, relying largely on diary entries for 1926 and 1927. He felt unable even to 'report' on the past, let alone 'recreate' it, and found that he was merely 'editing that other self'.[19] By Christmas, he had accumulated 25,000 words of dubious merit.[20] Though in the past the composition of memoirs had, in spite of its toll on his nerves, provided him with 'occupational relief',[21] he could draw no inspiration from his experiences in the 1920s. And so he finally broke off his explicit autobiography. The traumatic after-effects of his war experience, which lingered and disturbed his life in the 1920s, tarnished his attempts to reconstruct the past nostalgically as he had done with such satisfaction in *The Old Century* and *The Weald of Youth*. Versions of his self from these autobiographies are retrospectively blessed by virtue of their embodying spatial and temporal realms untouched by the devastation of modern war. For him, the period of the 1920s was barren of nostalgic possibility.

Certainly, his memory of climbing the stairs of 1 Raymond Buildings in 1941 to open the solid door and discover that 'the interior had vanished' marked for him a crucial moment in which the forces of history seemed to block dramatically his efforts to express his 'true self'. The Second World War shattered his capacity to gain access to a nostalgic personal past. This past, which he had once been able to conjure up in his writing with pleasure and conviction, was the past before the First World War. It was the experience of that war which changed his life forever, despite his attempts to reassure himself and others that he had not really been damaged and was 'right as rain' after all. As the telling narration of his 1941 return to his rooms of 1914 suggests, the 1939–45 war finally undermined his own private quest to integrate and capture his 'real state of mind', and disturbed his capacity to return to prior versions of selfhood integrated into consolatory and gentrified English social geography. But his need for meaning, which led to flirtations with spirituality, was keener than ever and eventually culminated in his conversion to Catholicism in 1957, which he came to call his path to peace.[22]

And yet it is also possible to see this conversion as a nostalgic gesture in a different register. In light of nostalgia's associations with communal order and a particular embodiment of Englishness, a conversion to Catholicism can be construed as a return to a social order that predates not just the world wars, but the upheaval of the early modern world. As Evelyn Waugh explained in 1949: 'England was Catholic for nine hundred years, then protestant for three hundred, then agnostic for a century. The Catholic structure still lies lightly buried beneath every picture of English life; history, topography, law, archaeology, everywhere reveal Catholic origins.'[23] In Waugh's terms, rural revivalists like Massingham, Leavis, Blunden and Penty did not go back far enough nor excavate deep enough to retrieve the essence of an English social order so imperilled by the modern world. Had they done so, they would have returned to a site of origin founded upon the singular and true vision of Christianity that underpins the landscape, institutions and history of England. To convert to Catholicism can be to return home. So it was for Waugh, so too for Sassoon.

While the Second World War obscured Sassoon's nostalgic vision, it did not impede other incarnations of modern nostalgia. Waugh's *Brideshead Revisited* amply demonstrates the resilience of nostalgia by tapping into the same period Sassoon found so barren; for Waugh and his narrator, from the vantage point of the bleak and enervating late war years, the 1920s became fertile ground for nostalgic reconstructions. In a technique Sassoon employed in his Edingthorpe and Raymond Buildings episodes, Waugh has his narrator revisit the particular space of his nostalgic past. On one of many apparently random army manœuvres, Captain Ryder's company strikes camp during a starless, drizzly night on the slopes of a property requisitioned by Brigade Headquarters. Hearing the name of the nearby country house announced by the second-in-command next morning, Ryder is transported instantly 'by a multitude of sweet and natural and long-forgotten sounds' that drew him back as he walks the grounds, 'the exquisite man-made landscape' of Brideshead he knew so well as a youth.[24] The languorous days of Sebastian and his family, of Oxford and of corporeal indulgences are figured as a golden Arcadia revisited by the recollecting narrator, now tainted by the deprivations of wartime and anxieties of mortality. Charles Ryder 'believed [him]self very near heaven, during those languid days at Brideshead'.[25] But Waugh does not look back with 'unalloyed affection',[26] and he manifests the spiritual emptiness of a modern world, however apparently languid, in part through the depiction of Brideshead house.

As a seat of Catholic aristocracy in England, Brideshead's days of glory are connected to a nostalgic vision of pre-Reformation England. It survived three centuries of Protestantism and a century of agnosticism, but the world wars have threatened its viability and continuity. The truly devout side of the family has reached the end of its line; Lady Marchmain's three brothers were killed during the First World War. Sebastian and Brideshead are unlikely to produce legitimate heirs, and the adoptive son to the Marchmains, Charles, has been blocked from joining the family through the intervention, or revisiting, of divine grace upon Lord Marchmain and Julia. In the Second World War, the army has invaded it physically, making mockery of its artistic grandeur, in effect vandalizing its civility. Brideshead still stands in 1944, but severed from its Catholic ancestry and battered by the war; its disrepair calls into question not so much its own social, cultural and religious validity but the validity of the contemporary culture that has reproduced world war and condoned the desecration of a symbol of glorious English past.

Before the end of the Second World War, the English country house symbolized an organic rural social order, with clear delineations of class and a foundation of community, nation state and culture.[27] The physical and artistic beauty of country house architecture became especially valued as a national treasure. Sacheverell Sitwell's *British Architects and Craftsmen* (1945) identifies the historic country house as a glorious tradition as integral to national identity as the canon of English literature.[28] As the fate of Brideshead (and Heytesbury House) attests, this social order could not survive the war intact. A Labour government swept to power, further weakening the influence of ancient seats. Waugh lamented the loss of aristocratic power and the crumbling of its most glorious symbol, and feared the social disruption arising from a destabilized class system, the concomitant ascent of Hoopers.[29] And yet Waugh was surprised by the curious, if altered, endurance of the country house. It was, by the late 1950s, no longer a symbol of organic English community, but a monument of the past, exemplary of the museumization of a social institution. 'Brideshead today [1959] would be open to trippers, its treasures rearranged by expert hands and the fabric better maintained than it was by Lord Marchmain.'[30] Nevertheless, in the midst of war, Brideshead had been rearranged by inexpert, clumsy hands, its disrepair representative of encroaching societal decay. Brideshead's Catholic chapel, however, 'showed no ill-effects of its long neglect',[31] and its burning flame attests to the hope, not of avoiding disaster, but 'that the human spirit, redeemed, can avoid all disasters', as Waugh explains in his 'Warning'.[32] This longing for the persistence of the aristocratically inflected Catholic faith within the rupturing forces of modernity is another embodiment of nostalgia during wartime.

The longevity of *Punch* magazine, founded during the heyday of the British empire and global English dominance and flourishing still during the world wars, is another testament to the resilience of nostalgia. In late 1944, around the same time that the poem 'Nostalgia' first struck Sassoon while he was editing *Poems from Italy*, *Punch* printed a cartoon that mocks nostalgia's idealizing tendencies. Two smartly dressed middle-class women, one equipped with a modern bicycle, the other a stylish lapdog, observe a jostling crowd of fashionable shoppers with empty baskets, pushing their way into a shop. One says: 'I suppose in about thirty years time people will insist on describing this as the good old days.'[33] The cartoon's message is obvious: a present no matter how bleak, even a present battered by modern war, can be transformed by time and nostalgic volition into 'the good old days'. And this is exactly what happened in England after the war. Yes, London was shaken by V1 and V2 attacks; yes, shops were often empty; yes, there were ration cards and food shortages. But what pluck those Londoners showed – 'some chicken; some neck', as Churchill had it in his speech to the Canadian parliament in December 1941. Nostalgic representations of Britain's finest hour during the Blitz and later bombings in the popular media in the latter quarter of the twentieth century are predicated upon an imagined act of remembering glory and resilience, and forgetting privation and trauma. Douglas Lionel Mays, the illustrator who drew the *Punch* cartoon, might have been surprised at his prescience. But Mays also had a more direct experience of nostalgia. A pacifist, he withdrew during the Second World War to his own country house where he installed a small herd of cows and tried his hand at farming.[34] Whether or not this return to a country lifestyle was intentionally nostalgic, it none the less embodies the bygone value system of the rural revivalists, practitioners of the ethos underlying Georgian nostalgics. John Drummond, also writing in 1944, asserted that 'No one is a true Englishman, or has lived a fully balanced life, if the country has played no part in his development.'[35] Drummond's assertion nicely captures the conflation of masculinity, fully balanced living and the prominence of the countryside that is behind the nostalgic recreation of the nation state, a recreation central to a revivalist movement seeking refuge from the trauma of modern war. Each in his own way, Mays, Waugh and Sassoon sought out the protective nostalgia that located him as safely as possible within an Englishness ruptured by modernity.

Modern Nostalgia, Absence and Loss

My contention that trauma and nostalgia are crucially linked builds on the ideas of important late twentieth-century scholars. According to Linda Hutcheon, nostalgia 'is the past as imagined, as idealized through memory and desire . . . but also [through] forgetting'.[36] This constitutive dialectic between memory and forgetting likens nostalgia to the underlying tension of trauma, which Andreas Huyssen locates 'on the threshold between remembering and forgetting, seeing and not seeing, transparency and occlusion'.[37] Dominick LaCapra argues compellingly that trauma is intimately bound up with absence and loss, categories which he insists are fundamentally distinct, even if the distinctions between them are commonly, and misleadingly, elided.[38] Loss has very much to do with specific historical events, which LaCapra connects to 'historical trauma'.[39] The losses of one's comrades or of those one has slain in modern war produce trauma; Sassoon's 'fair-haired Cameronian / Propped in his pool of blood', from 'A Footnote on the War' (1926),[40] resides in the liminal space between remembering and forgetting, a memory sometimes transparent, sometimes occluded. The traumatic experience may be occluded, as it certainly was for Sassoon, but it may also become transparent. In spite of Rivers's psychoanalytically inflected intervention, Sassoon's capacity for working through his trauma was complicated by the powerful nostalgic impulse that animates his writing, which derives as much from the lingering after-effects of his war experience and its attendant losses as from an underlying sense of absence.

Absence is more general than loss. LaCapra offers an illuminating literary analogy. The world of Milton is paradise lost; the world of Beckett is paradise absent.[41] Absence is associated with narratives of origin, which LaCapra calls 'transhistorical', in so far as a range of different cultures, different societies in different periods of history have in common various intimations of absence at their origin.[42] Nostalgia, similarly, is not about what was, but what can be forgotten, what might have been (but was not). Hofer's late seventeenth-century Swiss nostalgics suffered loss: loss of home, to which they could be returned and cured. But nostalgics after the nineteenth century longed for a sense of home connected to the time and place of childhood that could not be accessed. From the pressing and anxiety-provoking concerns of the present, the distant past of one's childhood, or one's nation, assumed increasingly idealizing contours. Homecoming was impossible, as Boym suggests, because home, in these retrospectively reconstructed terms, never existed. Home as such was not lost, but absent. 'In terms of absence', LaCapra argues, 'one may recognize that one cannot lose what one never had.'[43] Yet one can certainly long for what one never had, even, or especially, if one converts absence into loss.

To return to Mays's cartoon, the caption implies the power of nostalgia to remember the national resolve of wartime, which might even be traced to a sense of English national origins, and to forget the shortages, the ration cards, the squabbling in queues, the bombings, the trauma. Nostalgia is a response to the occluded recognition of absence, without being an acceptance of absence. Nostalgia is so persistent in the modern period, in various guises, because it adheres to a myth of origin, a past of glory that is not lost, but absent. The traumatic historical losses of the world wars obscure the transhistorical nature of the absence surrounding the pre-war golden age. This elusive golden age was constructed differently by high modernists, who looked far back to the Renaissance for originary order; the Georgians, who looked to the English countryside; the rural revivalists, who saw authentic, organic community in a rigidly structured rural social order; and Sassoon, whose solipsistic construction of a private idyll of childhood and youth represented a privileged English social geography jeopardized by modernity. But all of these golden ages are posited in response to a persistent longing for a past order to evade a present emptiness. They have in common modern nostalgia's sense of absence, erroneously converted to loss. When this conversion happens, LaCapra claims that it 'increases likelihood of misplaced nostalgia or utopian politics in quest of a new totality or fully unified community'.[44] This is an impossible and dubious quest, as the political implications of the modern nostalgics attest, from the high modernists to the Georgians, the rural revivalists, Waugh and Sassoon.

The nostalgia of Sassoon's poetry and prose strikes me as a response to a particularly modern absence of origin, an origin closer to Beckett's than to Milton's, despite Sassoon's late conversion. His persistent return to an imagined and reimagined paradisal childhood in his writing strives towards a melancholic absence[45] that can never be fully worked through, because it was never really there in the first place. As Robert J. Lifton has explained, the survivor of war looks backward in time to create a nostalgic vision that predates his traumatic losses, a vision of origins that provides the present with 'life-sustaining imagery',[46] but is distorted and illusory. Nostalgia, like trauma, is a response to what is missing, except with nostalgia what is missing is not lost, but absent. The modern nostalgic's entry into traumatic history at once motivates the establishment of home as an Edenic unity of time and space, and assures its elusiveness. Sassoon's compulsive revisitation of his pre-war selves is a voyage home without arrival, because the home of spiritual and physical unity is absent; in other words, it never was. Sassoon's later work manifests modern nostalgia, a phenomenon unavoidably linked to the aftermath of world war and a survival both incomprehensible and inescapable.

Notes

1. Siegfried Sassoon to Sydney Carlyle Cockerell, letter, 23 January 1946, Papers of Siegfried Sassoon, Manuscript Department, Cambridge University Library.
2. James F. Stewart, *A Descriptive Account of Unpublished Letters of Siegfried Sassoon in the University of Texas Collection*, diss, University of Texas, Austin (Ann Arbor, MI: UMI, 1972), p. 67.
3. Siegfried Sassoon, *Meredith* (London: Constable, 1948), p. 99.
4. Ibid. p. 99.
5. Ibid. p. 99.
6. Ibid. p. 99.
7. Constable initially published 10,000 copies to generally positive reviews (Stewart, *Unpublished Letters*, p. 283).
8. Ibid. p. 288.
9. J. R. Ackerley, *My Sister and Myself: The Diaries of J.R. Ackerley*, ed. Francis King (London: Hutchinson, 1982), p. 167.
10. Stewart, *Unpublished Letters*, p. 290.
11. Ibid. p. 290.
12. Siegfried Sassoon, *Diaries 1920–1922*, ed. Rupert Hart-Davis (London: Faber, 1981), p. 15.
13. Siegfried Sassoon, 'Prelude', ts. Sassoon Collection, Manuscript Department, Cambridge University Library, p. 1.
14. Sassoon, *Diaries 1920–1922*, p. 15.
15. Sassoon, 'Prelude', p. 2.
16. Sassoon, *Diaries 1920–1922*, p. 17.
17. Ibid. pp. 17–18.
18. Stewart, *Unpublished Letters*, p. 292.

19. Ibid. p. 300.
20. Ibid. p. 301.
21. Ibid. p. 313.
22. Siegfried Sassoon, *Siegfried Sassoon: Poet's Pilgrimage*, ed. Felicitas Corrigan (London: Gollancz, 1973), p. 187.
23. Evelyn Waugh, 'Come Inside', in John A. O'Brien (ed.), *The Road to Damascus* (New York: Doubleday, 1949), pp. 10–16, p. 15.
24. Evelyn Waugh, *Brideshead Revisited* (Boston: Little, Brown, 1945), pp. 15–16.
25. Waugh, *Brideshead*, p. 79.
26. Evelyn Waugh, 'Warning on dustjacket of Brideshead Revisited, 1945', in Maurice Cowling, *Religion and Public Doctrine in Modern England* (New York: Cambridge University Press, 1980), p. 339.
27. Laura Coffey, 'Evelyn Waugh's country house trinity: Memory, history and Catholicism in *Brideshead Revisited*', *Literature and History*, 15.1, 2006, pp. 59–73, p. 60.
28. Sacheverell Sitwell, *British Architects and Craftsmen* (London: Batsford, 1947).
29. Coffey, 'Country House', p. 59.
30. Evelyn Waugh, Preface, in *Brideshead Revisited*, 2nd edn (London: Penguin, 1962), p. 8.
31. Waugh, *Brideshead*, p. 350.
32. Waugh, 'Warning', p. 339.
33. Douglas Lionel Mays, cartoon, *Punch*, 4 October 1944, p. 299.
34. Artist Profile: Douglas Lionel Mays (1900–91), Chris Beetles Art Gallery, London, <http://www.chrisbeetles.com/pictures/artists/Mays_Douglas-Lionel/Mays_Douglas-Lionel.htm>
35. John Drummond, quoted in Malcolm Chase, 'this is no claptrap, this is our heritage', in Malcolm Chase and Christopher Shaw (eds), *The Imagined Past: History and Nostalgia* (Manchester: Manchester University Press, 1989), pp. 128–46, p. 142.
36. Linda Hutcheon, 'Irony, nostalgia, and the postmodern', in Raymond Vervliet and Annemarie Estor (eds), *Methods for the Study of Literature as Cultural Memory* (Amsterdam: Rodopi, 2000), pp. 189–207, p. 195.
37. Andreas Huyssen, *Present Pasts* (Stanford, CA: Stanford University Press, 2003), p. 8.
38. See Dominick LaCapra, 'Trauma, absence, loss', in *Writing History, Writing Trauma* (Baltimore, MD: Johns Hopkins University Press, 2001), pp. 43–85.
39. Dominick LaCapra, *Writing History, Writing Trauma* (Baltimore, MD: Johns Hopkins University Press, 2001), p. 80.
40. Siegfried Sassoon, *The War Poems*, ed. Rupert Hart-Davis (London: Faber, 1983), p. 147.
41. LaCapra, *Writing History*, p. 67.
42. Ibid. p. 48.
43. Ibid. p. 50.
44. Ibid. p. 46.
45. Here I refer to Freud's distinction between mourning and melancholia. LaCapra links trauma and loss with the process of mourning and working through, offering the possibility of amelioration and return to normative practice (LaCapra, *Writing History*, p. 66). Nostalgia, on the other hand, is drawn to absence (especially an absence converted to loss). Nostalgia and absence tend towards the recalcitrant fixity of melancholia, which resists amelioration, locking one in patterns of compulsive repetition, impasse and aporia.

    LaCapra's account of Freud bears a striking resemblance to the manner in which Sassoon's critics condemn his nostalgic inclinations:

> Freud, in comparing melancholia with mourning, saw melancholia as characteristic of an arrested process in which the depressed, self-berating, and traumatised self, locked in compulsive repetition, is possessed by the past, faces a future of impasses, and remains narcissistically identified with the lost object. (LaCapra, *Writing History*, pp. 65–6)

The point is not that Sassoon's writing should be condemned because of its parallel with LaCapra's reading of Freud, as previous critics have been inclined to do. The point is that by exploring the parallels between Sassoon's autobiographical project and psychoanalytic discourse, one is offered another glimpse into the modern culture that has produced both.

46. Robert J. Lifton, *The Broken Connection* (New York: Simon & Schuster, 1979), p. 178.

INDEX